Consumption and Growth

Recovery and Structural Change in the US Economy

by

Davide Gualerzi

University of Pisa, Italy

Edward Elgar
Cheltenham, UK • Northampton, MA, USA

Published by
Edward Elgar Publishing Limited
Glensanda House
Montpellier Parade
Cheltenham
Glos GL50 1UA
UK

Edward Elgar Publishing, Inc.
136 West Street
Suite 202
Northampton
Massachusetts 01060
USA

A catalogue record for this book
is available from the British Library

ISBN 1 84064 710 8

Printed and bound in Great Britain by MPG Books Ltd, Bodmin, Cornwall

Sun is the same in a relative way,

but you're older...

Contents

Introduction		ix
1	Economic development, technical change and demand	1
2	Pasinetti's structural dynamics and demand theory	18
3	Consumption theory	32
4	Consumption and growth	46
5	Towards a theory of the consumption–growth relationship	67
6	Empirical analysis and the recovery of the US economy in the 1980s	87
7	Macroeconomic trends and the evolution of the industrial structure	96
8	Consumption expenditure composition	107
9	Market development and output composition	120
10	The structural dynamics of the 1980s: recovery and the transformation of the consumption sphere	126
11	Consumption deepening and intensive growth: a new hypothesis	138
Appendix A: macro variables trends in the post-war period		159
Appendix B: industries grouping		169
Appendix C: expenditure categories, trends and ex-post forecast		180
Appendix D: data sources and data series		200
Bibliography		205
Index		213

Introduction

This is a theoretical and empirical book focused on the reciprocal determination of consumption and growth within advanced market economies. In the framework presented here their interaction accounts for the pattern of structural change and fuels the long-run course of economic growth.

Though it is one of the most fundamental questions studied by economic theory, the relationship between consumption and growth is rarely discussed from this point of view. Growth, at least in the long run, depends on saving while saving struggles with consumption. Thus consumption and growth are mostly understood as opposites, depending on the same process of determination: given the growth rate, the per capita consumption is determined as well. The fundamental idea presented here is that consumption and growth feedback on each other in a process of determination which accounts for structural transformation and the pattern of economic growth. Removing the assumption of a given technology allows us to explore a second relationship, that is the positive feedback between consumption and growth, which determines, through the growth of production, a shift of the frontier along which the constraint of the consumption–growth tradeoff operates. Transformation is indeed necessary and is driven by the social construction of the need structure and realized by the evolution of the consumption sphere.

Thus the book attempts to establish a systemic link between the theory of consumption and the principle of effective demand considered in a long-run perspective. The consumption–growth relationship is at the center of the particular view of the *long-run theory of effective demand* presented in the book.

OVERVIEW

Approaching the growth process from a Keynesian perspective the importance given to Schumpeter's work may seem surprising since, in the history of economic thought, Schumpeter appears to be in some respects opposite to Keynes. The study of the consumption–growth relationship, however, calls for a focus on the endogenous mechanism sustaining the expansion of the market. While largely outside Keynes' research agenda, this question is central to Schumpeter's concern with the long-term perspective of the market economy and its inner development dynamics. This book attempts to show that the reciprocal determination of consumption and growth patterns fits quite easily in Schumpeter's analysis of economic development and that it can address some of the issues left open in his work.

This is why the book begins with the discussion of Schumpeter's views on economic development and proceeds to examine the role of demand in the growth process, with respect to both the theory of structural change (Pasinetti's model) and the theory of consumption at the micro and macro level. It then develops a theoretical framework to analyze the consumption growth relationship and its implications for the process of structural evolution.

In the approach presented here the theory of consumption evolution incorporates the criticism of traditional static consumer theory and becomes the demand side of the growth process involving structural change and demand growth; the latter depends on an endogenous process of market creation which is part of the theory of effective demand in the long run and of a reformulation of demand-led growth.

The focus on theory guides the investigation and shapes the argument about the consumption–growth relationship. The theme of the book, however, reflects also the concerns about the actual trends of economic development within advanced market economies. After a period of rapid growth and low unemployment rates advanced industrial economies entered in the 1970s a new phase of relatively low growth rates. It is open to question whether the recovery of the 1980s has reversed this phenomenon, restoring the conditions for high growth rates and long-term prosperity. *This is indeed the question underlying the interpretation of the recovery of the 1980s in a long-term perspective* and it is immediately relevant for the analysis of the expansion of the US economy in the 1990s.

Many economists seem to think that the overall positive effects of technological advances and the growing integration of world economies, combined with a more flexible economic structure and social organization, constitute a growth potential capable of counteracting the tendencies towards low growth rates. According to this view, the economic forces unleashed in a new, impressive round of innovation and broad structural transformation would shelter industrial economies from stagnation tendencies. The steady pace of expansion of the US economy in the 1990s has given new strength to these arguments, which now enjoy a large consensus.

It may indeed be argued that the 1980s recovery was the beginning of a phase of economic change and structural evolution which can be described along these lines. Nobody denies, however, that a more sustained pace of growth is desirable. Those more outspoken on this account, like Nobel Prize Winner Robert Solow, stress that high growth rates are indispensable to ensure economic stability and social cohesion in market economies. But then the question is: what is growth about in advanced market economies and what are the factors capable of sustaining it in the long run? This appears a central theme of investigation precisely because of the new phase of development the world economy has entered. Thus the inspiration for the investigation comes from the persisting difficulties of the advanced industrial economies to maintain sustained growth rates and pursue successful income and employment policies, that is policies capable of increasing employment *and* real wages. This is the real challenge of economic development as Schumpeter saw it.

The recent Keynesian theory (Mankiw and Romer, 1991) has directed his analytical efforts to develop an alternative to the frictionless, market clearing view of labour markets, giving microfoundations to the notion of wage and price rigidities. Segmented labour markets, non-competitive behavior and the like are the characteristics of a view of the economy where imperfections are the norm and not the exception.

On the other hand, the analysis of growth has been enriched by what is known as New Growth Theory. The main focus of this strand of theory consists in endogenizing the factors of growth, overcoming a view of growth associated with exogenous technical change. However, removing long-held convictions appears to be just a first step and the extent to which the new theory is a real break with the previous theory is open to question (Kurz and Salvadori, 1998). Nevertheless it opened up a new research agenda, especially for the reference made to increasing returns.

Though sharing the stress laid by New Growth Theory on the endogenous nature of the growth process, the book approaches the question in a different perspective. It focuses on the central issue stemming from Keynes' original contribution: the question of the level of aggregate demand in the long run and of the forces that govern the long-term evolution of output, independently from market imperfections and asymmetric information, which has become the hallmark of the recent Keynesian theory.

The approach presented in the book brings this question to bear on the early theory of growth, based on a Keynesian perspective of the Harrod–Domar model. In particular it starts from the fact that the composition of output and its relationship to the level of output are unexplained, except for the recognizing that demand and supply must be in balance along a path of steady growth, which is inherently unstable. That is why the theory of growth *needs a theory of demand.* To insist on demand, however, may obscure the fundamental issue. It may suggest that the answer lies in a theory of demand which is in some sense independent from the theory of investment and income creation, whereas it must be first of all *a theory of demand consistent with the analysis of the growth process.* It must be a *theory of demand growth.*

The approach presented here focuses on the forces endogenous to the market economy which determine the structuring and expansion of the market, a fundamental issue for the long-run theory of effective demand. To be sure, market expansion cannot take place without the evolution of consumption patterns. A theory of demand appropriate to the analysis of growth must explain both aspects, that is be indeed a theory of output. In particular it must explain how spending contributes to and follows from investment decisions, not just how income is allocated and consumption decisions are made. This follows precisely from the idea of extending the principle of effective demand to the long run.

It can be concluded that: (i) a theory of the growth of demand must be a theory of how new markets are endogenously created by the growth process; (ii) the theory of demand appropriate for the analysis of growth has at its core a dynamic theory of consumption. Thus the basic theoretical scheme presented here consists of a circular process of determination in which the investment in market development, that is the 'autonomous' component of investment, determines, through changes in the 'consumption sphere', both the form taken by consumption evolution and the conditions for market expansion.

Structural evolution, which is regarded as a result either of supply factors or/and of exogenous shocks, attains in this framework a different meaning. On the one hand, change in consumption represents the stimulus to investment. On the other, investment contributes to the creation of new markets, not only because it creates additional income, but also because it fuels structural dynamics and changes of output composition. Indeed the internally generated stimulus to market creation is intertwined with structural dynamics. New markets are the result of the drive to market creation. Investment determines structural change and market creation and then it is sustained by market expansion and structural evolution.

The structural dynamics connecting consumption and growth is driven by the endogenous transformation of the sphere of needs satisfaction, the consumption sphere, which involves firms and socially molded individuals. In particular, the deliberate effort of firms to shape the market for growth, that is their strategy of market development, and individuals' drive to self-seeking lead the process of change of the sphere of social life which, in a market economy, sustains the existence and development of needs. Consequently the evolution of the consumption sphere determines the conditions for the realization of the growth potential of the economy as a whole.

METHOD

Given the characteristics of the investigation, it is important to say something about the method pursued in the analysis, which is that of the critical examination of theoretical arguments concerning the long-run process of economic development, highlighting and discussing in particular the role played by demand.

Contrasting Schumpeter's and Pasinetti's schemes, I formulate a set of interrelated questions. The critical evaluation is carried on to the theory of consumption, to highlight the advancement with respect to standard neoclassical demand theory and the extent to which it can be the basis for the analysis of the consumption–growth relationship. I then proceed to lay out the basic structure for a theoretical treatment of the question following the analysis of the growth process of Levine (1981). I incorporate the results of the previous chapters in a scheme centered on potential demand, the evolution of the consumption sphere and firms' market development strategies.

This theoretical framework is not designed for empirical testing of competing theories of the long cycle. It is nevertheless conceived as a framework capable of guiding more focused empirical studies. In general, empirical investigation must determine the concrete form taken by the evolution of the consumption sphere and help to read into the actual patterns of transformation the process of market creation. Indeed market creation, that is the expansion of the market, proceeds from the structural dynamics associated with the stylized facts of specific phases of economic development.

The empirical analysis focuses on the 1980s. I present some statistical evidence and some econometric exercises to illustrate the structural dynamics of the years of the recovery with particular reference to consumption evolution. Its results are then used to discuss the structural transformation of the period within an interpretation centered on the notion of a new consumption–growth regime. Such interpretation takes into account also a series of stylized facts and tendencies pertaining to structural change, industrial transformation and labour markets. It is a hypothesis on the new characteristics of the growth process after the exhaustion of the expansion potential of the long phase culminating with the 1960s cycle.

Thus, from the point of view of its internal structure, the book has three parts: the conceptual framework, which is general and theoretical in purpose; the empirical evidence, specific to the 1980s recovery; and the interpretation of the period, which addresses the larger question of the long-term pattern of the consumption–growth relationship.

STRUCTURE

In order to further clarify its logic and structure, let us consider in more detail the organization of the book. I have pointed out the importance of contrasting the Schumpeter and Pasinetti schemes and especially their views on structural change and the role of demand. In Schumpeter's view investment in new industries leads to industrial transformation and changes in the volume and structure of output. This implies reversing the causation going from final demand to production which is typical of the 'static' approach of economic theory.

At the center of the theory of economic development is the role of the entrepreneur's view and the effects of innovation on growth. The reading of Schumpeter's *Theory of Economic Development* suggested here is instead centered on the notion of potential demand, a notion which is implicit in his view of entrepreneurship and capitalism's long-term viability. Schumpeter's emphasis on the endogenous nature of the growth mechanism is most significant precisely when linked to a notion of demand latent in the process of economic development. This refocuses the attention on demand within the analysis of growth.

The centrality of demand evolution for the growth process is neatly exposed by Pasinetti. His contribution clarifies the relationship between demand and structural change, an issue hardly discussed within most growth theories. When technical progress, and therefore productivity growth, are uneven among sectors, structural change is ultimately governed by demand composition, which evolves following a non-proportional expansion path driven by per capita income growth.

Indeed Pasinetti goes a long way in the formulation of a new theory of growth and structural change. He may, however, have overlooked the possibility of developing some of the insights contained in Schumpeter. At the same time his investigation is constrained by the premise he starts from: Pasinetti's main concern is a rigorous discussion of the implications for the long-run dynamic equilibrium of changing industries' proportions. As a consequence his demand theory cannot do away with exogenous preferences, which end up determining the composition of output. Structural dynamics in the end is governed by demand, but the overall dynamics of the model depends on exogenous factors.

These limitations may not be relevant for Pasinetti's purposes. Still they suggest that a different approach to demand can endogenize the process of consumption evolution and give direction to the analysis of new markets formation. This is what I meant in arguing that 'economic theory should develop a theory of demand consistent with an analysis of growth' (Gualerzi, 1996, p.159). In this respect the most important result of Pasinetti's scheme is that productivity growth results in a potential for new consumption which must be used if full employment is to be maintained. In the scheme new markets represent only this necessity, but do not emerge as a result of the operation of growth process itself.

It then becomes necessary to focus on the theory of consumption as such. Here we find the well known distinction between micro and macro analysis. In the field of consumer theory the limitations of the rational choice model are the topic of a vast literature; ultimately they depend on the fundamental characteristic of the rational choice model, to be a purely allocative, static theory of consumer decision making. The criticism led to distinct theories of consumer behavior and to several alternative views of consumption and of consumers, but has not been able to confront directly the issue of taste formation. Even less has it elaborated the connection to the growth process. This is so despite the variety of the criticism and the recognition of some scholars (Amartya Sen in particular) of the role played by economic development. To move forward in the direction of a dynamic theory of consumption is necessary, not only to remove the presupposition of given tastes and given means to satisfy them, but also to begin to examine directly the relationship between consumption and the growth process.

In this respect the book reconsiders the work of Duesenberry. He argued that the criticism of the microfoundations is the only way to address the question of consumption at the macro level and analyzes their connection. Admittedly he is not concerned with the consumption–growth relationship as such, but, much in the same vein, he argues that the necessity to go beyond exogenous taste and study instead the forces which in a modern market economy determine consumption spending is in the very nature of the problem of consumption. Consequently Duesenberry's analysis of consumption sets the stage for that study of the relationship between growth and consumption at the macro level, primarily because it shows that consumption spending is not independent from social interaction and economic change.

Thus the criticism of consumer theory indicates the difficulties of the rational choice and exogenous preferences to be an adequate foundation for a dynamic theory of consumption and suggests that the theory should shift from the question of consumer choice to the question of consumption evolution. On the other hand, the macro theory of consumption is concerned with the level of spending, not with its composition. Consequently it cannot elaborate the connection with the process of structural change and economic development either. The change of perspective is then marked by the necessity to articulate a view of structural change where consumption evolution represents an active, rather than passive, force and potential demand is a part of the economic development process.

Levine's analysis of the growth process, centered on the notion of 'structure of expansion', is part of a more general appraisal of the objectives and the method of economic theory. This may be the reason why it contains the notions needed for a theoretical treatment of consumption appropriate for our present purposes. The structure of expansion accounts for the successive determination of the rate of aggregate growth through firms' market development strategies, while the consumption sphere evolution responds to the process of development of individual needs.

Combining the notion of potential demand, which motivates the view of the entrepreneur, with the idea of an economic structure exploiting the latent potential of socially determined needs, I have defined the core of the process which governs, through the transformation of the sphere of consumption, consumption patterns' evolution and the creation of new markets. In particular, changes in the modes of satisfaction of socially determined need feed the observed evolution of consumption patterns, while the interaction of firms' market development strategies and the constitution of individuals within a mode of life acts as a stimulus to market creation. This accounts for the process of self-expansion while determining the conditions for its replication on an extended scale.

This scheme is quite distinct from Levine's analysis of systemic growth. It is much smaller in scope and has a more specific objective. It is designed to analyze in general the form of the consumption–growth relationship and read in the structural dynamics of specific phases of development the process of market creation with its impact on growth patterns. Specifically, in the book, it helps to identify *the main discontinuity in the pattern of transformation and structural change of the US economy,* that is the transition to a new consumption–growth regime, which is the peculiarity of the 1980s recovery and the key to its interpretation.

The relevance of the empirical analysis in the book is thus twofold: it highlights the pattern of structural change associated with the recovery and it permits us to discuss on a factual basis the characteristics of the new consumption–growth regime and its implications for growth patterns. The empirical analysis also enables us to qualify some often unquestioned claims about the profile of the recovery and the nature of the 1980s expansion.

The fact is that this decade is widely considered a period of boom, driven by new products and the expansion of new industries, and a return to prosperity after years of low growth rates (Bartley, 1992). My use of the term 'recovery' instead simply stresses that in the middle years of the decade there was indeed an upturn in GNP growth rates. A brief examination of macro trends suggests, however, that it was a peculiar kind of recovery, weak by post-war standards and marked by a deep process of uneven development within manufacturing and between sectors.

Furthermore, the process of transformation emerging from the empirical analysis cannot be easily reconciled with a view of the recovery led by investment and new products that fills the most enthusiastic accounts of the period. This suggests that the process of change is considerably more complex and contradictory, leaving open the search for other explanations. Thus calling into question some commonly held notions serves to enhance the alternative interpretation presented in the book.

The pattern of transformation of the consumption sphere is consistent with a regime of '*consumption deepening*', associated with the differentiation of consumption patterns and the concentration of spending in certain areas of consumption. This implies and is sustained by a process of industrial transformation best described in terms of growth around a few dynamic sectors and pervasive technology changes. Combined with economic and social polarization, this leads the process of '*intensive growth*' of the market. The change in the structure of consumption in particular highlights the existence of significant phenomena of market creation in certain areas of need. With all its limitations this interpretation of the 1980s is relatively successful in explaining the characteristics of the recovery in the US economy and traces the broad lines of a process which may be the general trend of industrialized economies.

To conclude, it is useful to present a brief summary of the content of the individual chapters. The first chapter examines some textual evidence from Schumpeter's *Theory of Economic Development* on the role of demand in dynamic analysis. It then discuss the implications and the questions it raises for Schumpeter's view of the long-term viability of capitalism. The notion of potential demand is implicitly contained in such a view. It permits us to go beyond the limits of the neo-Schumpeterian perspective, but also of the notion of 'demand-creating technical change'. Chapter 2 presents an examination of Pasinetti's approach to growth and structural change. It is precisely within this theoretical perspective that the question of an endogenous determination of the growth process *and* of consumption patterns appears fundamental. It leads to a reformulation of the problem of demand within the growth process for which current consumption theory, examined in Chapter 3, is by itself insufficient.

Chapter 4 goes on to show that underneath the distinction between micro and macro approaches to consumption lies the static nature of consumption theory and that the criticism of consumer theory cannot become a truly dynamic theory of consumption, which is in essence based on the relationship between consumption evolution and the creation of new markets, flowing out of the internally generated process of structural change. This idea is an essential aspect of the long-term pattern of 'transformational growth' (Nell, 1998). The chapter then introduces the theoretical scheme centered on the relationship between consumption and growth by presenting the main characteristics of the theory of transformational growth and of the approach based on the notion of structures of expansion (Levine, 1981).

Chapter 5 goes on to elaborate Levine's theoretical framework in the direction of a theory of the mutual determination of the growth potential of the economy and the sphere of need satisfaction, where individuals define their social identity through the forms of satisfaction of needs. It concludes by presenting a reformulation of the theory of demand-led growth. Chapter 6 discusses the relationship between this framework and empirical analysis, introducing the question of the 1980s recovery and its interpretation.

Chapter 7 shows that, considered within the cyclical pattern of the US economy in the post-war period, those years hardly represent a strong upsurge and that the recovery has indeed some peculiar characteristics. Focusing on the growth rates of output further highlights quite distinct patterns of growth and decline within US manufacturing. These self-contained results identify the crucial aspects of the recovery and give a first picture of the structural transformation of the period. This analysis is pursued in Chapter 8 which examines the long-term evolution of the consumption structure and then tests the accuracy of the predictions of consumption composition generated by an income-led model. The results raise the question of the structural determination of consumption patterns beyond the income-driven dynamics and the role they played in the 1980s. Quite clearly the test is not capable of saying much about this, which is the topic of the discussion of the process of transformation of the consumption sphere in those years.

The following chapter conducts an econometric testing of the hypothesis according to which investment in market development and new products led structural transformation. Despite the limits of the testing model, the conclusions are quite interesting. There is no evidence of a strong correlation between sales and the variables which are part of the fairly traditional view of firms' market development strategies. The test tentatively confirms that the main force behind the expansion was not an investment push driven by innovation, leaving open the question of the characteristics of the process of market creation.

Chapter 10 draws some conclusions from the main results of the empirical analysis and elaborates on their interpretation considering some general trends of industrial transformation and consumption sphere evolution. The characteristics of the transformation suggest that the recovery is associated with the transition to a new regime of consumption deepening and intensive growth of the market. Such an interpretation is discussed in the last chapter, which then speculates on the long-run prospects of the structural dynamics associated with the transition.

The nature of the structural break did indeed become clearer in the 1990s. In fact, the general framework centered on the consumption–growth relationship helps us to understand the current trends of transformation. The conclusions in particular elaborate on the questions raised by the development of the information and communication technologies (ICT) and the new Internet scenario emerging at the end of the 1990s.

THEORETICAL PERSPECTIVES

The approach presented in this book, though not comprehensive, has the advantage of focusing on the fundamental process of expansion of advanced market economies. Thus it may be described as a theoretical and empirical contribution to the theory of growth and structural change (Baranzini and Scazzieri, 1990). In this respect it attempts to pursue empirically the analysis of 'the structural dynamics of a growing economic system' which Pasinetti indicates as a research topic arising from his appraisal of growth and structural change (Pasinetti, 1981, ch. X; 1993, ch. VI). To be sure this is done with respect to the characteristics of a specific phase of expansion, but this in turn clarifies the relationship between theoretical and empirical analysis of structural change. The latter should illustrate the main trends of the actual structural dynamics which are then interpreted with reference to a set of theoretical concepts and an overall view of the growth process.

Two other contributions shape the investigation and are discussed at length in the book. The main differences with Levine's approach have been indicated above: the concern with the actual pattern of growth is possibly the sharpest distinction. Levine's most recent research instead goes on with the theoretical analysis of the fundamentals of the theory of consumption (Levine, 1998).

With respect to the transformational growth approach the analysis of the growth–consumption relationship can be located between the level of the general theory (Nell, 1998) and the empirical studies of historically determined instances of transformation. The analysis of the structural dynamics of market creation contributes in particular to an understanding of the growth of demand in the long run, therefore addressing the central issue of the process of growth.[1] Furthermore the elaboration of consumption theory, and in particular the analysis of innovation in consumption, helps us to better understand the role played by technical change within the pattern of transformation.

More generally, the focus of investigation suggests a comparison with those theories that share the same interest in the causes and nature of the long-run process of expansion of market economies. A careful assessment of similarities and differences should be pursued elsewhere. It is sufficient to highlight how the approach presented here can contribute to addressing some open questions.

Neo-Schumpeterian theory has elaborated Schumpeter's scheme into a theory of the long wave centered on the interaction between innovation and industrial system. Though surfacing here and there, the issues of demand and of consumption patterns never become central to the explanation of the process of cyclical expansion. This is relevant per se, but has relevance also for the structure of the theory. Neo-Schumpeterian theory has been criticized in so far as it relies too much on technological push. The discussion around 'technological determinism' has led to an interesting, but at times inconclusive, debate. One could suggests that these limits may depend on a partial understanding of the message contained in Schumpeter's *Theory of Economic Development* and that a theory of demand growth may be a key issue. This seems to be the case when we notice that also the recent development of the Schumpeterian tradition in the direction of an evolutionary approach lacks any systematic treatment of the demand side. Addressing this open issue may contribute to a more satisfactory theoretical perspective.

Other long-waves theories, in particular the US Social Structures of Accumulation approach (Gordon, Reich and Edwards 1982; Bowles, Gordon and Weisskopf, 1990; Gordon, 1998) and the French 'Regulation School' (Aglietta, 1979), have instead stressed mainly the role of socio-institutional dynamics in determining macroeconomic results. The study of the regimes of accumulation, typical of the Regulation School, is interspersed with references to consumption changes. Some of them can indeed fit quite well in the view of the consumption–growth relationship presented in this book. However, similar in this respect to the Schumpeterian tradition, neither the Regulation School, nor the scholars who make reference to what is at times loosely labeled 'Post-Fordism',[2] have engaged in a detailed discussion of consumption evolution.

Consequently, there are limits to what they can accomplish in terms of articulating the growth process in distinct phases of development. This affects in particular their capacity to analyze the structural dynamics following the years of rapid growth and the *decline of mass production*, and to address the main issues pertaining to the long-run prospects of advanced market economies.

NOTES

1. The effort of placing demand at the center of the analysis of growth is quite consistent with the focus on policies capable of preventing stagnation tendencies from taking over the world economy (Halevi and Fontaine, 1998).
2. For a broad overview on the issues raised by the transformation see Harvey (1992).

1. Economic development, technical change and demand

1. SCHUMPETER'S THEORY OF ECONOMIC DEVELOPMENT[1]

1.1 Economic Change and Consumer Demand

In the theory of economic development, Schumpeter's main concern is to highlight the fundamental mechanism of growth and transformation on which the long-term viability of the market economy rests. Thus, not the facts of economic history, but the essence of the process of change accounting for the cyclical path, is the focus of the theory. For this very reason Schumpeter considers inadequate the method used by economic theory to analyze change. In his view comparative statics can at best be used to analyze the slow process of adaptation which follows from disturbances of the static equilibrium, or changes in the 'non-social data (natural conditions)' and 'non-economic social data (... the effects of war, changes in commercial, social, or economic policy)' (Schumpeter, 1934, p.62). But the essence of the problem of economic development is rather the occurrence of 'revolutionary' change, that is qualitative change, which cannot be analyzed in reference to equilibrium positions.

The distinction between comparative statics and dynamic analysis is also fundamental for Schumpeter's discussion of the role of consumers' demand in the process of economic development, an aspect that has received little attention in the literature. He states (ibid., p.12):

> Production follows needs; it is so to speak pulled after them ... This second 'side' of production makes it at the outset an economic problem. It must be distinguished from the purely technological problem of production. To be sure, we must always start from the satisfaction of wants, since they are the end of all production.

However later on he also says (ibid., p.65):

Yet innovations in the economic system do not as a rule take place in such a way that first new wants arise spontaneously in consumers and then the productive apparatus swings round through their pressure. We do not deny the presence of this nexus. It is, however, the producer who as a rule initiates economic change, and consumers are educated by him if necessary; they are taught, as it were, to want new things ... Therefore while it is permissible and even necessary to consider consumers' wants as an independent and indeed the fundamental force in a theory of the circular flow, we must take a different attitude as soon as we analyze change.

The recognition of the static nature of the model on which demand and consumer choice theory rest implies its irrelevance for the analysis of the process of change on which economic development depends. Changes in the direction of consumers' taste are causes of disturbances of static equilibrium (ibid., p.60n); as such they are not a form of qualitative change and do not need any new method of treatment. Qualitative change arises 'from within' economic life and 'in the sphere of industrial and commercial life, not in the sphere of the wants of the consumers of final products' (ibid., p.65). Schumpeter is then quite clear in this respect: consumers are not initiators of change.

1.2   Innovation

At the center of the process of change is instead the disruptive appearance of innovation, a 'new combination' of factors of production, which creates the conditions for profits above the average for the innovator, therefore inserting new dynamism into the competitive process. Innovation can indeed take many forms; its essential feature is the break with established structures and practices.

The conception and realization of new combinations is the social function of the entrepreneur, who, per se, is neither a capitalist nor a manager. His special function is the capacity of overcoming the obstacles which hamper the introduction of innovation: the uncertainty involved in moving outside the 'accustomed channels', which prevents him from relying on established data and rules of conduct; the psychological reluctance to overcome the habits of thought and action ingrained in the routine of running business; finally, the 'reaction of the social environment against one who wishes to do something new'. In one word the entrepreneur must be capable of 'leadership', a special kind of function distinct from a 'mere difference in rank, which would exist in any social body' (ibid., p.87).

There is certainly something very specific about the Schumpeterian notion of innovation, and of the entrepreneur, despite the broadness of its definition. Indeed, it suggests that it is not its form per se which is relevant, but rather its effects on the pre-existing productive structure. Schumpeter seems to think that, from the point of view of economic development, the fruitfulness of innovation is the amount of displacement it creates and the amount of structural adjustment it calls forth. The stress laid on the discontinuous and 'revolutionary' character of the changes is reflected in his characterization of entrepreneurship.

Focusing on the necessity of disruption, he leaves largely uninvestigated the question of structural transformation following such changes, though it is essential to determine the meaning and scope of innovation itself. The problem emerges even more clearly when examining the relationship between types of innovation and cycles. Van Duijn (1983) speaks explicitly of a Shumpeterian long wave containing cycles of shorter length. The idea comes from Schumpeter, who, analyzing business cycles, distinguishes innovations on the basis of their effects on investment (Schumpeter, 1935). Basic innovations have large and long-lasting effects such as to sustain the long wave.

To be sure, he considers the diffusion process and its effects on the cyclical pattern of the economy, what he calls the swarming and bandwagon effects. This, however, cannot substitute for the analysis of the systemic effects of the innovation throughout the economy. In particular, the magnitude of structural adjustment, and therefore the stimulus of innovation, depends on the patterns of substitution or complementarity of new and improved products. The point is that the effects of innovation cannot be analyzed in any satisfactory way without explicit reference to market creation, that is, an increase in the size of aggregate circulation, which follows and propels structural adjustment. This aspect remains implicit and Schumpeter certainly does not develop it.

In the end demand plays little or no role in Schumpeter's theoretical scheme. This is true in the sense that there is no space either for shortages of aggregate demand or for market limits to accumulation.

1.3   Mass Consumption and Accumulation

Indeed Schumpeter's views about the long-term viability of capitalism differ from the underconsumptionist strand within Marxian theory, though the latter also insists on the role of new products and new markets in the periodical renewal of the expansion process.

In *Capitalism, Socialism and Democracy* (1942), Schumpeter dismisses the reasons provided for an inevitable collapse of capitalism as speculations untenable in a truly scientific analysis. Neither the tendency towards stagnation, associated with the transition to monopoly capital, nor the disappearance of the historical circumstances which have sustained accumulation into one of the most astonishing periods of development of material wealth is in fact sufficient, he argues, to rule out the possibility of a repetition of the growth rates of the sixty years from 1870 to 1930. The demise of capitalism is, on the contrary, predicated on its internal contradictions, not on its incapacity to overcome the limits to accumulation indicated by its critics.

Schumpeter has his own explanation of such contradictions. He maintains that they originate in the character of the social class which is not identified with but is eventually the social location of the entrepreneur, the bourgeoisie. The roots of the declining spiral of the otherwise self-sustained process of creative destruction are in the incapacity to manage an increasingly complex social and political framework. In other words, it is the very character of entrepreneurship, its dynamism and efficiency, that makes the bourgeoisie less and less capable of political control, an art which requires tools and values different from those bred by the economic spirit of entrepreneurship. It is not the suffocating strength of monopolies, but rather the 'non-heroic' character of the entrepreneur which ultimately prevents him from maintaining control. The bourgeoisie is increasingly inept politically; eventually, that is fatal to entrepreneurship itself.

The mechanism which in principle could sustain capitalism into long-run expansion consists of two parts, connected to the phases of the cycle. On the one hand, innovation creates periodically new investment opportunities; on the other, the improvement of the living conditions of the working class, through mass-produced commodities and price competition, assures market expansion. Schumpeter consequently seems to identify in the penetration of capitalism into new spheres of production the condition for the internal generation of new markets. This in turn sustains accumulation. The improvement of living standards appears to be the socially beneficial effect of innovation, but also the condition for market expansion.

Submitted to the test of efficiency, he says, capitalism passes it with high grades and, if the conditions for entrepreneurship could be retained, there would be no real long-run tendency to stagnation or collapse.

1.4   Unemployment

There is, however, one aspect which is dealt with, to say the least, unsatisfactorily: unemployment. According to Schumpeter, if the economic system could sustain the high rate of growth it experienced, there would be the resources to face the poverty which arises with unemployment. In this respect capitalism could prove itself capable of achievements that even the most optimistic social reformers could not think of. And yet, this is no answer to the waste of resources that unemployment implies. The point is that, within the process of creative destruction, the mechanism accounting for employment of the labor force in the long run is far from convincing.

First, one must assume full employment from the start, otherwise there is no reason for displacement, which is essential to the process of creative destruction.[2] The assumption ties Schumpeter into maintaining that there are no aggregate demand deficiencies and that the compensation mechanism will ensure full employment as the process of creative destruction runs its course. In this framework it is possible to reintroduce factors substitution to ensure the result. Second, unemployment reabsorption depends on the pace at which new industries can pick up the labor force freed by the declining industries.

This compensating tendency must be linked to the 'swarming' and 'bandwagon' effect. Compensation will be easier when some products have entered the phase of expansion which is the most favorable to employment. Therefore it depends on the industrial composition of the macro economy. It seems clear, however, that once the innovation has been fully absorbed into the system, there are more opportunities for automation and rationalization of production, which are labor-saving and potentially harmful to employment. The same applies to the process of consolidation of firms, which is the other characteristic of the downswing. In sum: though a compensation argument is hard to disprove, its credibility as a mechanism accounting for full employment within a scenario of rapid technological advances is dubious. This leaves basically unanswered the question of technological unemployment, treated as a transitory, cyclical phenomenon, one more example of the painful aspects of the process of development.

The assumption of full employment is by far the weakest point of Schumpeter's analysis. The second most disturbing aspect of the scheme is the possibility that a persistent and possibly growing rate of structural unemployment may undermine the purchasing power of the working class and jeopardize market expansion, even if real wages are growing.

2. NEO-SCHUMPETERIAN THEORY[3]

2.1 Technological Systems

The greatest influence of Schumpeter's work has been in the field of industrial organization. This may explain the partial understanding and the scarce attention paid to the macro implications of his theory. In the last twenty years a growing body of literature has overcome this limit, developing the analysis of technical change and long-term growth patterns in a Schumpeterian perspective. We can make reference to this body of literature as neo-Schumpeterian theory.[4]

For my purposes it is sufficient here to make reference to the line of research centered on the notion of technological systems and in particular to the one contribution which lays out the essential features of the analysis of output and employment (Freeman, Clark and Soete, 1982).

Christopher Freeman has repeatedly maintained that the dynamics of technical change cannot be studied but in connection with the empirical study of innovation in specific industries. This point of view implies that there is limited scope for theoretical generalization in a Schumpeterian perspective. The notion of a technological system seems to represents the furthest one can go to capture in abstract terms the relationship between innovation, structural change and macro variables: income, investment, employment.

The notion of technological systems is indeed designed to explain the macroeconomic, long-term effects of basic innovations,[5] and, at the same time, the clustering of innovations, for which neither Schumpeter nor Kondratiev had a good explanation. There are in this respect similarities with the notion of 'natural trajectories' (Nelson and Winter, 1977), which indicates the 'cumulative exploitation of new ideas', some specific to an industry, some of general relevance.[6] When a new pattern of investment, based on these innovations and intended to exploit scale economies, is generalized in many industries, it leads to a productivity boom. The enlarged scale of investment may fuel further process and instruments innovation.

Typically innovation is not an isolated phenomenon. It is rather an interconnected process, in which innovation breeds innovation. The rapid entry of imitators into the industry, the swarming effect, has multiplier effects on the economy and provides the stimulus for related innovations. On the other hand, the diffusion process, the bandwagon effect, which represents 'the steep part of the S-curves' of the product cycle is 'associated with inter-related basic innovations, some social, some technical, concentrated very unevenly in specific sectors'. This emphasizes that diffusion is not a linear, but rather an interactive, process. Further runs of innovation emerge from the interaction between users and suppliers and from the evolution of the business environment. Incremental changes are endogenous to the technological system, that is, they represent its capacity for sustaining itself, regenerating the dynamics of innovation. Discontinuity in the process of technical innovation is then 'more than the statistical fluctuation in the number of basic innovations'. It is rather the burst of activity which takes the form of a 'technological web' of new industries and activities, with the emergence of 'groupings of firms with their subcultures and technologies', combined with changes in the patterns of consumption.

Throughout the stress is on 'managerial and organizational changes', which must accompany the process of development of new technology if the technological system is to exploit and uncover all its potential. The automobile was firmly established only by means of a basic innovation, the assembly line, and the Tayloristic social organization of production, which allowed a dramatic cut in the cost of the gasoline engine. The drastic price cut and wage increases created a market for a product in that particular form, not the steam or electrical engine automobile, but the gasoline engine automobile. This product specification implies specific multiplier and induced innovation effects.

The life-cycle of innovation typically proceeds from new products, to new processes, to product/process improvement. Increasing standardization and economies of scale associated with the maturing of innovation tend to increase capital intensity and narrow down changes to limited improvements and product differentiation. In this way the technological system is approaching its limits. 'An intelligent economic and social policy' may, at this point, be more effective than entrepreneurial initiative to create favorable conditions for the development of a new technology system. Policy can therefore play an important role in determining the turning point of the cycle.[7]

It can be concluded that the viability of a technological system and the course of the long wave, rather than being technologically determined, are the result of many related influences. In particular, the reliance on specific circumstances, the feedback effects and social and institutional evolution suggest that not much of a deterministic model is really possible. This is consistent with Schumpeter's claim that no upswing is equal to another, and the stress laid by neo-Schumpeterian theory on the empirical study of innovation within industries.

2.2   Employment and Investment

Contrary to the little attention paid by Schumpeter to the pattern of employment and wages associated with creative destruction, the question of unemployment is a central theme of Freeman, Clark and Soete (1982): 'we have chosen to focus our discussion on the forces which prevented total labor demand from keeping the pace with the increased supply of labor [from 1973 to 1979]'. Their conclusions, however, do not add much to well established views. The most important force is the deficiencies of aggregate demand. A second reason is the mismatch between labor supply and labor demand and that of capital stock characteristics and requirement of production.

The link between innovation, growth and employment is investment. In the first phase the displacement of workers from old industries is presumably compensated by the demand arising from the capital goods sector and the greater complexity of new products. Then it is the process of diffusion of the new technology and the associated demand for capital goods which sustains the expansion of employment. Accordingly investment is directed first to the creation and expansion of new capacity, then to rationalization and reorganization. It is quite clear that, as the technology system approaches its final stage of development, the employment-generating effects of the innovation become weaker and weaker. Ultimately the volume and characteristics of investment along the cyclical pattern of expansion affect employment, while short-run fluctuations are explained by the trade cycle volatility of investment and the capital stock rigidities.

This approach departs from the accelerator–multiplier model, but the motivation for innovative investment is not contradictory to the notion of 'animal spirits'. Indeed Freeman, Clark and Soete say (p.28):

> Disappointingly, he [Keynes] did not investigate the role of innovations in generating the revival of animal spirits and raising the level of expectations for future profits. But the aphrodisiac effect of a new wave of investment opportunities based on a cluster of innovation is quite consistent with his general approach to expectations and investment behavior.

'Thus, the emphasis is *on the supply side*, that is, autonomous investment rather than on "demand induced accelerator investments or multiplier processes ... as driving forces in economic development"' (p.31).

2.3   Productivity, Output and Demand

The effects of technical change appear as differential rates of productivity growth in fast growing and slow growing industries and in the rise of new industries. Rapid productivity growth implies both booming rates of growth of output and lower prices, which, in turn, reinforce output growth.

Much of the transmission mechanism between productivity growth and output growth rests on relative prices changes. Demand is led by productivity increases, depending on productivity elasticity of price and price elasticity of demand. These two parameters ultimately account for the overall rate of growth of output. The first depends on the market structure, which evolves from less concentrated to more concentrated, along the process of maturation of the new technology. An oligopolistic structure prevails in mature industries. As a consequence the productivity elasticity of price decreases in step with the degree of monopoly: 'over the fourth Kondratiev long wave, and with the flattening out of growth – at least with the "maturing" of some of the crucial main Kondratiev carrier industries – the structure of these industries (as well as overall industrial structure) has become more concentrated, with firms having become gradually more ready to distribute the productivity gains to their employees', in the form of higher money wages, 'rather than to the consumer ... in the form of lower prices' (p.139). In declining industries productivity growth will not be accompanied by expansion. Even if productivity gains are passed on in the form of price decreases, demand will not pick up. Output growth will remain stagnant. The outcome will be unemployment.

In general, 'the weakening of the relationship between employment, output and productivity growth over the post-war period relates directly to a possible fall in the price elasticity of demand' (p.140). Here the role of changes in demand pattern is recognized as one of the issues which 'has received little attention in economic theory'. The exception mentioned is the generalization of the Engel law into a general rule of non-proportional growth of demand, formulated by Pasinetti (1981), which suggests that patterns of consumption are evolving through time quite independently of price elasticities:

> In a situation of rapid income growth such as occurred in the 1960s and early 1970s there is little doubt – from a purely theoretical perspective – that price elasticities might have fallen ... With rapid income per capita growth it is the development of new products corresponding to new consumer wants that is the crucial factor in maintaining the balance between the rate of growth of productivity and the rate of growth of output, and by implication full employment.

Freeman, Clark and Soete hardly elaborate on this issue.[8] The question of demand comes up again when they examine the contrast between Schumpeter and Schmookler, under which lingers the question of the direction of causality between innovation and market. They warn against an 'illegitimate over-simplification' of Schmookler's insistence on the role of demand in determining innovation. They then distinguish two models of innovation contained in Schumpeter's work, labeled mark I and mark II. The second endogenizes innovation within the R&D department of modern large industrial firms. Thus the growing importance of the R&D sector effectively becomes the filter through which demand is integrated in the supply model of innovation.[9]

3.   TECHNOLOGY-DRIVEN ECONOMIC GROWTH

Neo-Schumpeterian theory has been criticized for the excessive reliance on technology as the key factor explaining the long wave. Rosenberg and Frischtak (Freeman, 1986) observed that Kondratiev maintained that the long wave sets the stage for innovation, not the opposite. Consequently capital accumulation is the independent variable of the long-term pattern of expansion and contraction. An approach to the long wave alternative to that of neo-Schumpeterian theory is based on the analysis of institutional change. According to Gordon, Reich and Edwards (1982) it is the stability and dynamism of the 'social structures of accumulation', a set of institutions reflecting social conflicts and forces operating in the labor market, which determine profitability, investment and therefore the cyclical pattern of the economy. Gordon (1987) argues the influence of these social determinations is much more effective than technology to explain the long swing, as shown by his empirical testing of the two hypotheses.

Nevertheless, one must recognize the advances contained in the elaboration of Schumpeter's views on the role of innovation and cyclical development of industrialized economies. The notion of technological system and in general the vast neo-Schumpeterian research program on the study of industrial dynamics, clearly enriches Schumpeter's theoretical scheme. In particular, it definitely goes a step further in overcoming a rather sterile contrast of the supply and demand side, arguing that both have to be considered for an understanding of growth and structural transformation. A good example of that is elaboration of the role of R&D activities. And yet, in this research agenda the demand side has received little attention.

Freeman, Clark and Soete (1982) maintain that 'economic growth is not only accompanied by the rapid expansion of new industries, it also primarily depends on that expansion' (p.32). A technology system is indeed associated with the rapid growth of one or more industries, the 'Kondratiev carriers'. Innovation-led investment is the key to the analysis of economic growth and the stress lies ultimately on the capacity of technological advances to recreate the stimulus for expansion. The more intimate relationship between firms' R&D effort and market is used to explain the development of the large multi-product enterprise, rather than extended to the process of market development and its macroeconomic consequences. Demand influences the clustering of innovation and market saturation marks the upper limit of the process of maturation of the technological system, but the fundamental forces of change are located elsewhere.

In fact, the main theoretical advance for the analysis of growth is inserting technological push into Keynesian investment theory, which gives the long-run perspective to the process of capital accumulation. The

'Schumpeterian' part of the model, with its focus on technology advances and R&D activities, is inserted in an aggregate demand framework, where demand management, combined with industrial policy, has an important part to play. Consequently neo-Schumpeterian theory simply builds much of its macro analysis on Keynesian concepts. This approach to demand is distinctively different from the one presented in this book. It focuses on the level of aggregate demand, not on the process of market creation as part of the theory of economic development.

4.   DEMAND-LED GROWTH

4.1   Autonomous Demand and Growth

Despite the advances, neo-Schumpeterian theory remains, to a large extent, an elaboration of technology-driven growth.[10] The positive effect of technical progress on productivity growth is the source of the process of change and the transmission mechanisms rely on market signals. The relationship of productivity and output growth is therefore analyzed following Salter's (1966) approach: 'The problem is basically to fit productivity and technical change into the context of prices and cost'. When the analysis proceeds to consider the relationships between 'changing productivity and other economic variables', the major problem is 'the absence of a suitable framework in which to organize our factual knowledge of productivity' (p.4). From this point of view the Neo-Schumpeteriam perspective seems to provide precisely a framework where that relationship can be discussed in a more articulated and meaningful way.

In another theoretical view, that of Kaldor (1966), the strong positive correlation between output and productivity is explained by a reverse causation: the rate of growth of output, spurred by autonomous demand, creates the stimulus for productivity increases. Quite independently of the controversy on the order of causation between productivity and output, which is discussed in a large literature and has been hardly solved by recourse to empirical testing,[11] what is relevant here is to emphasize that this approach contains the elements of an alternative perspective on the relationship between technical progress and development.

Kaldor's view is based on Young's seminal work on increasing returns (1928). The most original and far reaching aspect of Young's argument is that the economies of scale associated with increasing returns are of a quantitative nature, that is, increased productivity, but also embody qualitative aspects, that is, changed composition of output. The idea of market expansion and division of labor leading to increasing returns contains, at least implicitly, the idea of structural change. Still, rather than developing this aspect, demand-led growth has remained dominated by the focus of an exogenous demand stimulus which drives the sequence of productivity and output increases. Typically such a stimulus could come from exports (export-led growth). But then, of course, this poses the question of the sources of demand growth, that is a theory of its endogenous determination.

4.2   Demand–creating Technical Progress

A recent development of this approach is of particular interest in the present context. Hiroshi Yoshikawa (1995) discussed the Japanese growth experience using a model centered on the interplay between technical progress and demand constraints. The theoretical parts of the book discuss demand-constrained growth and the implications for Keynesian theory, both old and new (p.19). There one finds an elaboration of the relationship between technical change and demand.

The first step in the analysis is the introduction of an exogenous demand component in a Harrod–Domar growth model (p.399). This highlights 'an awkward feature of the implicit investment function in the Harrod–Domar analysis ... the *higher* the growth of exogenous demand, the *lower* the growth of investment' (p.400). This is so, argues Yoshikawa, because no real attention is paid to investment. It would be otherwise clear that embodied technical progress has also a demand–creating effect.

> Investment is customarily identified ... on the supply side. I argue, however, that investment embodies the demand-creating technical progress ... Specifically, investment would expand future demand for the firm's product, perhaps through the introduction of new products (*products innovations*), an improvement in the quality of existing products, or a reduction of their prices (*process innovation*). (Ibid., p.400)

In this way the demand–creating effect of technical progress shifts upward the (downward sloping) demand curve facing firms and lifts the demand constraint. Consequently demand-creating technical progress is a crucial determinant of the growth rate.[12]

It is interesting to note that Yoshikawa's main theoretical argument is the rejection of the attempt of much of current economic theory to explain business cycles in terms of consumers' preferences and changes in the elasticity of intertemporal substitution (p.397). To lend support to his view he makes explicit reference to Schumpeter, quoting the exact same passage of the *Theory of Economic Development* used in this chapter to illustrate Schumpeter's point of view on the role of consumers' demand.

This confirms that indeed Schumpeter's remarks on consumers' role in economic development lead not to a denial of the role of demand, but, on the contrary, to the elaboration of a notion of demand appropriate to the process of economic development, an aspect which has remained largely uninvestigated by Schumpeter. Yoshikawa's demand-led model goes beyond the technology-driven scheme of economic development that remains the benchmark of the Schumpeterian perspective. In particular, it turns the Schumpeterian focus on technical progress and investment away from the supply side, showing that it is consistent with a demand-led view of growth, and gives full relevance to the notion of industry-driven market growth which is the positive statement contained in Schumpeter's remarks on consumers' demand.

And yet his demand-led approach to growth falls short of an explicit discussion of a theory of demand growth. This becomes apparent once we proceed to the final stage of the argument: 'The search for markets has no place in standard neoclassical theory, but it is, in fact, vital for the growth of the economy' (p.394). Indeed the question of new markets is a crucial issue for demand-led growth and for Yoshikawa's model. The exogenous rate of growth of demand must be explained, otherwise it remains hanging in the air. But, having gone this far, Yoshikawa does not follow through with a theoretical discussion of this issue. He quotes Young[13] and proceeds to presents his explanation: 'I argue that historically the following sources of demand growth were important in many countries, including Japan: (i) population growth, (ii) Lewisian dual structure, and (iii) exports' (p.413). Earlier he had made reference to the importance of wars for Japanese growth (p.17; p.393–4).

This confines Yoshikawa's theoretical analysis to a combination of stylized facts. The first is, in Schumpeter's view, a fundamental 'non-economic' factor; the second makes reference to a well established mechanism of long-run industrial development; the third is the reassertion of an external stimulus to domestic growth. These causes may indeed be historically the core of the explanation of Japan's growth path. They are certainly susceptible of being integrated in a mechanism relevant for an interpretation of the development experience of industrialized economies. But they are not sufficient for a theoretical analysis of the growth of demand.

The criticism is not concerned with the relevance of 'non-economic' factors, nor with the importance of singling out the economic forces which, in historically specific circumstances, determine the economy development path, but rather with their capacity to identify the inner mechanism of development Schumpeter sought. Such an investigation must follow a different path. Yoshikawa's model has the merit of showing how demand-led growth can be used to study long-term development and its relationship to technical change. He also mentions the distinction between structural and accidental factors.[14] His final remarks, however, confirm quite clearly that a theoretical investigation of demand growth is not what he is primarily pursuing. This, I would argue, should start from a full appreciation of the criticism of consumer theory contained in Schumpeter's work.

5.   ECONOMIC DEVELOPMENT, POTENTIAL DEMAND AND MARKET CREATION

Demand theory is based on non-satiation and diminishing marginal utility. Underneath is the non-economic nature of taste, which is a given for the economic analysis. Thus Schumpeter regards the determination of output by wants permissible only for purposes of static analysis. As far as economic development is concerned, innovation leads output composition and structural change, consumer demand follows. This criticism opens the way to a theory of taste formation alternative to that based on exogenous taste and consumer sovereignty and to a dynamic theory of consumption. In turn, this should be part of the analysis of the endogenous mechanism of market creation, which could explain the growth of demand and the rise of new markets, therefore completing the Schumpeterian view of economic development. It would also serve to integrate the idea of demand–creating technical progress, elaborated by Yoshikawa, into a theory of consumption evolution.

The irrelevance of the sphere of wants for the process of economic development leads Schumpeter to a view of demand evolution shaped by producers. This, however, leaves undetermined the sources of demand growth and the issue of new markets. It exposes even more cogently the need of a theory of growth of demand. It would also be misleading to conclude that taste is shaped exclusively by producers. The development of needs has an important component which is autonomous, depending on the development of the individual. It is then appropriate to think of changes in modes of life as the domain that can be brought to bear on the meaning of new combinations. In this context the consumer is indeed important, though not as an isolated individual.

Precisely because it is not concerned with any particular event, but rather with the abstract mechanism of change, Schumpeter's view of economic development is open to the integration of the demand into a theoretical scheme which otherwise remains dominated by the supply side. The point is to develop an appropriate notion of demand: not current demand, but rather the demand which is implicit in the very notion of development, that is potential demand, is relevant for a theory of economic change. The latter is latent in the existence of unsatisfied wants and must indeed be the variable which connects the entrepreneur's vision, which goes beyond and actually conflicts with the current economic structure, to structural evolution, ensuring the stimulus to growth from within economic life.

Consequently, integrating the demand side into a Schumpeterian perspective seems the most important development afforded by Schumpeter's theoretical scheme. I would argue that this is in line with Schumpeter's view of economic development and could complement, for general theoretical purposes, the approach taken by neo-Schumpeterian theory. The most dramatic instance where the notion of potential demand could be relevant may be precisely the analysis of the business cycle turning point, which has long been a point of debate among long wave theorists, especially if one thinks of guidance for the 'intelligent' policy intervention advocated by Freeman, Clark and Soete.

When looked at carefully, Schumpeter's 'creative destruction' fits quite well the notion of a progressive structuring of the market for its expansion, that is a process creating the conditions for further accumulation. This requires an approach to consumption alternative to that of traditional consumer theory and, in particular, a theoretical scheme where taste is endogenously determined and the expansion of the market rests on the capacity of technical change to exploit needs, while at the same time cutting cost and sustaining investment. These aspects come together in the firms' strategy of market development, in which innovation uncovers new needs, new markets and new investment possibilities, while price reductions create uncommitted income.

I have argued elsewhere that the Schumpeterian notion of entrepreneurship can be better understood if we look at the entrepreneur as the agent taking advantage of new opportunities based on a vision of 'the market to be' (Gualerzi, 1994). Consequently, even if the dynamic of the upswing originates in its initiative, the view of the potential demand is essential to the innovation process and market development concurs in determining its macroeconomic effects. Similarly, though innovation attains its distinct character from the discontinuity typical of the development of science and technology, it becomes part of economic development following the logic of market creation. There is, therefore, support for a view of the growth mechanism which, while not contradictory to Schumpeter's theory of economic development, is not supply-determined. To move in that direction, however, it is necessary to focus on the notion of market creation. This would relieve the theory of economic development from the search of exogenous stimuli as the ultimate explanation of the growth process. Potential demand is the necessary link between market creation and economic development. In turn that implies that a theory of consumption is indispensable for the analysis of growth and structural change.

NOTES

1. The main ideas in sections 1 and 5 of this chapter have already appeared in Gualerzi (1994).
2. Indeed, only if there is full employment does a new combination necessarily imply displacement.
3. The quotes in section 2 are from Freeman, Clark, Soete, 1982, unless otherwise indicated.
4. The early development of this perspective is due to Freeman (1974), who has, alone and with others, largely contributed to this literature; a second theoretical strand originates with Nelson and Winter (1977, 1982). A more recent development is due to Dosi (1984). For a more systematic presentation of the theory, which includes contributions of the main researchers, see Dosi (1988).
5. Basic innovations are those 'that create a new market and a new branch of industry'. They are distinct from major innovations, which 'give rise to new products and new processes in existing branches of industries', and minor and incremental innovations, which represent 'small improvements to existing products and processes'. The same distinctions apply to inventions, which, bearing with Schumpeter's original distinction, are the original ideas, sketches or contrivances of a new product or process. Innovation is the commercial and social introduction of inventions.
6. For example: the process of mechanization, electrification and automation are associated with basic innovations, such as the steam engine, the combustion engine and the computer.
7. However, Keynesian policies of demand management in the 1960s were implemented when the turning point in the business cycle had already occurred 'spontaneously'.
8. They observe instead that that technical change is seen by Pasinetti as a continuous process, though proceeding at different rates between sectors, and that there is no role for small innovative firms, which were crucial for the rapid growth of new industries in the 1970s.
9. 'The "coupling" between science, technology, innovative investment and the market, once loose and subject to long time delays, is now much more intimate and continuous' (p.41).
10. One should note, however, that the growing recognition of the importance of institutional dynamics, both at the level of the enterprise and at the level of the economy, may change this fundamental trait.
11. Though ultimately subscribing to Salter's view, Freeman, Clark and Soete themselves point out that the empirical results are less than compelling.
12. 'The preceding analysis of firms' behavior can naturally be carried forward to a theory of growth of the macroeconomy. Above all, it leads us to focus on investment as the key variable. It also suggests that the most important ultimate factors in explaining economic growth are the growth of exogenous demand θ, and the demand-augmenting technical progress which is embodied in investment γ. The long-run growth rate is $\theta / (1-\gamma)$' (p.408).
13. 'It is dangerous to assign to any single factor the leading role in that continuing economic revolution which has taken the modern world so far away from the world of a few hundred years ago. But is there any other factor which has a better claim to that role than the

persisting search for markets? No other hypothesis so well unites economic history and economic theory' (Young, 1928, p.536).

14. 'The growth rate of demand depends on many factors, some of which may even be accidental to the economy' (Yoshikawa, 1995, p.431).

2. Pasinetti's structural dynamics and demand theory

1. STRUCTURAL CHANGE AND NATURAL RELATIONS

1.1 Development, Structural Change and Demand

The main conclusion of Chapter 1 is that Schumpeter's *Theory of Economic Development* represents a good starting point to analyze the dynamics of market economies in so far as it addresses the fundamental question of the endogenous mechanism of growth and development on which the dynamism rests. Schumpeter, however, is hardly considered part of the theoretical literature on growth, both because of the broader, non-formalized approach it takes, and because of his focus on innovation and the cyclical pattern of expansion of the market economy. It is, in other words, a world apart from the traditional approach to growth of economic theory.

Indeed what he discusses is development, that is a process of uneven, cyclical expansion whose inherent feature is structural change. In his scheme structural change is represented by the emergence of new methods of production and of new industries; that is, innovation in the broad sense which drives the long-term pattern of expansion. Structural change is therefore not an additional feature which must be fitted into the growth path, which is the problem in growth theory, but rather the very source of extra profits and therefore of the form taken by the expansion path.

The comparison between Schumpeter's scheme and the approach to growth of Pasinetti is illuminating for the question of the relationship between growth and consumption evolution. Pasinetti's model not only overcomes many of the limitations implicit in the growth theoretics based on steady state models, but also addresses some of the questions of development of advanced economies. It does so in a distinctively different manner from Schumpeter. Most noticeable in this respect is the treatment of the demand side which is ignored by Schumpeter, and also by recent

Schumpeterian schemes. At the same time the limits of his approach raise new questions for the relationship between growth and demand.

Indeed the second conclusion of my critical examination of Schumpeter's *Theory of Economic Development* was that it is supply-dominated. That fundamental feature remains a characteristic of neo-Schumpeterian theory, despite the advancement contained in the notion of technological systems; nor is it addressed explicitly in the contributions which have taken an evolutionary approach or discussed institutional dynamics. And yet Schumpeter's remarks open the way to a discussion of demand in a dynamic setting which can be neither ignored nor reduced to the traditional static theory of consumer choice. The notion of potential demand is an almost natural completion of his theoretical view of development and new markets fit quite naturally into his view of advanced capitalism.

By contrast demand evolution plays an essential role in Pasinetti's model. The reasons for examining in detail his model are therefore both his rigorous analysis of structural change and the closely connected theory of demand he develops. These are the fundamental characteristics of the theoretical scheme, already formulated in the early 1960s, presented in great detail in Pasinetti (1981) and in its most refined and essential form in the book on structural dynamics (Pasinetti, 1993). In this chapter the critical appraisal of these characteristics leads to an evaluation of the limits of the approach to consumption evolution contained in the model and points in the direction of a new theory of consumption connected to the growth process.

1.2 The Theory of Structural Change

Pasinetti's contribution has been fundamental in defining structural change as a theme of theoretical investigation. His model is one of the most comprehensive and formally articulated approaches to the question, which is discussed in a relatively recent theoretical literature (Baranzini and Scazzieri, 1990).

In his introduction to the 1981 book, Pasinetti gives a brief history of structural change analysis. He does not give much space to Schumpeter's contribution, which is mentioned only a couple of times in the entire book. He acknowledges, however, his prominence as one of the very few economists who understood technical change as the 'prime mover' of industrial capitalism and the decline of some industries as an essential aspect of the growth process:

Perhaps, the economist who perceived this process [that of declining industries] more clearly than anybody else was Schumpeter. Unfortunately, he had no clear analytical scheme in which to put it. But he gave at least a descriptive analysis, which he tried to epitomise in a famous expression: 'creative destruction', applied to the disruptive effects of technical progress on some sections of the economic system. (p.230)[1]

Thus, though insightful, Schumpeter's work is limited by his marginalist premises. As a result it could not develop an analytical treatment of structural change. 'Unfortunately, [Schumpeter] failed to grasp the requirements of a theory of production. He adopted the marginal approach, and his sparkling insights died in a long description of a process which his analytical tools were unable to tackle' (p.19).[2]

Pasinetti also examines briefly the contribution of the development literature to the question of structural change. Structural transformation accompanying the transition from agricultural to semi-industrialized and then industrialized economy is indeed a main theme in the analysis of development (Kuznets, 1956 and 1967; Chenery, 1960; Chenery and Taylor, 1968; Chenery and Syrquin, 1975). Nevertheless development theory has mostly bypassed a general theoretical discussion of the issue, focusing instead on the underlying process of industrialization and its implications for development policies.[3]

1.3   A Multisectoral Growth Model with Technical Change

What Schumpeter failed to grasp is essentially the necessity of studying technical change within a structural model derived from the modern theory of production. Pasinetti instead carries on his investigation using a multisectoral linear model which is the analytical tool for the treatment of the most important (and neglected) characteristic of technical change, the fact that it is uneven across sectors.

Within steady state models the rate of technical progress is uniform among sectors. The steady path of growth theory is therefore a dynamic equilibrium which eludes the question of differential growth rates. It embodies the utterly unrealistic assumption that industries' proportions do not change and the demand and supply, growing at the same rate, are continuously consistent with each other. This conceals the fact that, as argued by neo-Schumpeterian theory, the rate of growth of the economy is dependent on a group of dynamic industries; that is, that the necessary condition for growth is the process of changing industries' proportions. Consequently the steady state is not an appropriate abstraction for the study of economic development, which is dominated by a pattern of uneven industrial development.[4]

One might say that the only elaboration on structural change within the theoretical literature on growth is the Von Neumann model. Taking the state of technology as a constraint, the model shows the set of industries' proportions required for the maximum feasible growth rate. However, this is hardly a contribution to the analysis of structural change per se, except for the explicit attention given to the rates of change of industries' proportions which arises in relation to the search for the maximum feasible rate of growth. Furthermore it can be noticed that such a rate is postulated on a passive adjustment of demand composition to the structure of supply.[5]

Pasinetti points out that steady state models appear to be special cases of his multisectoral model, obtained by means of simplifying assumptions. The first special case is that of expansion led by population growth, a 'Cassel–Von Neumann–Leontief theory of growth'. In this case each demand coefficient for new investments must be equal to the corresponding demand coefficient for consumption goods multiplied by the rate of population growth, that is $a_{k_{in}} = g\,a_{in}$ for each sector (p.53). All the physical quantities change at the same rate, g, the rate of growth of population. Consequently there is no change in the structure of the economic system. The same result holds in steady state models with technical progress only assuming a uniform rate of productivity growth in all sectors and that all demand coefficients expand at that same rate. We can then combine productivity growth (O), in the form of labor augmentation, and population growth (g), to obtain Harrod's natural rate of growth. In this case 'Each single sector and the economic system as a whole expand at a rate which is the sum of the rate of population growth and the rate of technical progress'. Accordingly new investment will grow at the rate ($g + O$), that is $a_{k_{in}}(t) = (g + O)\,a_{in}(t)$ (p.64). The 'constancy in time of all the proportions of the economic system' follows from 'the device of uniformity, both in technical change and in demand expansion' such that 'all movements of coefficients cancel out inside each sector' (p.64). Finally, a third special case is that 'in which the rates of change, although different from one sector to another, yet are such that, *in each single sector*, demand grows exactly at the same percentage rate of change as that of labor productivity' (p.88).

These assumptions can hardly rescue the steady state approach to growth; indeed they serve the purpose of maintaining the analysis within what Pasinetti calls 'proportional growth'. Only when these assumptions are removed does it become clear that maintaining the economy on the expansion path is far more complicated than is highlighted by steady state models. In other words, only by the abandoning of 'pseudo dynamics' does the issue of structural dynamics of the growth process come to light.

1.4   Structural Dynamics and the Natural System

Pasinetti's structural dynamics addresses exactly the lack of analysis of this growth–structural change link, which has long been the characteristic of growth theory,[6] going well beyond the results of the growth literature.

It does so, however, on the basis of a very specific understanding of the problem: identify, given the uneven nature of technical progress, the necessary process of adjustment which maintains full employment. A dynamic equilibrium is therefore an expansion path along which full employment is maintained while industries' proportions and resources' allocation change.

Consequently the essence of Pasinetti's structural dynamics is the investigation of how technical change, that is productivity growth differentials, affects the rates of change of output, employment and prices, with respect to a full employment growth path. Full employment, however, is not the result of market forces. It serves only the purpose of investigating the set of decisions which are 'necessarily imposed on the members of the community by the very existence of technical progress. This is a characteristic of any progressive industrial society, quite independent of its institutional set-up' (p.219). In other words, if indeed full employment is assumed to be 'a matter of general concern' then the pattern of structural adjustment can be determined on purely logical terms.

This is the most fundamental level of analysis, the level which, Pasinetti argues, 'Classical economists called natural' (p.xii), in so far as it is previous to any institutional set-up. The entire analysis is therefore concerned with what Pasinetti calls the natural system. The continuity between the latter and the level at which classical political economy pursued its investigation is redefined in the 1993 book by the new focus on the learning principle, which is now explicitly regarded as the fundamental force behind structural dynamics.[7]

As a result, whereas in the 1981 book capital goods were introduced at a second stage, the fundamental relations of the natural system can now emerge independently of any analytical treatment of capital goods. For that a pure labor production model, where labor is the only input, the l_i coefficients, and consumption the only use of output, the c_i coefficients, is sufficient. The condition for macroeconomic stability, $\sum c_i l_i = 1$ emerges directly from the structure of the model and implies that all available labor is utilized, that is implies the existence of equilibrium solutions.

The pure labor production model stresses that not capital accumulation, but learning, is the foundation of economic progress; at the same time it highlights even more sharply the fundamental issue of labor displacement and reallocation implicit in the structural change process, an issue treated in a rather cavalier way by Schumpeter and basically not addressed by steady state growth theory. Indeed proportional growth is a theoretical framework in which the macroeconomic condition $\sum c_i l_i = 1$ remains always satisfied. This is why Pasinetti speaks of 'pseudo dynamics'.

In general it appears that the nature and the objective of the theoretical approach are more fully brought out in the 1993 book, which is also noticeable for the developments in the analysis of the structural dynamics of prices and of the 'natural rate of interest', distinguishing a structural and a monetary component. For the purposes of this work, however, the interest is directed to the quantity side, since it highlights the central role assigned to demand structure evolution as a bridge between uneven productivity growth and full employment. Overall the many changes introduced in the latest presentation of structural dynamics do not alter the fundamental structure of the model and its premises.

The classical legacy Pasinetti claims for its approach is only one of the points which has encountered strong criticism. Possibly the most controversial contention is that the natural system is relevant to an understanding of the growth process of real economies. According to Harris (1982), Pasinetti describes a 'super golden age', in which, though everything changes, there still is full employment. He concludes that the significance of the natural system for the actual macrodynamics is very much in doubt.

I have already discussed in some detail the model in a comment where it was also argued that 'the fundamental aspect which has eluded previous criticism is its reliance on exogenous forces of change, which remains despite the centrality of the learning principle' (Gualerzi, 1996, p.156). Here I should note that especially the conception of equilibrium imbedded in the model and the suggestion that institutions can be added to the scheme of the natural economy have implications for the treatment of the demand side, which is the most distinctive aspect of the model.

2.   DEMAND COMPOSITION AND THE THEORY OF CONSUMPTION

Indeed Freeman, Clark and Soete noticed that Pasinetti basically stands alone within the literature on growth for integrating the demand side into the analysis of growth and structural change. A second distinguishing feature of the model, the use of 'vertically integrated sectors', is essential for that purpose.[8] This treatment of demand is of particular interest for my purposes since it contains a theory of demand evolution which is in essence a dynamic theory of consumption.

Pasinetti observes that there is one thing we know about demand: 'it does not expand proportionally'. Plotting the expenditure in three main groups of goods, necessities, other normal goods and inferior goods, against real income we can observe that the rate of change of expenditure is dramatically different within the same range of income variations. The effect of relative prices is relevant only in certain portions of the curve and is much less significant when consumption 'levels off', approaching the saturation level. After that per capita expenditure on one good, or group of goods, is bound to stagnate.

The treatment of the demand side is therefore based on a generalization of the Engel law, which as such is simply an empirically observed regularity, showing that as income increases the share spent on food decreases. This is the result of the recognition of the existence of a 'hierarchy of needs' such that demands for necessities and inferior goods are satisfied first 'if any other commodity is to bring in any utility at all' (p.72). On the other hand, when approaching saturation level, where neither changes in price nor income will affect demand, the increase of utility of each good or group of goods 'may fall dramatically and become negative', depending on the shape and the section of the Engel curve of the goods considered. In general, as income increases, the needs at the lower levels of the hierarchy, which are satisfied first, tend to become saturated. Consumption is then directed to the satisfaction of higher level needs and potential demand, that is disposable income shifts to commodities whose relative share in the consumption basket will continue to grow though they too are bound to approach saturation levels at some point. As a result 'the rate of change of demand for each commodity will be continually changing over time and will normally be different from the rate of change of demand for any other commodity ... a non-steady rate of change' (p.223).[9]

Needs hierarchy and the income-driven non-proportional law of demand expansion are the first element of the dynamic consumption theory contained in the model. They are the endogenous component since the evolution of spending patterns is internally generated by income growth. However it can at best explain shifts to areas of spending directed to satisfying superior needs; it is not sufficient to determine the consumption basket and demand composition in any finer sense. Indeed the rate of change of per capita demand for each good or combination of goods, r_i's, the unknowns the model must determine, cannot be found without reference to the 'exogenous process of consumers' preferences formation'. Using the 1981 notation (p.82):

$$r_i(t) = f_i\left\{a_{n1},...,a_{n,n-1},a_{nk_1},...,a_{nk_{n-1}}; \frac{d}{dt}\left[a_{n1},...,a_{n,n-1},a_{nk_1},...,a_{nk_{n-1}}\right]\right\}$$

The function f_i embodies the 'non-economic' process of preferences formation, which is another, yet exogenous, influence distinct from that exerted by technical progress. 'The technical coefficients ... influence the r_i's through the medium of two channels: the level and the rate of change of real per capita incomes and the variations in the structure of prices' (p.82).[10] In the 1981 book, taste exogeneity is explained with an explicit reference to the notion of 'human nature': preferences 'ultimately depend on human nature, which represents, in the same way as the technical conditions of production do, a fundamental external datum for any meaningful economic investigation' (p.68). It follows that the model retains consumer sovereignty as the ultimate determination of output composition.

The third aspect of Pasinetti's theoretical treatment of demand is the learning process. Technical progress is itself a learning process which turns new ideas into innovation. The model of a progressive society dominated by a pervasive trend of productivity growth, however, also requires learning on the part of consumers. Through learning their consumption basket grows bigger and more differentiated. In particular, consumers need to discover the utility of new products and to learn their new preferences. The necessity of speeding up consumers' learning arises with the 'periodic emergence of the necessity to find new outlets' and the appearance of new products and/or the revitalization of interest in old ones.

In sum: technical progress determines disposable income dynamics, the hierarchical pattern of need satisfaction and exogenous preferences determine final demand composition, via the rates of change of sectoral demands which enter the determination of the equilibrium conditions. As demand composition changes over time it ultimately determines the structural change pattern and the path of sustained growth, but also the possibility of maintaining full employment.

I have made reference here to the 1981 presentation of the model to stress that the theory of demand is almost unchanged in the 1993 version of the scheme, with a noticeable exception. The notion of human nature has disappeared and the focus is shifted to the notion of learning, both as technical knowledge and as consumption knowledge, as the very engine of the process of change. This new focus, however, does not change the substance of the theory. Rather it makes more evident the lack of analysis of the learning process. The fundamental similarity with the earlier elaboration is the idea that learning of preferences is the mechanism which accounts for changing patterns of consumption expenditure. This does not do much to dissipate the impression that preferences arise 'naturally' and consumers are held back, at least up to a certain point, because they do not know how to spend the additional disposable income which becomes available to them.

Therefore, quite independently of any notion of human nature, the task of maintaining full employment is entrusted to a process of determination external to structural dynamics itself and resting on the extraeconomic nature of taste formation. Preferences are handed down to the economic system without any connection to its own dynamic. Similarly, consumers' learning concerns preferences arising independently of the consumption experience and of the evolution of production. Consequently, 'the integration of the demand side into the analysis of growth, which is potentially the most fruitful step forward, does not lead to an analysis of the endogenous growth mechanisms because of a fully inadequate theory of demand' (Gualerzi, 1996, p.157).

3.   POTENTIAL DEMAND, NEW PRODUCTS AND INCOME CREATION

It should be stressed that these are the consequences of the very logic of Pasinetti's model, which is also manifested in Pasinetti's notion of potential demand.

He observes that 'the relevance of technical progress depends on potential demand' (p.68) and that 'any investigation into technical change must necessarily imply some hypothesis on the evolution of consumers'preferences as income increases' (p.69). However, in Pasinetti's scheme, since the very source of income growth, technical change, is itself fully exogenous, potential demand is identified only with available disposable income; as such it is a passive notion. It indicates just the possibility of consumption, which needs to be validated by the external determination of consumption spending. With potential demand defined as the growing pool of uncommitted income, expanding markets depend on drafting exogenous preferences into the non-proportional expansion path of the Engel law.

It could be argued that the lack of any discussion of the process accounting for the rate of change of income is mirrored in the necessity of an external datum to determine consumption decisions. It does not change much the structure of the theory to assume, realistically indeed, that there must be consumer learning.

The problem is that both technical change and taste are the results of processes external to the determination of the equilibrium conditions. In fact, if it were not so, there would be no equilibrium path to speak of. This in turn can be explained by the fundamental scope of the model: to develop a coherent scheme to study the effects of technical change on a balanced growth path, and the necessary conditions for maintaining full employment.

The model may indeed have the advantage of generality and rigor. But it can capture only some of the questions raised by the macrodynamics of innovation and structural transformation.[11] With respect to the endogenous process of determination and redetermination of the growth rate of the economy, the most useful conclusion which can be drawn from the model is that structural change, and therefore changes in investment composition, is needed to maintain full employment and that output composition has a role in determining growth.

On the other hand, given the theoretical structure of the model, what needs to be developed is the analysis of the relationship between causes of income growth, such as innovation, new products and, in general, structural change, and the recreation of the growth potential by means of changes in consumption spending. Pasinetti's natural dynamics seems almost inextricably linked to these issues, though they rest outside the reach of the formal model. New products are essential to the determination of consumption patterns in at least two ways: they contribute to a larger and more differentiated average consumption basket, that is they help to shape taste and determine the modes of satisfaction of needs and even the emergence of new needs; and they are part and parcel of the process through which technical progress and innovation determine new investment patterns and modify industrial structure and output composition. New products almost inevitably lead to the question of taste formation and to the question of an endogenous determination of consumption patterns evolution.

The dynamics of demand structure evolution investigated by Pasinetti suggests the importance of new commodities and taste formation. Furthermore, in both the 1981 and the 1993 publications, there are plenty of references to new goods and ways of shaping consumer demand which are at odds with the exogeneity of consumer preferences. Similarly Pasinetti not only acknowledges that new goods are an important aspect of technical progress (p.89), but talks about the effort of investors at 'making new models or new products for which they can promote demand'. The necessity that the decision makers in the economic system 'succeed in correctly finding out the new sectors that are to be expanded' raises a second aspect, that of the forces determining the creation of new markets and market expansion in the aggregate. But new industries and new products can only be represented in the model. They do not become forces of change and the model does not acquire dynamism from them. This only confirms that its motion must be determined from the outside.

It seems that precisely because of the theoretical structure centered on the notion of an equilibrium path these questions remains unexplored. Therefore it is appropriate to conclude that Pasinetti's theoretical scheme uncovers questions which can be answered only by going beyond some of its premises. This is indeed the research agenda which emerges from a careful appraisal of his model.

In particular, at the basis of a dynamic theory of consumption it must be recognized that the reference to the hierarchy of needs is not capable of giving determinateness to consumption evolution and it is barely sufficient to define broad categories of goods associated with the notion of necessities and luxuries. But there is indeed a great variety of ways to satisfy needs. The notion of need hierarchy cannot substitute for the discussion of the technological and social dimensions which influence the modes of need satisfaction and the forms taken by consumption activities. This in turn appears to be the consequence of an overly abstract notion of needs, which seem to arise, as preferences, as a result of nature and almost biologically. Consequently the connection with economic development vanishes.

This notion of needs is consistent with a view of potential demand which is solely a matter of income growth. In this respect it should be stressed that the notion of potential demand elaborated in the first chapter in close connection with Schumpeter's views of development appears quite different and more appropriate for the purposes highlighted by Pasinetti. The exploitation of new opportunities of market growth depends on an insight which is specific about need satisfaction and need development. Through research, innovation and new investment this potential demand becomes market creation, a condition for growth. More specifically, the degree of development of the aggregate sphere of circulation depends on the progressive structuring of the market. In turn the structuring of the market acquires specificity in connection with the degree of development of the industry or, more generally, of the productive system.

4.   A NEW PERSPECTIVE ON UNDERCONSUMPTION

It can be concluded that the work of Pasinetti raises two main questions: that of the evolution of consumption patterns, on the one hand, and the process of new markets formation, on the other.

Before pursuing these two questions it is of interest to examine how Pasinetti deals with 'the old controversy about the possibility of market gluts, underconsumption and overproduction', that is the inherent incapability of capitalism 'to develop sufficient demand to absorb the increasing production that technical progress was bringing about' (p.240).

According to Pasinetti, 'there is no inevitability about the slowing down of investment and the appearance of unemployment'. At the same time 'there is indeed an inevitability about the periodic emergence of the necessity to find new outlets' (p.234). To this extent Say and Ricardo were right to regard the concern for an insufficient level of demand as being essentially misdirected. The question is the 'appropriate structural composition' of effective demand, 'and not one of reaching any absolute level'.

The shift of the theoretical focus on demand composition may serve to re-examine the controversy and the merit of old and new underconsumptionist views, giving new perspective to the implications for the analysis of accumulation. However, emphasizing the importance of final demand composition, rather than its level, does not seem sufficient. In particular, it may seem to beg the question of whether there is a tendency towards a full employment equilibrium. The question is made more complicated by the issue of technological unemployment. In Pasinetti's model technological unemployment is a matter of possibility and not of necessity. This is completely true within that theoretical structure because of its very nature.[12]

Such a structure hinges fundamentally on the possibility of human learning. In Pasinetti's view, the difficulties of maintaining full employment are the result of the periodic saturation of certain needs, from which there follows the necessity of speeding up the learning process. Still, in the model, consumers' learning is 'called in' rather than analyzed. Furthermore, it should be noticed that there are circumstances in which learning would not be enough, since even implementing the correct decisions on the part of consumers and firms would not achieve the desired result. In this respect Lowe (1976), using a three-sector model, has shown how difficult, in the presence of technical change, it may be to maintain full employment, since it may require expanding the industry whose demand is falling. To have a structure of demand consistent with full employment would require planning, a decision-making process which does not rely on market signals. Pasinetti himself observes that the possibility of maintaining full employment rests ultimately on policy: 'There is nothing in the structural evolution of technical coefficients ... and of per capita demand ... that will ensure the maintenance of full employment ... it will have to be actively pursued as an explicit aim of economic policy' (p.90).

He is also quite clear on the nature of the problem. 'The point is that this process [of structural adjustment] is not one to be expected automatically. The learning process it entails can by no means be taken for granted ... Difficulties do arise because periodic accelerations of this process of learning are required' (p.242). These difficulties can be, no doubt, very serious, and still one should consider them short-run, non-persistent phenomena which do not prove any built-in tendency; consequently the underconsumptionist argument cannot be accepted.

However, one cannot fail to observe that Pasinetti's scheme leads almost inevitably to stagnation. Indeed the continuous decrease of technical coefficients and the limits set on per capita demand by saturation strongly suggest a tendency for the macro condition to be undersatisfied. Whether or not consumers' learning will be sufficient to ensure the appropriate expansion of per capita demand in new areas of spending is a matter of primary concern because there are few remedies to this potential situation of stagnation: on the supply side, the diminution of the activity rate and/or of labor time; on the demand side, external sources of demand, such as exports.

It should be noticed then that the idea of external stimuli to demand is precisely one of the answers suggested by underconsumption theory. Rosa Luxemburg put forward a somewhat crude interpretation of the schemes of reproduction, showing that the tendency towards overproduction could be offset only by tapping into new, external markets, like those of the Third World. She thought that to be the fundamental reason for colonialism and imperialism. More generally the underconsumptionist interpretation of Marx (Bleaney, 1976) and stagnation theory suggest that the demand generated by capitalist development is insufficient and that is the source of recurrent crises of accumulation. For this reason they have stressed the sale effort and consumer manipulation as ways to overcome an insufficient rate of growth of demand.

It therefore seems fair to conclude that there is some similarity about the theory of demand contained in Pasinetti's structural dynamics and the views centered on market limits, though the two are on opposite ends as far as the appreciation of consumer sovereignty is concerned. True, Pasinetti focuses on consumers' learning, which, however, remains largely unexplained. Aside from that, both are forced by the structure of their theory to make reference, in one form or another, to exogenous demand sources, this similarity revealing in the end the same lack of an endogenous theory of the growth of demand.

NOTES

1. The quotations in this chapter are from Pasinetti (1981) unless otherwise indicated.
2. He does not, however, fail to mention, in a footnote, Schumpeter's comment on marginal utility: 'Marginal utility theory may well have been, as Schumpeter puts it (*History of Economic Analysis*, New York 1954, p.888), "a purely analytic affair without reference to practical questions"' (1981, p.13n).
3. 'Although some broad patterns of industrial development emerge at successive levels of per capita income (in terms of both the level of industrialization and the composition of the industry by principal products), these patterns largely reflect the similarity of

industrialization strategies and policies. They do not indicate an optimal industrial growth path' (Cody, Hughes and Wall, 1980, p.21).

4. It should be noted that the steady state has a different meaning in different theoretical perspectives. It is a path towards which the economy gravitates only in neoclassical growth theory. Joan Robinson has suggested considering it purely a benchmark. Indeed there are reasons why steady growth is logically untenable for the study of economic development (Nell, 1982).

5. Derived from Von Neumann's model is the so-called 'Turnpike Theorem'. A set of proportions is used to achieve rapid growth of the system, to reverse later to another intended to maintain steady growth.

6. One may note also that this question is not touched by the research agenda of the so-called 'new growth theory', which however may help 'to formulate the question of endogenous growth within Pasinett's model' (Gualerzi, 1996, p.156).

7. 'The learning principle ..., which is at the root of the pure production (labour) model, ... goes down to a more profound level of investigation. The classical economists intuitively perceived the importance of moving down to this deeper level: they called it "natural". In the present work, the "natural" relations emerge as having pre-institutional characteristics, and thus as being even more fundamental than in classical analysis' (1993, p.xv).

8. 'Only final commodities will be considered. No intermediate stage and thus no intermediate commodity, is explicitly represented. All production processes will be considered as vertically integrated, in the sense that all their inputs are reduced to inputs of labour and to services from stocks of capital goods' (Pasinetti, 1981, p.29).

9. 'At any given ... income and price structure ... All goods and services may ... be classified into three categories: those goods for which demand is at the bottom of the corresponding Engel curves (zero demand); those goods for which demand is somewhere in the middle of the corresponding Engel curves; and those goods for which demand is at, or is near ... the saturation level' (p.73).

10. The function does not include the $a_{k_{jn}}$, the new investment coefficients, nor the $a_{k_{ji}}$ replacement coefficients. This only stresses what Pasinetti maintains explicitly later (p.176), that new investment demand is derived demand. They are not, strictly speaking, technical coefficients, but rather demand coefficients, but do depend on technology, since they reflect also the capital intensity of the production process.

11. This may not be the purpose of Pasinetti's scheme. But then of course the problem is the 'theoretical practices, purposes, and uses to which the model is put' (Harris, 1982). This criticism does not have to be confused with the lack of a theory of technical change, which, as Pasinetti notes, 'would pertain to a much wider field than economics' (p.67).

12. It suggests that natural dynamics, stripping the issue to the very essence, can only highlight how the question can be posed.

3. Consumption theory

1.   PASINETTI'S THEORY OF CONSUMPTION

The great merit of Pasinetti's model is that of addressing the question of demand within the analysis of growth and structural change. As a result the model directs the attention to the evolution of consumption patterns, that is to the issue of a dynamic theory of consumption, and to the question of the formation of new markets. These two questions arise precisely from the structure of the model and are the consequence of Pasinetti's main contention: full employment can be maintained only if demand composition changes and spending is redirected to new areas of consumption. This follows exclusively from the existence of technical change.

Within the scheme of natural dynamics the answer to these two problems is entrusted to a consumption theory based on the generalization of the Engel curve and on consumers' learning. Thus changes of demand composition follow a one-way process of determination due to income growth, that is exogenous technical change, and exogenously changing preferences. Learning itself, which should ground consumer's choice in social and economic dynamics, is essentially unexplained and brought in to show the possible consistency between demand and output composition. Thus Pasinetti's theoretical scheme, while useful to discuss the effects of technical change on macro–dynamics, uncovers questions which can be answered only by going beyond some of its premises.

To move in that direction we must first recognize the criticism of demand theory contained in Pasinetti's scheme. The existence of an order in the satisfaction of needs, such that a certain level of consumption must be reached if any other commodity can bring in any utility at all, already calls into question the notion of the rational consumer, busy determining his preferred basket of consumption, making marginal substitutions. Though both the hierarchy in need satisfaction and the Engel curve can be dealt with within the dominant theory, the criticism stresses the limits of a static approach to consumption and suggests that factors other than relative prices are far more important to determine choice. Indeed Pasinetti argues that relative prices become important only when the level of demand is approaching saturation levels. All things considered, the income-driven theory of consumption based on the sequential satisfaction of needs, which reflect biological, but also social priorities, and the limits set by market saturation suggests a picture of consumption and of the consumer quite distinct from that of traditional theory.

Precisely because of the questions posed so cogently by Pasinetti's model, the theoretical perspective centered on the consumption–growth relationship requires us to take this criticism further. It is then necessary to consider in more detail the logic underlying traditional demand analysis and the alternative approaches to the analysis of consumption which emerged from the research in the field.

2. CONSUMER THEORY

An overview of the problem is contained in a survey (Zamagni, 1986) which discusses the recent theoretical developments of consumer theory. The survey is particularly useful because it examines both the refinements and modifications of the Pareto ordinal utility paradigm and the approaches which depart from these foundations to develop alternative views.

Zamagni points out that the question of demand theory deals with the very foundations of economic analysis. In classical theory demand has no role to play in the determination of natural prices, whereas it is fundamental for the 'symmetrical' theory of value of neoclassical theory. In such a system utility indexes transform exogenous preferences into demand for products, determining the level and composition of output. The refinements of the Pareto ordinal utility paradigm have in common the effort to improve the coherence and generality of the theory, relaxing some of the assumptions necessary to obtain demand functions with the desired properties. The analytical developments in this direction led to a full-fledged analysis of the duality between demand and utility. The research has shown that the requirements imposed by the rationality principle on the utility function do not fit observed demand functions, but also that some of the axioms imposed on preference relations are unnecessarily restrictive. If one does not want to reject maximizing behavior as an appropriate foundation for the analysis of consumer behavior, it is necessary to loosen these conditions.[1]

However rationality, as defined above, is not the only possible foundation for a theory of choice. The notion of directional choice, developed by Georgescu-Roegen and further elaborated by Katzner, embodies a different notion of rationality, based on local preferences and a myopic consumer. It shows that, for the main purpose of demand theory, that is the generation of demand functions with specified properties, utility maximization is completely irrelevant.

An interesting set of results also follows from the abandonment of the completeness postulate (Gay, 1983). It makes explicit that there can be a number of theories, other than utility maximization, that ensure the respecting of the consumer budget constraint. On the other hand, since choice becomes dependent on a sequence of choices, the notion of demand as a function itself loses meaning. What becomes relevant is the notion of 'instrumental choice' and consequently the link between preferences and constraints. Finally, when choice is not uniquely directed to utility maximization the final objective of choice becomes relevant, so that we can speak of 'teleological preferences'.

The self-imposed limitation of choice options (Elster, 1979; Schelling, 1984) raises another type of difficulty, that of the 'return of preferences', which manifests the alternating pull of distinct value systems on the consumer. The problem illustrated by *Ulysses and the Sirens* (Elster, 1979), observes Zamagni, is not simply that there is no optimization in the computational sense suggested by the theory of rational choice. It lies deeper at the root of the paradigm, to the extent that the alternation suggests the existence of many subjects as agents of choice. Rather than the completeness of information, it calls into the question the notion of the self as a single agent, when instead it can be thought of as a series of many layers, each associated with a set of preferences (Steedman and Krause, 1985).

Within the modification of the rational choice model, Zamagni considers the 'characteristics' model of Lancaster (1971), the 'utility tree' (Strozt, 1957) and Becker's model of household production function (1965, 1976). The distinguishing element of Lancaster's model is the fact that choice concerns not goods directly, but their 'characteristics', some objective properties which make them valuable, and are associated with a certain 'consumption technology', defined with respect to the goods space. The interest of the model is in the possibility of taking into account new products in the formulation of the consumer choice problem. However, the maximization procedure, applied to something like a utility function, defined with respect to characteristics rather than goods, may not result in the desired simplification of the consumer choice problem.

An alternative approach to the same issue is that of the 'utility tree'. Here the separation of preferences related to areas of consumption (food, clothing and so on), which do not compete with one another, has the effect of redefining the problem of choice only within the specific area where the new product appears. The main shortcoming of the 'utility tree' approach is, quite obviously, the lack of any consideration of complementarities, which are at the core of a 'life style'.

The notion of life style can instead be incorporated in the 'allocative model' of time and consumption envisioned by Becker. The household production function model overcomes the separation, typical of traditional consumer theory, between work, as a way of obtaining income, and utility maximization, based on the expenditure of that given income. In particular the household produces the good 'consumption', combining time and goods under a technological constraint, which it later consumes to obtain utility.

The analysis of the time dimension raises new problems. What matters is not only *how much* but also *when* time is spent on the activities of work and consumption, an aspect which is overlooked in Becker's household production function approach. The search for optimal time profiles for work and consumption is the characteristic of the work of Winston (1982) and it is based on the idea that there are things which are pleasant to do and others that are pleasant to have done. Consequently there are different sources of utility. The distinction leads to the two notions of 'process utility' and 'goal utility'; the first follows from the consumption activity itself, the second from the use of the consumption goods. It is then possible to define a number of combinations describing the many possible situations arising from consumption activities. This question has become the matter of further research: Pollak and Wachter (1975) have examined the case of activities which remain internal to the household because of their positive process utility, such as cooking, while others become external despite their positive utility of scope (cleaning). Using the characteristics of domestic activities of consumption, Gronau (1977) has discussed the formation of new consumption markets.

Despite the effort to improve it, the weakness of the explanatory power of traditional consumer theory and the difficulties it encounters to prove its conclusions at the empirical level have stimulated the search for alternatives to the Pareto ordinal utility framework.

The adaptive approach to consumption is anticipated in the work of Simon of the 1950s. It is based on the realization that in the traditional model rational behavior is assumed, rather than derived. Consequently economic theory cannot discuss satisfactorily the consequences of violating the assumption. In particular it is not able to discriminate market outcomes (Debreu, 1974). It is therefore too weak to afford any theory of demand. As a result modern theory has developed models of adaptive consumption (Kornai, 1971; Cyert and De Groot, 1975; Cross, 1983; Parrinello, 1984[2]) in which consumers do not maximize any utility function, but rather adjust their choice on a trial-and-error basis.

A second alternative approach is instead based on preferences discontinuity.[3] Its characteristic is the hierarchical order in the satisfaction of needs, typical of the lexicographic models. The axiomatic statement of this approach is in Chipman (1960), following the seminal work of Georgescu-Rogen. It has been developed by Fishburn (1974), Ironmonger (1972) and Earl (1983). Ironmonger's work, in particular, is most interesting because it discusses how technical change can be incorporated in the analysis of consumption. The idea of hierarchy in wants satisfaction is also important for the notion of life style, which is the key word in the recent development of the behavioral theory of consumer choice (Earl, 1986).

Another line of research makes reference to the notion of endogenous preferences. Pollak (1969, 1970, 1978) elaborated the notion of habit formation and showed that preferences may depend on past consumption. Though demand functions can still be obtained from conventional utility functions, habit formation represents the abandonment of the idea that preferences can be taken as exogenous data.

Plausible as it may seem, the idea has had little impact on the way economists think of consumption, even on those who have been active in modifying the theory,[4] possibly because it requires a fundamental revision of demand theory. Zamagni (1986) points out three main consequences. First, it implies that preferences are not given independently of the means available to meet them. Second, preferences vary according to the relative economic and social position of the decision maker, and ultimately they are defined within the limits of its budget. Third, once we allow for consumption experience and preference interdependence to affect taste it becomes quite natural to consider the effects of the production system on taste, as argued by Parrinello (1984) and Schefold (1985).[5]

Another approach which breaks drastically with the traditional model is that of subject capabilities (Sen, 1985). Needs can be satisfied by different types of goods in different forms. Preferences, however, make reference to goods in the market, which are defined, in a market economy, by other economic agents. It follows that there is a discrepancy between preferences and needs. The notion of subject capability refers to what the subject can accomplish with the available goods. The characteristics of a good then are not independent from capabilities, since a good by itself does not say what the subject is going to get out of it with respect to his needs.[6] The notion of capability has the advantage of incorporating a sense of rationality which is defined more as systematic exploitation of information and of reasoning, rather than in the economist sense of axiomatic maximization.

3. CONSUMPTION IN MACRO MODELS

3.1 The Theory of the Consumption Function

Far from being exhaustive, this overview of consumer theory is sufficient to highlight the seriousness and variety of the criticism. It also points out the numerous elements useful for an alternative theory. And yet the criticism has not so far been able to lay out new foundations to the analysis of consumption patterns and displace the traditional theory.

This situation has its counterpart in the theoretical treatment of consumption in macro models, which is based on Keynes' consumption function. The Keynesian consumption function does contain a theory of consumption, though rudimentary: it is the psychological law embodied in Keynes' marginal propensity to consume. It concerns only the level of consumption, with no connection with its composition.[7] It raises instead a different problem.

Since by definition the propensity to consume is less than one, the law implies that there is a built-in tendency towards an insufficient growth of consumption spending as income grows.[8] If we maintain, as Keynes did, that the absolute level of income determines the level of consumption spending, then, given the short-run consumption propensity, the average saving ratio is bound to increase. This, however, contradicts the observed constancy of the ratio in the long run. In the early debate on the consumption function Keynesians attempted to rescue the proposition, known as the Absolute Income Hypothesis, introducing trend factors that could have, in the long run, a positive effect on consumption expenditure.

It is unclear whether the problem of the relationship between level and composition could be discussed in that context. What is certain is that the successive developments did not focus on this aspect. Both Milton Friedman (1957) and Modigliani (Ando and Modigliani, 1963; Modigliani, 1966) seem to think that the problem with the consumption function is really the lack of solid microfoundations, to be provided by a more adequately formulated and analytically consistent maximizing behavior.[9]

According to Modigliani's Life Cycle Hypothesis, individuals make their decisions about consumption with a time horizon which is that of their lifetime. Their decisions reflect the stream of income coming from their total resources (wealth, current and expected income), not just current income. Oscillations of the consumption ratio therefore follow from the level of expenditure in different periods of this lifetime with respect to current income. The upward shift of the short-run Keynesian consumption function is explained by the new intercept defined by the new and higher level of wealth of individuals.

In Friedman's permanent income theory, consumption depends on the stream of income originating from assets, such as the stock of wealth and human capital, determining permanent income. The contradiction between short-run fluctuation of the consumption ratio and its long-term stability is just the result of the oscillations of measured income, which diverge from permanent income. The difference, that is the transitory component of income, accounts for the short-term oscillation of the ratio and distorts the long-term trend.

3.2   The Relative Income Hypothesis

A different approach to the problem is that of Duesenberry (1949). His alternative to the Absolute Income Hypothesis, which has become known as the Relative Income Hypothesis, rests on the criticism of the microfoundations of choice. It is precisely by showing the connection between the micro level and the macro level of the analysis and the implications of the criticism of consumer theory that the contradiction internal to the Keynesian consumption function can be solved.

Given the contradiction between short-run and long-run consumption ratios, the 'sophisticated Keynesian', says Duesenberry, needs to introduce trend factors.[10] Trend factors, such as the introduction of new products or the effects of urbanization, originating in the process of structural transformation, exert their effect over time and are customarily taken as parameters. However, for reasons that he later examines, he does not find this type of solution theoretically sound. Alternatively, one must reconsider the question of the microfoundations of consumption theory.

'By now ... Hicks and others have shown that the Keynesian consumption function is a special case of the general theory of consumer behavior and can be deduced from it by making certain assumptions'. Questioning these assumptions, Duesenberry argues that individuals do not determine their level and composition of consumption in isolation from the social context, but following the lead and choices of upper income groups. Once they develop certain 'habits' of consumption, and consequently a certain proportion between income and consumption expenditure needed to support these habits, which they regard as normal, they will not adjust them in response to a reversal of income dynamics. There is a 'ratchet effect' at work (p.115).

To fully appreciate the importance and the originality of this contribution let us consider it in some detail. The argument is based on three sets of considerations. Duesenberry develops first a criticism of demand theory, then the implications for the theory of saving. The third step is to test whether the alternative theory fits the factual evidence better than the standard theory.

4. DUESENBERRY'S THEORY OF CONSUMPTION AND SAVING

4.1 The Criticism of Consumer Theory

Tastes have been considered for a long time as 'data of economics'. Even so that does not mean that they 'are constant in time. But it does mean that the parameters of preference systems are substantially independent of the other economic variables. In particular ... independent of the actual purchases of others. Otherwise it would be impossible to obtain aggregate demand curves by the simple addition of individual demands' (Duesenberry, 1949, p.13). The question is of course how can we take tastes as data if their change is '(at least partly) due to economic events? In particular are the preferences of one individual affected by the actual behavior of others? If that is so, the preference systems in existence are the consequence of actual purchases in the past. We cannot say that our problem is to find how the system adapts to the data if the data are changing with the adaptation' (ibid., p.14). Consequently in which sense can we regard them as autonomous from economic analysis?

Preferences interdependence may be known to economists, observes Duesenberry, but it never became the object of their analytical efforts. This has long hidden the fact that if tastes are interdependent the separation between maximizing exercise and the individual and social psychology dimensions breaks down. Even if you are convinced that rational choice cuts through culture and psychology, preferences interdependence undermines the very foundation of the separation between psychology and economics. 'If no changes in taste except autonomous ones occurred, the preference system scheme would serve its purpose [that is to stay away from psychological assumptions]. But if tastes are interdependent, a dynamic development in taste is implied. Analysis in the dynamics of tastes requires an analysis of the driving forces in the development' (ibid., p.17).

Duesenberry dismisses the analysis based on shifting preferences.[11] His conclusion becomes categorically negative when considering that 'both sets [the preference parameters and the parameters 'of the relation governing the shift in preference parameters'] are subject to autonomous changes' (ibid., p.18) and are both unobservable measures. On the other hand, using 'generalized preference systems', that is assuming that each individual has ordered preferences 'for different combinations of goods for himself and for other people' needs knowledge of the shape of the preference functions, which in turn requires precisely those kinds of 'psychological bases of consumer choice' (ibid.) which economists are trying to avoid.

We need instead to assume that the 'central tendencies of the relations between economic variables and consumer choices' (ibid.) result from the operation of certain forces, derived from 'some definite commitments of a psychological and sociological nature' (ibid., p.19) and are captured by the movement of some variables. The gains, Duesenberry argues, no doubt outweigh the loss of perfect generality of the theory.

4.2   The Theory of Saving

If such a theory is successful in explaining 'the facts about saving,' the importance of tastes' interdependence is demonstrated and 'at the same time we lay the groundwork for a general theory of consumer choice' (Duesenberry, 1949, p.19). In other words, the theory should be able to explain consumers' choice and also 'variations in saving', (ibid., p.8). Either it can do both, or neither.

Assuming that 'physical needs are a given datum' and that 'most of the activities carried out by an individual can be predicted if we know his age, occupation, social status, and marital status' (ibid., p.23), the choice between consumption and saving is ultimately a choice of 'the quality of the goods and services [the consumer] uses for any purpose'. Granted that the quantity can be seen as different aspects of quality, 'a decision has to be made as to the quality of the goods to be purchased' in face of the budget constraint and the desire for saving, that is the desire for future welfare. However, 'the mechanism which connects consumption decisions is not that of rational planning but of learning and habit formation. At any moment a consumer already has a well-established set of consumption habits' (p.24). Habit formation is the result of an 'experimental behavior' which may lead to 'regret' for some purchase; the establishment of a pattern of consumption is consequently also the result of the attempt at avoiding this type of disappointment.

He continues, 'our problem is to explain the resolution of a conflict – the struggle between desires to increase expenditure and desires to save or balance the budget. To do this we have to discover the nature of the forces in both sides' (p.25). The analysis of these forces will also lead to establishing whether in our society there is indeed an inherent drive towards higher consumption. The question to ask is: what drives the search for quality? '... we now have to find the source of a drive sufficiently strong to account for the amount of work people do, and for the small size of their savings in face of considerable insecurity'. The point is that 'Ours is a society in which one of the principal social goals is a higher standard of living.' According to Duesenberry, culture and public policy both concur in reinforcing this goal 'as an end in itself'. Consequently 'the desire to get superior goods takes on a life of its own' (p.28).

A way of life includes both needs and ways to satisfy them. A consumption pattern is a 'temporary adjustment', taking into account the income constraint and the rival forces of consumption and saving. This struggle is continuously renewed by the contact with high quality goods 'which makes the latent preference for these goods' manifest. 'Habit formation' is a defensive tool to resist such a pull by restricting our purchases to those we have defined as acceptable. The consumption expenditure of others, through the 'demonstration effect', is a powerful habit breaker. The resistance to giving up saving depends on the frequency of the contact with superior patterns of consumption and the intensity of the desire for saving.

Such a demonstration effect 'need not depend at all on consideration of emulation or "conspicuous consumption"'. Many features of our society work as a powerful mechanism to the hastening of consumption by making it part of the goals of the individual, quite independently of its prime, natural purpose, the satisfaction of needs. For Duesenberry this is 'the social significance of consumption'. Essentially when 'any end becomes a generally recognized social goal ... the importance of the attainment of this goal is instilled in every individual's mind by the socialization process' (ibid.). The pursuit of this goal becomes part of the self-esteem of the individual. Consequently, 'our social goal of a higher standard of living ... converts the drive to self-esteem into a drive to get high quality goods' (p.31).

The stability and smooth functioning of this mechanism depends on the forces of social mobility and the hierarchy of social status. Though 'formally classless', society is characterized by 'a system of differentiated social status'. At the same time there are not 'strong barriers against association among individuals of different status'. Consumption and the demonstration effects are all the more important in a society where status is largely identified not with birth or behavior, but mainly with income. Moreover, since prestige and success are highly correlated with income, the drive towards consumption can hardly be exhausted.[12] It follows that the utility index of a consumer is a function of his consumption level over the weighted average of consumption of individuals with whom he compares himself.

But what is the desire to save? '... attitudes toward future consumption depend on current consumption standards ... [which are] influenced by other people's consumption behavior, and desires for future consumption will be influenced in the same way'. Formally it is a matter of expressing the argument of an intertemporal utility function as ratios to the consumption of other individuals. Duesenberry then derives the foundations of his 'relative income hypothesis': (a) the equilibrium solution of the set of equations representing the intertemporal choice is independent from the absolute level of income, and (b) despite the lower propensity to consume at higher levels of income, as indicated by budget studies, such equilibrium is stable since the interconnection of preferences tends to increase consumption until a new equilibrium position, characterized by proportional increases in consumption, and therefore a stable saving ratio, is reached. This result is not undermined by the fact that it must hold in a dynamic analysis, in which variables, usually treated as parameters (interest rates, income expectations, preference parameters), are not constant any more (ibid., p.39).

4.3   The Empirical Test of the Relative Income Hypothesis

The testing first concerns the main proposition of the alternative theory, 'Our basic theory shows that the saving ratio for an individual family is a function of its position in the income distribution. This result is produced by social factors which are local in character'. The empirical evidence used by Duesenberry is in general favorable to the idea that desired income increases depend, not on absolute income, but rather on who you compare to in terms of social status, and the level of saving depends on the contiguity with people with high income.[13]

Next Duesenberry turns to the problem of changes in saving over time to show that the hypothesis is 'consistent with such facts as are known in the field'.[14] He examines three sets of data: the series calculated by Kuznets for the 1869–1929 period, families' budget studies for two periods 1935–6 and 1941–2, and the Department of Commerce data on saving and income since 1929. He concludes that 'the alternative hypothesis that the propensity to consume is dependent on absolute income and trend factors is shown to be at least implausible ... instead of seeking for trend factors we can reexamine the assumption which leads to the contradiction (between short-run fluctuations and long-run constancy of the saving ratio)' (Duesenberry, 1949, p.48).

Specifically, with regard to new products, he observes that 'Even a hasty glance at the make-up of consumers' outlay in recent decades will indicate how large a portion of it is commodities and services that are distinctly results of modern technology and relatively recent technical innovations.' The listing of innovations can then be a guide to the changing in consumption patterns, but cannot be the answer. On the one hand, 'It can easily be seen that the principal element in the shift of output is the automobile.' At the same time, 'Undoubtedly there were new product developments in other fields but short of tabulating Sears Roebuck catalogues it would be difficult to find them.' We can conclude that 'the major developments in new goods were in the field of consumer durables'. This is as far as we can go. Some more definite answer to the question at hand can be obtained if historical trends can be used to show what has happened to the saving ratio in the absence of such a trend factor.

Using Kuznets' data, Duesenberry shows that while real income per consumption unit had increased by 50 per cent expenditure for durables remained virtually constant until 1909 and so did the percentage of income saved. Consequently, even though in the following decades that expenditure grew considerably, it does not warrant the conclusion that, in general, the savings ratio remains constant because of it. 'If the automobile had not been invented people would have bought pianos and large houses, as they did before when they received higher incomes' (p.61).

5.   THE NON-NEOCLASSICAL THEORY OF SAVING

Duesenberry's book had little impact on the theory of saving. The non-neoclassical theory of saving, however, incorporates much of his argument, as confirmed by the survey contained in Marglin (1984). Comparing alternative traditions of economic analysis, he observes that, 'Outside the neoclassical camp, economists have had surprisingly little to say about the determination of saving propensities' (p.143). Most of the theory that does not make reference to intertemporal maximization of utility relies on what Marglin calls the 'disequilibrium hypothesis'. In equilibrium 'the pressures to spend are supposed to be too great for a typical household to resist'. Saving would arise therefore as a disequilibrium phenomenon, as a residual 'that occurs only when income is increasing at a faster rate than households can learn to spend' (ibid., p.144). This is consistent with the view that 'consumer is a creature of habit who requires time to adjust his consumption to changes in income' (ibid., p.361).

In Marglin's view saving is the result of two 'cultural pressures', that of spending and that of saving, exerted on households and individuals by the system of values embedded in society. Regulating factors are then those connected to the structure of social and cultural beliefs. On the one hand, 'consumption is never enough' as a measure of 'prestige and esteem'. Advertising and the image-producing industries are therefore the tool for enhancing conspicuous consumption in modern capitalism. There is more to it than simply consumer manipulation. 'Advertising is not the villain ... Thus the emphasis on consumption which characterizes the West is not a problem of false consciousness ... Far from being false, belief in the power of consumption is distinctly appropriate to individual survival in our society as it exists' (ibid., p.364). On the other, the 'undermined, but hardly eradicated cultural belief in the virtue of saving' remains. The point is that 'commodity-based solutions to problems of social life' are the only ones available. And this cannot change unless the institutional framework itself becomes a variable.

The latter is what determines the two parameters of the consumption function drawn from the disequilibrium hypothesis. The change in consumption spending is a function of previous level of savings, current income, and the first difference of income, weighted by two parameters, representing the learning of consumers and a measure of unmet wants.[15]

> In the disequilibrium view, the household will, with constant income, just maintain its assets. However, as income varies ... the household will find itself with more or less income than it is accustomed to. Saving takes place when income rises in the average and households are on balance facing the relatively easier and more pleasant task of learning to spend income rather than the harder task of pulling in their horns. (ibid., p.365)

NOTES

1. The revealed preference theory exposes in the clearest terms the central issue discussed in the literature: it solves the conflict with the observed demand functions by inferring the underlying preference relation from market outcomes. If it can be demonstrated that a utility function exists and yields, if maximized, the observed demand function, then we could conclude that the consumer behaves as if he was a utility maximizer.
2. Parrinello's argument is developed in connection with Sraffa's analysis of production. He argues that consumer responses to changes in production cannot be neglected or forecast, because of the endogenous character of consumers' preferences. That is, there is no axiomatic answer to the problem.
3. Sen (1977) has shown that the use of utility indexes rests on the continuity of preferences, which in turn is indispensable for the principle of substitution. However, the plausibility of preferences continuity becomes much less obvious if we abandon the example of trading apples for oranges and instead think in terms of life styles, that is alternative systems of preferences individuals evaluate and choose from.
4. See, for instance, Stigler and Becker (1977).
5. He also points out that the autonomy of preferences from the economic process is essential to the welfare approach and for retaining Pareto optimality as the guideline in devising economic policy (Marschak, 1978).
6. Gibbard (1986) clarifies the point by saying that Pareto ordinality focuses on satisfaction of preferences, not of needs.
7. As noted by Zamagni, Keynes' focus on the aggregate level of economic activity and the nature of consumption spending, a 'passive' component in the process of income

determination, has diverted attention away from the forces accounting for output composition.

8. A regressive income distribution would have an effect similar to an income increase, since it would shift purchasing power towards the wealthy who have a lower marginal propensity to consume, depressing the average propensity. A change in the income distribution in the opposite direction should have an expansionary effect on consumption expenditure.

9. Interestingly this is combined, at least in Friedman, with the abandonment of the notion of income as a flow.

10. An example of that is the early work of Modigliani (1949) where he argues that consumption spending depends on both current and previous highest income. The fluctuations of the consumption ratio then originate in unemployment and income distribution changes, which accompany the downward phase of the cycle. The long-term constancy of the ratio is ensured by the appearance of new products and the improvement of old commodities on which income increases are spent.

11. 'Until a well-developed general demand theory is available, analysis in terms of shifting preferences is a little difficult' (Duesenberry, 1949, p.17). However his model of new products introduction in Chapter VI is an example of such an analysis.

12. 'Success is a goal without a satiation point, and the desire for it, instead of abating, increases with achievement' (p.31, footnote 6).

13. The test is based on a study on income aspiration, a comparison between saving rates of blacks and whites, and BLS (Bureau of Labor Statistics) budget studies, 1935–6, for individual cities.

14. 'All we can do is to set up a theory which seems plausible in the light of general observation and of psychological considerations ... No amount of data can prove a hypothesis, but they can disprove it. All we can do is to take the available materials and see whether they are consistent with our theory' (Duesenberry, 1949, pp.46–7)

15. The Cambridge theory of saving contains distinct saving propensities for two social classes. In the same way these parameters may vary for different social groups.

4. Consumption and growth

1. THE RELATIONSHIP BETWEEN THE MICROECONOMIC AND THE MACROECONOMIC THEORY OF CONSUMPTION

The theoretical literature examined in Chapter 3 summarizes quite well the general approach of economic theory to the analysis of consumption. In particular it highlights the split between micro and macro analysis. The macro approach is concerned only with the level of spending and the choice between saving and consumption. The 'macro choice' between saving and consumption addresses the question of growth, though within the traditional approach of an allocative model in which saving comes first and investment follows. The focus on the aggregate level of spending instead is much more Keynesian in spirit. It certainly follows from the stress laid by Keynesian theory on income determination, but also from the short-run type of framework in which Keynes discusses such a determination. The passive role of consumption appears in that framework justified by the fact that autonomous investment is considered only in its potential for larger output and employment. It is well known that the extension to the long run of Keynesian analysis has brought to light the additional inherent problem of the capacity-creating effect of investment. The inherent instability of the growth path and the tendency of the system to run into overcapacity if investment does not grow at an increasing rate are the main results of the contributions of Harrod and Domar. However that leaves us quite far from posing the question of the relationship between investment and consumption composition.

The reason for that may be the concern with the aggregate level of economic activity, which overshadowed the question of investment composition and structural change, though the latter becomes, quite obviously, a proper topic of investigation in a long-run perspective. Hidden in Keynesian growth theory is, then, as pointed out by Joan Robinson, a steady state path of growth, which carries the implication of constant proportions within sectors.

Pasinetti's analysis uncovers this aspect of the theory, starting precisely from the fact that productivity growth requires changes in final demand composition; as a consequence either we assume a full adjustement of demand or investment composition must change over time. Pasinetti's model is then really important, for reasons, which go beyond 'natural dynamics'. If structural change is an inherent feature of growth, an idea common to both neo-Schumpeterian theory and Pasinetti's model, then the relationship between the pattern of investment and the evolution of final demand becomes a central question for the analysis of the growth process. This does not call into question the central role of investment and of the multiplier in determining output and employment. Simply it calls attention to the structural component of the growth process, that is changes in the volume of spending in new areas of market expansion. We do not have any theory of this crucial aspect, but it certainly involves the process of consumption evolution.

So, how can we be satisfied with a theory of consumption concerned only with spending as a pure, 'passive' component of income growth? Indeed, without reference to a short-run perspective or an assumption of constant proportions, this appears no longer justified and the question of consumption composition takes on a different meaning.

The reason why macro approaches, with the exception of Pasinetti's model, never quite saw this problem may be that they never considered analytically the notion of potential demand, that is the potential for market expansion implicit in the development process of market economies, and did not elaborate its implications for investment.[1]

The recent developments of macro theory have not touched on this issue, which remains outside the reach of intertemporal models of allocation between saving and consumption. Indeed, most economic theory has directed its analytical effort to the search for solid microfoundations for macro choice following a research agenda similar to that of consumer theory. Micro choice is concerned with the allocation of a given income between different goods, macro choice with the optimum allocation between consumption and saving. Therefore the approach of economic theory to consumption rests squarely on this micro–macro distinction, with the two aspects held together by the common reference to the maximizing behavior of independent, self-conscious, rational agents. From this point of view intertemporal optimization appears as yet another application of the same rational choice paradigm. Thus the entire burden of determining output and consumption patterns falls on the optimizing procedure.

The sharp distinction between micro and macro choice, however, breaks down once we recognize that consumers do not determine their choice in isolation from one another and/or independently from economic factors. This is precisely the result when we allow for habit formation and adaptive behavior to influence choice. Duesenberry shows the link between criticism of microfoundations and its macro implications. Preference interdependence and habit formation cause what he calls the 'ratchet effect', which in turn explains the aggregate level of spending.

We can conclude that the micro and macro aspects are interrelated. But this is as far as we can go. Otherwise we ought to discuss more explicitly the relationship between taste formation, consumption spending and growth. Duesenberry, fifty years ago, had prepared the terrain for this type of investigation. At this stage we can only suggest that the separation between the micro and macro aspects is the manifestation of the failure of most of the theory to investigate the structural dynamic which connects the basket of consumption with the level of saving as a residual.[2]

2.   CONSUMER THEORY: LIMITATIONS AND ELEMENTS FOR AN ALTERNATIVE THEORY OF CONSUMPTION

This stands in sharp contrast with the considerable amount of criticism directed at the rational choice model of consumer theory. Both its internal coherence and its relevance have been questioned and the search for alternatives has developed in several directions.

One of the main strands of criticism argues that rational choice is not the only possible theory of choice and hardly the one more appropriate for the analysis of consumption.[3] On the other hand, moving away from goods being directly a source of utility, the attention focuses on goods being able to satisfy wants, and wants are satisfied sequentially.[4] More generally, a hierarchy in wants satisfaction suggests that there is no abstract utility, or human nature, to command the demand for commodities, but rather a fairly stringent sequence of priorities, determined by the logic of reproduction of social life.

Hierarchy of wants, however, does not mean hierarchy of goods, something obscured by the income-driven dynamics of the Engel curve. Ironmonger's (1972) contribution points out that new commodities are an independent determination, distinct from prices and income, of consumption demand through time.[5] We can conclude that there is an ordering in the introduction of consumer durables which is not explained by sole reference to the existence of a hierarchical structure of wants.

Thus the existence of separate wants has opened the way to consider the forms taken by consumption and their variability, since the attention is much more concretely on wants and social forms of their satisfaction. Therefore consumption choice almost naturally appears to depend largely on the evolution of production and the social acceptability of the solutions.

At the same time the issue of changes in the forms of satisfaction of wants cannot be solved purely on the technical ground of products' characteristics. Both Lancaster and Ironmonger in the end have to make reference to a subjective element and to the sphere of wants as something which must be taken as given to the analysis of consumption patterns. This is in essence the meaning of exogenous preferences. They make it possible and plausible to analyze choice independently from the economic process. This presupposition, however, becomes less obvious when we consider preference interdependence.

Preference interdependence, habit formation and adaptive behavior have all in common, rather than a narrow sense of individual choice, the reference to social interaction and the interplay of choice with economic variables, recognizing that they are essential to the formation of taste. As such it is never the consumer in isolation, but rather the social process, which brings into existence a certain mode of satisfaction of wants. Preferences depend on the relative economic and/or social position of the consumer, who develops, within the relative homogeneity of an income group, a pattern of consumption associated with a specific life style. On the other hand, the conception and production of the commodities that make possible and even define the ways in which wants are satisfied depend on the development of the system of production. There is therefore interdependence between taste and the system of production. All these arguments imply some notion of endogenous preferences. Indeed we can conclude that preference endogeneity is a common thread which runs through much of the critique.

These conclusions seem to vindicate Veblen's analysis of consumption. Consumption spending is not just dictated by natural necessity and biological need; it follows rules translating personal and social values into choice. Indeed Veblen's leisure class is important for economic theory, because it is an example of this social mechanism, which can be enhanced by new products and innovation in general.

A last remark concerns the notion of life style. This term appears in several contributions, but it is the cornerstone of the 'behavioral' approach to consumer theory which goes back to the work of H. Simon (Earl, 1986). This notion is useful because it is capable of incorporating much of the new perspective developed by the consumer's theory critique. At the same time it is possible to redefine such a notion in a way more appropriate to the theory of consumption articulated in the next chapter.

In Earl's approach the problem of choice in consumption is analyzed along the lines of a strategic approach to a turbulent and ever-changing environment. From another point of view, the main interest of this notion, which is broadly used also in the marketing literature, consists in the fact that a life style can then be thought of as a socially rooted criterion of choice reflecting a set of 'standards' for the satisfaction of separate wants, ranked according to social priorities and associated with specific modes of satisfaction of needs. The setting in of a life style represents an adjustment designed to cope with wants and available means to satisfy them.[6]

We can conclude that the research on consumer theory has opened the way to a systematic rethinking of the notion of the consumer and of consumption choice. It has also made plain how little we know about the consumer, or, at least, how little is the relevant knowledge on this topic developed or incorporated by economic theory.[7] There is an entire new research agenda on the consumer. Still it addresses only partially the question of an alternative framework for the analysis of demand and output composition, which is instead the main focus of the present work.[8]

The central issue in this respect is the inherently static nature of the rational choice model, the fact that traditional theory assumes that preferences are given and can be expressed with respect to given goods.[9] The notion of life style and the elements leading to an endogenous theory of taste formation take us a step forward in the direction of a new approach to consumption theory, but are not sufficient to develop a theory of consumption evolution within advanced market economies.

If we are to take seriously the challenge implicit in the static nature of consumer theory, it is necessary to begin to articulate the relationship between consumption and the process of economic development. Instead most of the critical literature focuses on agents' behavior and decision making; it is therefore at best capable of explaining the internal logic of consumers' demand. It may open up to broader considerations, which ultimately involve economic development, but does not develop its contribution in that direction. Nor can the problem be solved focusing solely on the consumer. Although important for the process through which consumption patterns emerge and evolve, the fundamental process of determination can be adequately analyzed only with respect to a relevant notion of economic development, which is not that of development economics, but rather the Schumpeterian notion of the endogenous mechanism of growth of advanced industrial economies. This limitation is not overcome in the critical literature, which has addressed a substantially different question and therefore has not felt the need to confront the question of consumption evolution within an analysis of the growth process.

The limitations are apparent when we consider the two most important advances spurred by the critical analysis and based on the notions of life styles and of endogenous taste. Grounding the evolution of consumption in the evolution of life styles may be a far more socially rooted and interesting approach. But it remains to a large extent unable to build on the relationship between consumption and investment, between income and income creation. What accounts for structuring, change, multiplication of life styles? Similarly what is the key to the process of 'change' of endogenous taste? An answer to these questions implies a reference to the unified conception of the process of change, involving production, market structuring and the evolution of consumption patterns. Within that framework it becomes possible to study also choice and consumers' behavior.[10]

This perspective highlights the other side of the problem of consumption evolution: can the evolution of consumption determine endogenously market expansion and therefore sustain growth in the long run? Unless we discuss this question, the growth rate of the market in the aggregate, that is the rate of growth of the economy, is left hanging in the air, or entrusted to a process of determination dominated by exogeneous factors.

3.   MARKET-LIMITED GROWTH

It is useful in this respect to observe that the limitations of the critique of consumer theory are mirrored in an opposite difficulty, which is the characteristic of an altogether different approach: the theoretical literature on market limits. Here the starting point is precisely the analysis of the accumulation process in advanced industrial capitalism, which leads to the conclusion that the rate of market growth is the factor limiting growth. Advanced capitalism, in both the Marxian and institutionalist perspective, can at best manage to keep it under control, but never quite fully overcome this problem. This dictates the entire relationship between growth, consumption and market expansion.

Thus, on the one hand, consumer theory has no theory of development in which to articulate the notion of consumption evolution; on the other, some long-term views of capitalist development argue that growth is limited by the expansion of the market. And yet there is not much elaboration of the issue that is at the core of the problem, the relationship between the process of change in consumption and market expansion.

To be sure, the focus of much of the literature on stagnation stresses the progressive concentration of market power of large corporations and the ensuing growth of profit margins as the main cause of the problem (Steindl, 1952).[11] What is more important is the stress laid on the idea that the growth of markets represents the internally generated barrier to the process of capital accumulation, since sales cannot keep pace with productive capacity.[12]

We have already seen that there is an underconsumptionist strand within Marxian theory, which goes back to Rosa Luxemburg and includes Sweezy's interpretation of Marx in *The Theory of Capitalist Development* (1942). His later work with Baran (*Monopoly Capital*, 1966) insists on the difficulties capital encounters in reinvesting accumulated surplus and argues that the sales effort is one of the ways to overcome this self-created limit. It is, however, insufficient to contrasts the tendency towards overproduction and the recurrent crises of accumulation.

A similar conclusion is at least implicit in the literature focused on the rise of modern corporate capitalism. J.K. Galbraith (1967) argues that the effort of the modern corporation to shape consumption is part of its planning for growth. That is why determining consumer taste is indeed an essential aspect of marketing strategies of large, multi-product firms. Consumer sovereignty is therefore a notion void of meaning in modern industrial capitalism. This is only the result of a stringent necessity. Firms must struggle to maintain and enlarge their market, while market growth in the aggregate is necessary to sustain the corporate structure of industrial capitalism. This leads to a pressure on consumption spending which is at the basis of consumerism. This social phenomenon is the fundamental way in which affluent society relates to consumption spending.

The critics of this process, which accompanied the establishment of mass consumer goods markets, have argued that product differentiation and the manipulation of taste through advertising and the media are the essence of the marketing of 'waste'. The latter, however, has a specific economic function: overcoming the tendency towards overproduction, that is, in the words of one of these critics, the 'nagging prospect of saturation' (Packard, 1960).

Regardless of the role one is willing to recognize in the 'hidden persuader' the hardly disputable conclusion of this literature is that in large mass markets more and more sophisticated efforts at shaping consumption are necessary to maintain demand at levels consistent with productive capacity and productivity growth. This echoes the question of the inherent tendency of the system to run into overproduction. Thus the same problem arises: the system creates its own limits, which manifest themselves as an insufficient rate of growth of sales and of market expansion in general.

I would argue that an oversimplified view of consumption has an important role in leading the theory of market-limited growth to dispose of the possibilities implicit in market evolution and structural adaptation. In other words: though it is important to pose the question of stagnation tendencies present in advanced capitalism, it accords too little relevance to the consumers and to the evolution of consumption. In turn, this impedes a closer consideration of the process of change and of its effects on market growth.

The theories discussed here are noticeable for the little consideration given to taste formation and consumers' demand, which are thought to be essentially unimportant as such, since in the society of corporate capitalism the sales effort, consumer manipulation and consumerism dominate the expenditure for consumption. These phenomena, though important for the criticism of consumer sovereignty and the recognition of the active role of firms, are not by themselves a satisfactory theory of consumption. In particular, they cannot account for the forces constituting a pattern of consumption, except in very general terms, that is referring to the way of life associated with consumerism.

Thus the theory of market-limited growth did not elaborate on the relationship between the process of change in consumption, the internal generation of new markets and the rate of growth of the market in the aggregate. As a consequence the endogenous potential for market creation remains basically uninvestigated. The emergence of new markets is explained solely by the appearance of inventions and new products. Indeed, since the efforts at shaping consumption are remedies constantly running out of steam, ultimately the remedy resides in external stimuli, either in the form of 'external markets', that is sources of demand capable of maintaining demand growth in line with productivity growth, or in the form of technical change, which periodically can recreate the conditions for a new cycle of investment.

These are the 'epoch-making' inventions of Sweezy, reminiscent of the Schumpeterian new combinations generating the long wave of capitalist development. However, production systematically tends to grow at a rate greater than that of market expansion. Consequently the rate of growth of the market sets the limit to accumulation.[13]

4.   THE CONSUMPTION–GROWTH RELATIONSHIP

The contrast between the opposite problems raised by the theories examined above is indeed quite striking. On the one hand, the focus on the limits imposed by market growth on the process of accumulation of advanced industrial economies does not lead to the study of consumer demand and consumption evolution. On the other, even the discussion of new products does not address within consumer theory the question of the interdependence of the process of change in consumption and the pattern of economic development.

It is appropriate to recall that we are dealing with theories that have very different premises and aims. My critical assessment serves only to highlight two opposite and symmetrical shortcomings. As it stands, consumption theory needs some hypothesis about the pattern of economic development and the process of structural evolution, while the theories of market-limited growth need a proper analysis of consumption. This is why the critique of consumer theory cannot articulate a truly dynamic theory of consumption[14] and the theories centered on market limits, though focusing on the dynamics of capital accumulation and corporate strategies, lose sight of the possibilities implicit in the structural dynamics of growth.[15]

It appears that theories considered above, rather than answering the two questions raised by Pasinetti's model,[16] repropose them. Focusing on their basic structure, however, helps us to understand better the nature of the problem and further articulate these questions. In this respect one may notice that, while at opposite ends with respect to the research agenda and the appreciation of consumer sovereignty, they have in common the exogeneity of the ultimate determinations of the process of change and of output composition.[17]

This is a fundamental similarity to Pasinetti's approach.[18] The step forward, however, was to consider both ends of the growth process, which allowed for an explicit discussion of structural change. It is important at this stage to recognize that the dynamic component of Pasinetti's theory of demand is the *endogenously* generated rule of non-proportional expansion of the Engel law. That, however, neatly exposes the fact that there is no feedback of the consumption structure dynamics on income creation.[19] In other words, precisely the element of endogenous determination of the theory of demand suggests a circular, self-determination of the growth process, in which change in consumption may foster and feedback into technology and productivity growth. This aspect of the problem is muted by the reference made to the exogeneity of the ultimate determination of taste and productivity growth.

Consequently, the reference to exogeneity prevents the analysis of the circular process of determination, which is the characteristic of an expanded reproduction approach. But only by taking this approach can the question of the internal generation of new markets be addressed. In fact exogeneity displaces the issue of market creation and makes its analysis impossible. We have therefore an explanation for the lack of any investigation of the issue of the growth of demand, which is a second characteristic common to the theories considered so far.

Within consumer theory, given its static nature, it is less than surprising that it remains entirely outside the research agenda; it emerges quite clearly from the structure of Pasinetti's model. It is the change in the structure of consumption, which leads to considering the possibility of overproduction. The latter may occur if consumers' learning does not accelerate as required by productivity growth. Pasinetti, however, concludes that it is a matter of possibility, not of any built-in tendency. The theories of market-limited growth argue precisely the opposite. Indeed consumers do not even exist in their analysis. And yet, as was pointed out in Chapter 2, the theories on market-limited growth, and Pasinetti himself, must ultimately subscribe to an exogenous stimulus coming from technical change or external markets to explain the growth of demand.

The examination of consumption theory and of market-limited growth permits us now to grasp these questions more clearly and put in perspective Pasinetti's criticism of consumer theory and his answer to the problem of underconsumption. It becomes clear that the fundamental problem lies indeed deeper, at the level the theoretical structure used to analyze what is really the twin problem of the change in consumption and of market expansion. To discuss the issue we have to go beyond a theoretical treatment, which relies on exogeneity to explain the process of change within consumption and in the structure of economic growth. The process of change itself must become instead the focus of the analysis.

An alternative approach should start from the recognition that a theory of consumption evolution, that is of the structure of consumption spending and the choice of items, can be based only on a conception of the development process. On the other hand, this conception must be based on a theory of the growth of the market, that is a theory of its structural determination, capable of explaining the growth of demand in the long run, thus becoming the demand side of the growth process. Indeed a theory of demand appropriate to the analysis of growth process should be able to discuss both aspects of the issue.

The fundamental issue for a theoretical development in both directions is the investigation of the mutual determination of the consumption structure and the structural dynamics of growth. This calls forth a research agenda focused on the consumption–growth relationship. In particular, it implies a study of the basic mechanism connecting the two sides of the process of change and of the form taken by their interaction, in this way overcoming the exogeneity of the stimulus to growth and of the ultimate determinations of consumption evolution.

To give determinacy to the theory of consumption it is necessary to analyze the form taken by consumption evolution and then explain whether and how this process of change sustains market creation and therefore the long-term growth of demand. In other words, it must clarify how the process of change in consumption originates and ensures the reproduction of the system at an expanded scale. In this way the relationship of consumption to economic development loses its generality and can be linked to the pattern of transformation in specific historical circumstances.

5.   TRANSFORMATIONAL GROWTH

In order to develop the analysis of the consumption–growth relationship along the lines indicated above we must turn to a type of literature which is not focused specifically on either consumption or growth, but rather on long-term patterns of structural change and demand evolution. The approach of the theory of transformational growth (Nell, 1988, 1991, 1998) is particularly relevant for these purposes precisely because technical progress and structural evolution are discussed, with attention given to the issue of the growth of demand.[20]

The notion of transformational growth (TG) represents the culminating point of a criticism of steady growth. Steady growth, Nell argues, would inevitably lead to stagnation; transformational growth is thus the process by which capitalism can, at least up to a certain point, sustain itself in the long run:[21] 'To work properly the system must grow, and to grow it must continually transform itself through the introduction of new products and new processes, creating new life-styles, redistributing income and generating new markets' (Nell, 1988, p.159). Growth, therefore, depends on a complex process of change, which involves innovation, income distribution and market expansion.

The starting point of such a process is the introduction of a 'new principle' which means 'a new way of accomplishing some general social purpose' (ibid.) identified with the fundamental necessities of social life, such as food, clothing and shelter. The application of this new principle 'tends to generate an interlocked set of new products and processes, which create new activities and new social patterns, which in turn combine to create new ways of living, new forms of social life'. The result is 'the development of many new industries, and the expansion and modification of many old ones, to supply the needs of both new industries and new ways of living' (ibid., p.160). Thus transformational growth 'tends to be expansive' since it stimulates investment, though that does not rule out problems on the side of employment. Along with changes in the structure of the economy due to the growth of new industries and the new technological requirements of production, the result is 'creating new markets in the process' (ibid., p.161).

However, the direction of transformational growth is not technologically determined. The very pressure on technological change and investment is indeed driven by the social and institutional dynamics, which accompanies the transformation of family-based artisan and domestic production into modern industrial production. Therefore transformational growth is the process underlying the actual structuring of industrial capitalism and in particular it is 'the kind of growth the US experienced during the 1920s, during the war and for the twenty years after the war' (ibid., p.162).

It is based on a process whereby expansion tends to be self-sustaining.

> With new products and new processes coming on line generating new ways of life and new markets employment will be high, productivity and real wages will be growing, profits will be high and capital will be accumulating rapidly, while prices will tend to be stable as cost cutting will tend to offset increases due to high demand. A high level of investment spending means a boom in the investment goods sector; with high employment and high wages in the capital goods sector, the consumer goods sector will also prosper. And the effects will be cumulative. ... Transformational growth, then, tends to encourage a boom. (Ibid., p.163)

In this framework a fundamental role is played by consumption evolution and market creation.[22] In an Engel curve perspective:

> So long as social positions remain unchanged, a rise in income will lead only to minor changes in basic and established patterns of spending, and the additional income will go on new products or on non-basics like luxuries and entertainment. Adapting this to the aggregate, if the social structure is given, a rise in income will lead to greater *discretionary* spending.

Similarly new products which are 'merely improved versions of existing ones' will not reverse the tendency towards a saturation of the markets for consumers' durables.

The argument highlights how the consumption structure is part of the long-term process of transformation. Without major changes in the hierarchy of social status or fundamental discontinuities in the patterns of consumption, even an increase of income may have limited effects. In these circumstances the evolution of consumption is constrained. In other words, without the rise of new ways of life and their extension to a considerable number of people there would be little transformation to speak of. Consequently neither income growth nor innovation by themselves lead to transformation. Growth proceeds from change, but only from change associated with a potential for transformation.[23] What comes to light is that the transformation which matters implies market creation. Indeed 'growth requires transformation and the transformation has to ensure that markets will expand' (ibid., p.167).

Income distribution, but also changes in 'social parameters', such as 'the urban–rural division and the pattern of marriage and family formation', may have a fundamental impact on the rate of new market formation. These factors, combined with major innovations, have indeed marked the development of mass markets in the years of rapid growth of capitalism. Still, though important in an historical perspective, they cannot constitute the main theoretical explanation of the rise of new markets. Similarly, the structural implications for market growth of such pervasive innovations, like the automobile, cannot by themselves be a theory of market growth either. The development they have originated is contingent on a process that is more fundamental of these phenomena.

Indeed, 'the problem in fact lies much deeper' (ibid.). The reasons why 'The transformation draws to an end' depend on the direction of structural evolution and the closely connected issue of the growth of demand. 'It is not a matter of a "shortage" of new inventions or of new technologies; in fact we are in an era of almost unprecedented technological innovation, coupled, paradoxically, with stagnation in investment. This is because many of these innovations tend to be labor displacing or market destroying, rather than expansionary' (ibid.). Why is it so? The explanation goes back to the transition from craft- and family-based production to modern, factory-based mass production: 'For the past century perhaps the chief impetus to growth has been the progressive invasion by industrial capitalism of the traditional province of the family. This has created the great consumer markets of the advanced West ... The market and the state ... have taken over most of the functions previously performed by the family' (ibid., pp.168–9).

In this process technology guided by capital has substituted modern, mass-produced products for those of domestic and handicraft production. It has transformed the industrial structure and sustained market creation and accumulation. There are, however, a number of reasons which suggest that the peak of this type of development was reached during the boom of the 1960s. 'That, for better or worse has been the process of transformational growth. And, evidently, it has come to an end. Given the distribution of income, and in the absence of a major attempt to create new incomes for the poor, there is nothing left to transform' (ibid., p.170). Furthermore the alternative to industrial mass production, which had entered its stagnation in the 1970s, 'the setting up of the information economy, had hardly begun' (ibid., p.171).

We can conclude that the TG approach makes it possible to specify further the nature of the problems involved in the analysis of the consumption–growth relationship. The stylized facts and long-run course of TG are connected to an endogenous process of market creation, anchored to the penetration of capitalist production into productive activities and new spheres of social life. Thus it suggests that the sources of market expansion must be sought in the internal dynamics of advanced capitalist economies. Innovation and new products have a positive effect on growth because of the transformation of the ways of life and that feeds back into the industrial system. In fact, the extension and generalization of capitalist production and market growth are associated with the rise of new ways of living and new forms of social life, not purely with technical change. It is not just a matter, simply put, of new ways of doing things replacing old ones, rather of the role of change in consumption in determining the structural dynamics of expansion.

Income distribution and changes of the social structure have a central role in the process of transformation. They both affect the process of market creation. Income distribution is fundamental for the diffusion of new products and new ways of life, which is the characteristic of the 1960s expansion. Since wages are not rising and there are no social programs to sustain the income of the poor, nor any other mechanism sustaining income redistribution, the spending power and the potential for transformation are constrained, and consequently so also is the process of market creation.

Changes in the social structure are a powerful force ensuring endogenous change and the pressure leading to technology progress and innovation. Indeed, along with the transformation of the structure of production and consumption, entirely new social classes emerge, determining the rise of new ways of life and an increasing complexity of the market for consumption goods. Quite clearly the evolution of the social structure is part and parcel of the process of transformation and therefore it is located at the deepest level of determination of the growth process.[24]

Finally, TG suggests that economic rules, adjustment processes and institutional forms change according to the phases of the process of transformation. They help to shape the concrete form taken by the rise of new markets and new opportunities for investment, but also the limits within which transformation may continue.

6.   LEVINE'S APPROACH TO CONSUMPTION AND GROWTH

6.1   The Structure of Expansion

The TG approach clarifies that growth through transformation occurs by means of a process of change involving innovation, income distribution and market expansion. At the same time it offers a historical perspective to the question of market creation, grounded on the stylized facts of long-term development. It is now possible to focus more narrowly on the relationship between changes within consumption and the process of market creation.

To develop the analysis of this crucial aspect a decisive step forward is the approach to the growth process of D. Levine, whose *Economic Theory* (1981) is an attempt to redefine the object and method of economic theory.[25] The theoretical task goes well beyond my purposes, but, for this very reason, the approach is very helpful to addressing the main theme of the present investigation. The two aspects most relevant are the central position occupied by the 'system of consumption' (Levine, 1981, vol. II, p.226), which implies a reconsideration of the role played by need and individuality, and the notion of 'structure of expansion' (ibid., p.179).

The structure of expansion is responsible for determining the rate of growth of aggregate circulation, that is the growth of the market in the aggregate. 'Investment is the activity of building the structure of expansion. But the peculiarity of capital is to be found in the fact that the building of the structure is also the purpose of the structure' (ibid., p.184).[26] The building of the capital structure, that is of the producing and marketing structure, must be validated by its realization as a structure of expansion. This requires the establishment of the product of the particular capital within the consumption structure. Thus the structure of expansion, while accounting for the internal logic of systemic growth, is the other side of the process of determination of the system of consumption.

From the point of view of the capital structure, and of the accumulation process, the realization of the growth potential of the economic system appears from the start as a problem concerning the relationship between new and established products.

> It is necessary to consider explicitly the determination of that market structure capable of sustaining the growth of the particularized capital structure rooted in the symbiosis of new and developing commodities. Put in a more general language, it is necessary to answer the question: what kind of market is capable of sustaining the capital structure in its most advanced forms? (Ibid., p.203)

What comes to light is therefore the 'mutual determination between the market-creating effects of investment, and the market determination of the form and extent of capital accumulation on the part of the firm'. Indeed private accumulation on the part of firms depends on 'the exploitation of the latent structure of the market, and therefore the realization of its developmental potential' (ibid., p.204). Thus 'the *rate* at which the market as a whole expands, enters into the determination of the rate of growth of particular capitals, while the growth strategies of the particular capitals jointly determine the rate of overall market expansion' (ibid., p.216).

It follows that, while market growth is the result of the deliberate effort of firms to structure the market for their expansion, it ultimately depends on the interplay of firms' growth strategies and the rate of growth of aggregate circulation. Expanded reproduction then depends on the 'structural development of the market' (ibid.); it is the result of occupying a space, economic in nature, which must itself proceed from the structure of production and consumption.[27] Crucial to such a process is the generation of uncommitted income.[28]

Levine defines uncommitted income as the income which is not fixed to sustain a given structure of consumption. That calls into question pricing policies and their role within the overall process of market development. On the other hand, it raises the question of the level of the wage. However, while the wage bargain may have an effect, the generation of uncommitted income 'is always the work of competition and accumulation' (ibid., p.224). This stresses that the creation of uncommitted income is primarily part of the effort to develop the market.

We can conclude that market growth in the aggregate is the result of net investment, determined by the current rate of market expansion and by the market development effort. The latter, however, is the force ultimately responsible for the rate of market growth through a continuous process of structural redetermination.[29] We could say that growth is therefore pulled by the rate of market expansion, but market creation crucially depends on net investment in market development.

Though the demand-creating effects of investment may be depressed by higher profit margins, it is the potential for market development that sustains the expansion process. 'Sustained rates of accumulation of firms require that the potential increase in the productivity of capital be offset by the sales effort and the prospects for market development. Extensive growth can create a developmental potential, but it is the realization of that potential which sustains the process of extensive growth' (ibid., p.228).

For this reason new products and developing commodities are essential to the process of market growth. 'Widespread development of new products may stimulate aggregate demand in such a way as to assure that the demand-creating effects of investment aimed at new product development may absorb those products without diminishing demand for existing products' (ibid., p.226). This calls into question 'the conditions which determine the system of consumption' (ibid.). Specifically Levine argues that interdependence of needs creates the potential for 'a system of interdependent products'. Therefore it 'underwrites the capacity of new product development to act as a net stimulus to investment' (ibid., p.227).

In the next chapter we will see how this happens. Here it is important to point out another aspect of the structure of expansion: while the development of the market, and indeed its structural determination, is entrusted to the growth strategies of firms and to the process of determination of the system of consumption, 'the structure of systemic growth' is the result of the symbiotic relationship of the innovation sector and the developing sector 'defining and exploiting a region of economic space – a structure of need' (ibid., p.232)

The developing sector of the economy is responsible for 'redetermining the growth rate of aggregate circulation ... The multiplier effects set in motion by investment directed to the work of market creation ramify throughout the aggregate circulation' (ibid., p.230-31). In turn, the locus where opportunities for innovation are discovered and exploited is the innovation sector. The two 'constitute a structure of reciprocal determination' (ibid.). Here again the relationship between the developing and the mature sector brings to the fore the question of consumption evolution and its role in determining the rate of growth of the economy. In particular, the establishment of a 'mature sector', lowering the aggregate rate of growth, reflects the necessity that 'new modes of life not only grow within their own economic space, but, in so doing, bring about the displacement of the older modes of life' (ibid., p.233). Indeed, only under particular circumstances does the evolution of the system of consumption imply expansion.

Thus the 'structure of expansion' is substantiated by uneven industrial development driven by innovation, the creation of uncommitted income and evolution of the consumption structure. And yet the system of consumption is far from being determined. This requires discussion of need and need development.

6.2   Socially Determined Needs

Levine discusses need and the development of individuality at the beginning of his restatement of the object and method of economic theory and returns to the topic at the conclusion, discussing the 'social purpose of the market' (ibid., p. 275).

> The attempt on the part of social theory to move beyond the immediate natural determination of the social being and to constitute his concrete condition as a social reality entails first the opposition of the social being to the mode of existence of the species within the 'state of nature'. In society according to Rousseau, 'man becomes other than he is' ... But, having first grasped this independence which is characteristic of the social life of man, social theory displaces it to the 'state of nature'.

That is, the social determination of the abstract person is made dependent 'upon the basis of their different natural endowments' (Levine, 1981, vol. I, pp.32–3). The concrete social determination of the individual

> is first accomplished by classical political economy ... the object of the science of economics is precisely the conception of this sphere within which the free self-seeking of the individual becomes the process of his self-constitution as a social act ... Need is not a quality attributable to the otherwise abstract property owner. It is instead the content of his self-determination, and the objective of his self-seeking. (Ibid., p.45)

It is precisely the freedom according to which social needs are developed which makes them indeterminate, that is impossible to determine a priori. This is in sharp contrast with the notion of needs 'by which the species renews itself within a determinate system of natural relations'. Classical political economy, though insisting on the social determination of need, is not capable of going beyond a conception of need which remains 'relegated to the life of the individual outside society ... since [it] entails the element of constraints and determination which is connected to a requirement of life but not to an individual whim' (ibid., p.47).[30] Consequently, though 'the logical content of classical theory argue forcefully in favor of the necessity of a conception of a sphere of need not determined by any natural interaction' it cannot articulate 'the idea of a distinctive sphere for the development and subsistence of needs, a sphere of economic life' (ibid.).[31]

As opposed to subsistence needs 'which are imposed on the individual' (Levine, 1981, vol. II, p.280), socially determined needs contribute to the individual self-seeking and personal identity. This implies change and variety in the forms of satisfaction of needs. Uniformity over time and space and/or across individuals would be contradictory to the very notion of individuality and then to the notion of socially determined needs.[32] Thus it would call into question the existence of the market. 'No matter how complex the structure of production and consumption, if it is unchanging, then the market is superfluous to its process of renewal ... Change ... poses the economic problem' (ibid., pp.283–4) and is, we may add, the source of dynamism.

In fact, the dynamic force immanent to the structure of production and consumption is the development and the multiplication of needs implied by the constitution of the individual personality within a system of persons. The development of need, latent in the idea of its social determination upon the basis of individuality, is the potential exploited by the growth process and the source of market creation. The notion of 'socially determined needs' is then the basis of the growth potential of the market economy and a constant stimulus to change.

The institutional form which makes that possible and, incidentally, has proved to be rather successful at thriving on 'change', is a system of market relations where the means to the satisfaction of need is wealth. This fundamental characteristic of the market system has itself implications for need development. On the one hand, wealth makes possible the satisfaction of individual needs; on the other, it limits the neediness of individuals. In fact, the process which creates the potential for market expansion clashes with the hierarchy of wealth and income it generates.[33] The question strikes at the very basis of the process of need development and market expansion; it raises the question of the 'social purpose of the market' which, quite appropriately, concludes the analysis. According to Levine, 'While the satisfaction of a particular need can be contingent on the market, the existence of the needy individual as such cannot be made contingent on the market' (ibid., p.305). Thus 'It is precisely the assumption of this contingency, which vitiates the central conclusions of modern economic analysis, and social science more generally. The conception of the market must be consistent with its determination within a social totality not exhausted by specifically market relations. This determination does not eclipse the distinctive character of the market, but allows that character full expression' (ibid.).

NOTES

1. We have seen that in Pasinetti's model the analysis of that potential is confined to the learning process of consumers.
2. Indeed the insight contained in Duesenberry's criticism has been almost completely lost.
3. Herbert Simon has argued that rationality is too narrow a concept to analyze consumer psychology and decision making. Therefore neoclassical demand theory has nothing really to offer in the way of analyzing behavior.
4. This is the far-reaching implication of Lancaster's (1971) characteristics model.
5. His analysis of diffusion processes stresses the importance of the parameters controlling the sequence of related new commodities. In particular the inclusion of a lagged value of consumption seems to work well at isolating the effects of new commodities in the early stage of diffusion and of outmoded commodities in the final stages of decline.
6. As clarified by Sen's notion of subject capability (Sen, 1985), there is a distinction between what is available in terms of commodities and what can be done with them for purposes of satisfying individual needs. A life style may be seen as the result of these two forces, which may be more or less stable and subject to change.
7. In particular the focus on rational choice has led to a remarkable contradiction between the importance formally recognized to the consumer and the extremely simplified view of its role as a utility maximizer, typical of economics (Gualerzi, 1998).
8. As could be expected, there is overlapping between these two themes of investigation. Indeed, this is a topic for further research.

9. As pointed out by Zamagni (1986), this may not be a serious limitation when confronting problems of allocation, but it is clearly insufficient when the focus is on choice within the process of economic development.

10. This approach can also push forward the research agenda on consumption of Post-Keynesian theory. As observed by Lavoie (1994) 'Although there have been few contributions, even few comments, about consumer behavior by Post-Keynesian authors, there is a certain degree of coherence among the few contributions. Indeed, 'The common ground of Post-Keynesian consumer choice theory' can be the starting point for a theory of consumer choice largely consistent with the approach suggested in this book. The analysis of consumption occupies a significant role in Eichner (1987). He shows that the hierarchical pattern of the Engel curve can be combined with a desegregation of consumption to construct a model of households' behavior. The latter distinguishes between needs and products and elaborates on the role of habit formation and non-routine expenditure in determining consumption patterns. Eileen Appelbaum (1992) later developed some of Eichner's ideas on the modeling of the household sector.

11. In this respect it is interesting to note that, 'In Steindl's work, the derivation of a tendency towards secular stagnation associated with a tendency for profit margins to increase is crucially dependent upon the assumption that firms are constrained to invest profits in existing lines of production' (Levine, 1981, vol. 2, p.227n).

12. I prefer to use the term 'market limits' precisely because I want to focus on this aspect of the theory, which is common to both the Marxian and the institutionalist traditions.

13. It is interesting to note that, despite the similarities, Schumpeter was more sanguine about the capacity of innovation and entrepreneurship to ensure long-term viability to capitalism, though he put the issue of market expansion at the center of the investigation.

14. Choice and consumer behavior should be analyzed consistently with the process of change determining, together with taste and life styles, the structure of consumption

15. They neglect the possibility that the process of change can fuel market growth and therefore lack any analysis of endogenous market creation.

16. The evolution of consumption patterns on the one hand, and the process of new markets formation on the other.

17. Consumption theory argues its results on the basis of exogenous changes of taste, while in the theory of market limits the possibility of accumulation depends on the stimulus of exogenous technical change.

18. I stressed earlier that the analytical results of Pasinetti's natural dynamics depend on assuming exogenous the process of determination of both consumers' demand and productivity growth.

19. In general, if the evolution of demand depends on income growth, the question of income creation almost automatically arises.

20. A full account of the theory of transformational growth theory goes beyond the purposes of this book. I am here following the analysis contained in Nell (1988, ch. 7), which specifically seeks to analyze the reasons for the slowdown of economic growth.

21. 'A capitalist industrial system, being inherently dynamic, has two and only two long-run options – transformational growth or stagnation ... These two choices tend to alternate, giving rise to the appearance of "long waves" in economic life' (Nell, 1988, p.163).

22. Indeed one of the reasons why steady state growth is not an acceptable abstraction and it must inevitably result in stagnation concerns consumption.

23. This is why 'A transformation is required that will change the income distribution so as to create new markets' (ibid., p.165).

24. Its relevance is most dramatically highlighted by the transition from family-based to capital-based production.

25. 'The object of economic science is to construct a conception of the system of economic relations established within its generative cycle ... In effect, the condition of self-renewal can be made to replace that of equilibration in characterizing the process within which the system of economic relations is determined' (vol. I, pp.14–15)

26. 'It is as if the putting up of a house, rather than living in it, were the purpose of a house (which is, appropriately enough, the case so far as the contractor is concerned)' (ibid.). Thus, the structure of expansion is ultimately rooted into the process of self-expansion of capital.

27. 'Expanded reproduction of the market is the expanded reproduction of a structure of production and consumption' (ibid.)

28. 'Capital accumulation must create uncommited revenues of firms and uncommited income of consumers' (ibid.)

29. From the point of view of 'the economy as a whole, the rate of market growth which is generated by current accumulation is determined by (1) the current rate of market expansion and (2) the net investment stimulated by the development of new markets. The first factor, however, is itself the result of past operation of the second. That is, the long-run rate of growth of the capitalist economy is the outcome of the realization of its potential for market development' (ibid., p.225).

30. 'Within society the individual can at best articulate a set of preferences, which as such cannot be considered to constitute any real determination. Ultimately the idea that there are needs articulated exclusively within society stands as a reproach to the whole of the history of social theory' (Levine, 1981, vol. I, p.47).

31. According to Levine, classical political economy identifies the concrete determination of the person with the notion of subsistence and makes it the basis for the realization of the person's freedom.

32. Indeed 'Uniformity of need makes individuality purely formal' (Levine, 1981, vol. II, pp.280–81).

33. 'To the extent that the pursuit of individual self-determination comes to dominate over enterprise, the measure of relative social position provided by the stratification of income and wealth ceases to constitute the necessary component of personality structure, and the social rationale for that stratification weakens' (p.303).

5. Towards a theory of the consumption–growth relationship

1. NEED DEVELOPMENT AND THE SYSTEM OF CONSUMPTION

The interest of Levine's contribution is precisely the focus on the logic which governs, in the abstract, the expansion of the market economy and the operation of the system of consumption. He identifies the potential for market creation and growth in the development of socially determined needs, a notion which permits a theoretical treatment of the consumption–growth relationship. In order to proceed in this direction it is necessary to further analyze the working of the system of consumption within Levine's theoretical scheme.

This task is made difficult precisely by the general purpose of his work: that is to reformulate a general theory of the operation of the market economy. It is hard to work with Levine's concepts without being continuously forced back to consider the connection of the single parts to the whole. It is therefore necessary for my purposes to deconstruct to some extent this whole.[1] This is to a large extent a preliminary step with respect to the main purpose of this chapter: to present a theoretical scheme where (1) a new approach to consumption theory incorporates the results of the critical appraisal of consumption theory and (2) the theory of market creation is specified with respect to the initial question of potential demand and to a reformulation of demand-led growth.

It is first appropriate to clarify that the notion of socially determined need is not intended to identify any particular category of needs, but rather the very social character of individual needs. What is at the basis of individual identity and personality structures is indeed the fact that individual needs are socially determined. Development of needs then proceeds on the same basis of individuation and determines the consumption choice.

> The object obtained by a given pattern of consumption is the social recognition of the individual personality in and through its relations with others. Individual personality expresses its particularity through identifying itself with a structure

of needs implying a specific pattern of consumption. So far as the identity of the individual comes to be bound up with a pattern of consumption, for the individual to sustain his identity he must sustain, through repetition, his pattern of consumption. (Levine, 1981, vol. II, p.218)

However individuation, and the development of personality implied in it, is only a potential, is the opportunity implicit in the system of market relations. New products and market development, that is investment on the part of firms, bring out that potential which in turn can disrupt established forms of needs satisfaction. Thus, while individual identity and personality structures come to the fore as determinants of the structure of need, the ultimate reason for its development, and the evolution of consumption patterns, follows from the fact that the forms of needs satisfaction are constantly changing. Investment therefore can promote needs development because it reveals that potential, making change possible.[2]

In order to trace the process of change in consumption and read into it the effects on market growth it is necessary to refer to new concepts, which embody the critical aspects of this process. Levine makes reference throughout to a mode of consumption, that is the way of satisfaction of individual needs, which is at times associated with a form of life,[3] and to a mode of life. A mode of consumption corresponds to a need, a mode of life to a structure of needs: 'The needs satisfied through consumption of commodities constitute a structure which corresponds to a mode of life. It is the mode of life taken as a whole which determines the particular needs, and it is the structure of needs which defines its individual components' (ibid., p.141).

The notion of mode of consumption is designed to take into account the variety of ways in which needs can be satisfied. However, it is 'just because the individual's orientation towards his needs has been generalized, or made abstract, and ideal, that this problem arises' (ibid., p.139). The variety of modes of consumption is the result of the social process by which the system of market relations dissolves the identification of need with fixed forms of satisfaction rooted in custom and tradition.[4] Consequently, 'Consumption is a mode of individuation, but its particular form must be determined by the individual as an element of his self-determination within society' (ibid., p.140). Similarly, the rationalization of the social practice of consumption, that is the capacity of distinguishing between need, social utility and the capability of commodities to satisfy them, 'allows the consumer to fulfill his needs in different ways, and use the commodities which he acquires to construct an integrated mode of consumption expressive of his personality' (ibid., p.141).

The notion of mode of consumption implies then both the existence of the needy individual searching for individuation and the possibility of change in the means of satisfying needs. Precisely because the domain of consumption lost his fixity, rooted in custom and tradition, we have the potential represented by personality development. New products realize and reproduce that potential. It would not exist without a system of market relations governing expanded reproduction, nor would innovation have the capacity to create more then a limited displacement of the form of needs satisfaction. Instead, to the extent that it affects not just the form of needs satisfaction, but their structure and development, it can act as a stimulus to net investment, and therefore as a stimulus to market expansion.

Levine illustrates the role of new commodities within this process using the example of a new writing instrument:

> the typewriter is substantively different from the pen, and, while it defines itself within a mode of life within which the pen is the preeminent writing instrument, it also adds a dimension to that mode of life. So soon as it is perceived to satisfy certain needs previously satisfied by the pen, it is also perceived as a stimulus to the development of altogether new needs. Its potential is also a stimulus to the development of new modes of consumption, and the new dimension it adds to existing patterns is only the starting point in the process of redefining, more or less radically, the very structure of needs which first made the new product possible. What is really new about an innovation can only be known when experience of the social practice associated with its use uncovers its real potential. The starting point must be the unity of old and new; the movement into the unknown world of a new structure of needs starts out by masquerading as a part of the prevailing structure. (Ibid., pp.141–2)

The importance of new products development must therefore be read through its effects on the structure and rate of growth of the market. In fact 'New product innovation is the process of the structural determination of the market ... Innovation, while operating strictly within the quantitative limits of the growth of the internal market, acts to qualitatively alter the structure of the market' (ibid., p.138).[5]

As pointed out in Chapter 4, these effects depend on the characteristics of the system of consumption. 'This system has an inherent structure defined upon the basis of the interdependence of needs. ... the success of a new product may depend upon its ability not simply to replace some existing product, but to stimulate an alteration within a system of interdependent products' (ibid., p.226).

Thus the evolution of the system of consumption appears linked to the process of market creation. The latter is the result of the structural development of the market[6] caused by firm's growth strategies. In fact, in the logic of expansion, individuation through consumption has its counterpart in the firms' exploitation of the potential implicit in the development of socially determined needs, by means of new products and the strategy of market development. Innovation, in particular, disrupts the pure reproduction of established patterns of consumption, changing the modes of consumption and the structure of need identified with a mode of life.

To the extent that the development of need, which reflects that of the individual personality and its social identification, is realized by the strategies of investment, and by new products in particular, it appears that individuality is not independent from the growth process itself and the dynamism of the 'structure of expansion' is contingent on its development.

The evolution of the structure of consumption is therefore a matter of successive specification of modes of consumption within a system of modes of life. This evolution results in new market creation as a consequence of firms' strategies of market development. The latter must do more than introduce new commodities; it must pursue a combination of product development and pricing strategies such as to realize the potential for market expansion. In particular it must establish new commodities within the structure of consumption and create uncommitted income in the process.[7]

Thus, within Levine's theoretical scheme, the development of the structure of consumption is the condition for the realization of the productive structure as a structure of expansion. At the same time change in consumption is not just a zero sum game. It proceeds and implies change in the structural dynamics of growth. In fact, the notion of structure of expansion combines the idea of expansion with that of a changing structure. Investment breeds structural evolution and creates new markets in the process. It can do so only transforming the sphere of economic life which sustains the existence and development of need, the sphere of consumption.

Firms' investment in innovation, given the symbiotic relationship between the innovation sector and the developing sector of the economy, expands the market and creates change, which is the condition for the market structural determination. The evolution of the structure of consumption validates the process of change and recreates the conditions for further market development.[8] Introducing 'structure' into expanded reproduction, the internally generated dynamics of change becomes the mechanism of self-expansion of aggregate circulation. In the logic of systemic growth the self-determination of the growth process is thus a possibility, implicit in the reciprocal determination of the structure of expansion and the system of consumption. The crucial point is the realization of the potential originating in the intensity and direction of need development, which is the force inherent to the system of market relations. The latter, however, must confront also the barriers generated by its own internal dynamics.

It was pointed out before that within a system of market relations the mean to the satisfaction of needs is wealth.[9] Therefore also the creation and realization of the potential engendered by need development depend on the structure of wealth. More specifically, 'The self-development of wealth carries on a symbiotic relation with the development of needs and of the structures of individuation of personality expressed throughout the structure of needs' (ibid., p.174).

In Levine's theoretical scheme the contradiction between socially determined need and self-seeking, as opposed to enterprise and social status, is the contradiction between self-realization through consumption and the limits imposed by the hierarchy of wealth, which is itself a result of market relations. We could say that what makes individuals a potential for market expansion, their self-seeking based on individuality, is both stimulated and constrained by the system of market relations.

This pressure, Levine argues, must be felt also within the labor market. As a necessary input labor cost must be consistent 'with the expansion of capital at a rate determined within the accumulation process'. As a source of income 'it must also be determined in such a way as to be adequate to the needs of the laborer'. Consequently 'laboring must set a limit to the neediness of the laborer consistent with profitability'. In fact it is the wage rate which defines a mode of life and 'the neediness of the worker is, in effect, established given that wage' (ibid., p.297). Accordingly, the laborer is identified not with labor being necessary, but with a determinate 'mode of consumption'.

2. A NEW APPROACH TO CONSUMPTION AND GROWTH

2.1 The Transformation of the Consumption Sphere

Though itself the result of the systemic approach to the analysis of the growth process, the centrality of need development and the system of consumption is the distinguishing feature of Levine's theoretical contribution. This is also the reason why Levine takes a critical view of classical theory.[10] In successive writings he further elaborated the theoretical approach examined above, most notably in his study of subjectivity (Levine, 1998). This certainly allows for a refinement of the theory of need development and the analysis of choice in consumption. The

present investigation, however, goes in a different direction: it develops the
implications of Levine's approach for a theory of the demand side of the
growth process focused on the consumption–growth relationship. The latter
serves to discuss the twin question of consumption patterns evolution and
the structural dynamics of market creation.

The question is now grounded in the analysis of the sphere of economic
life which ensures the subsistence and development of individual need, the
sphere of consumption, a notion which eluded both classical political
economy and modern economic theory. It is a decisive step forward in the
way of endogenizing consumption patterns evolution and the process of
market creation.

The consumption sphere (CSPH) is the sphere of economic life which
realizes the existence of the individual and the development of personality.
This process, however, attains the character of a social determination, that
is the realization of the individual as a social product. Within the CSPH the
social determination of individuals interacting with other individuals is
combined with their realization through consumption spending. The
concrete determination of the structure of consumption is then the result of
the realization of the individuals' need development by the socially shaped
forms of satisfaction of needs. This determines the transformation of the
CSPH, which is sustained over time by the interplay between present forms
and the new ones emerging from the process of change. Change creates the
conditions for long-term evolution and, in presence of the appropriate
conditions, for market creation. Consequently the CSPH contains not only
the structural determinants of consumption patterns, but also the
endogenous principle which sustains the creation of new markets and
therefore the process of market expansion.

In particular, the transformation of the consumption sphere, along
directions which become a proper object of empirical investigation, acts as
a stimulus to net investment. From the latter the stimulus to investment is
propagated into the rest of the economy. It can be noted that, precisely
because it concerns the sphere of subsistence and development of socially
determined needs, the transformation is associated with an 'economic
space', that is with the creation of new opportunities for market expansion.
This space, however, is only a potential. To become market creation, and
then further stimulus to net investment, it must be exploited by firms
through the strategy of market development. This regulates the expansion of
aggregate circulation.

The social process of need development, resting on individuality and its
constitution within a mode of life, guides the transformation of the sphere
of consumption and involves taste formation and the constant incentive to
invent what Levine calls 'forms of life'. On the other hand, the direction of

the transformation and the possibility of innovation in consumption depend on the development of the system of production, whose purpose is to make actual the potential implicit in the needy individual in a definite pattern of consumption. Thus the transformation of the CSPH is the representation of the process of social construction of need and accounts for the internally generated dynamic of change driven by the reciprocal determination of the production system and the constitution of individuals within a mode of life. This is a circular, self-sustaining process, which depends on the recreation of the potential which is at the basis of the stimulus to investment, that is the endogenous creation of potential demand. That potential – that is the possibility and indeed the necessity of the development of socially determined needs – is now specified as the characteristic attribute of a system of market relations. In other words, it is the source of the demand latent in the process of economic development of market economies.

It should be noted that, while the deliberate strategies of firms, together with the identification of individuals through particular modes of consumption and within a mode of life, determine the transformation of the consumption sphere, its overall evolution depends on factors which are not under firms' control. Firms are not in control of the conditions of social reproduction at large, though they have an essential role in determining them.[11] While the role of the system of production is fundamental,[12] the feasibility of a mode of life depends on an adequate development of the system of production, but also on a number of physical infrastructures and social conditions. Thus the evolution of the consumption sphere is contingent on the development of public sector as well as on the rules of civil society.

2.2.   A New Approach to Consumption Theory

We are now in a position to discuss the question of consumption structure and evolution from a rather different perspective. Indeed Levine's contribution provides the theoretical framework and set of concepts which help to articulate the notion and content of a dynamic theory of consumption.

The approach to consumption analysis based on the notion of consumption sphere suggests first of all how to locate and understand the relevance of taste formation, which Levine does not discuss per se. Socially defined needs are requirements of social life, but also the manifestation of the self-seeking of individuals. Consequently they are neither simply an attribute of human nature, nor purely the result of the agency of individuals. They reflect rather their constitution in a system of persons and market relations. Personality development is similarly a result of the interaction of the self with these determinations. The needy individual is neither the result of biological necessity nor the simple replication of a social uniform pattern. He is the result of socially shaped personality development within a system of market relations. This is the fundamental difference with a notion of needs arising from 'nature', which can no longer serve to displace the issue of taste formation into the domain of an extra-economic determination.

The development of socially defined needs is therefore inextricably linked to taste formation. In this perspective the latter appears not only the bridge between need and purchase, that is taste as criterion choice, but also an aspect of the process of identification of individuals and therefore also of new needs. Consequently taste formation depends on the development of the needy individual and proceeds on the basis of the same constitution of individuals within social life. Consumption choices flow from individuals' self-seeking and socially molded identity.

As suggested before it is possible to read into the notion of life style, typical of the behavioral approach to consumer theory, the social manifestation of individual taste, taking the form of a set of social standards for the satisfaction of needs. Now these social standards, defined by income levels and groups' self-image, attain a new meaning: they are defined by the specific forms of needs satisfaction, which in turn depend on need development and new commodities. Focusing on the ways needs are satisfied permits us to discuss also the role of new products and product differentiation, an issue which constantly comes up in consumer theory.

The analysis of consumption patterns evolution must start from the rather obvious recognition that in a market economy needs are satisfied by means of commodities. However, the problem cannot be solved simply by postulating an independent determination of taste by new commodities. It could appear that what accounts for changes in the forms in which households and individuals choose to satisfy their needs is technical change. For instance, it is rather obvious that electric appliances have a fundamental role in changing the production of domestic services. However, this should not take us to hasty conclusions.

Technological feasibility is insufficient to establish this or that alternative as the prevailing form of satisfaction of a particular need and therefore also as the opportunity for new investment. That may depend on the identification of individuals and groups through consumption and the establishment of social norms for the satisfaction of needs, as much as it depends on products' technical content. In turn, identification and social norms are developed through learning and are part of what we can call innovation in consumption. The latter consists of the invention and selection of the 'modes of use' and the appropriate consumption practices which establish the usefulness of a product and the social feasibility and desirability of a certain form of consumption.[13]

Each of these elements contributes to the structuring and evolution of the consumption sphere. What they have in common is some subjective attribute, typical of learning and invention, and a social dimension, that is the interaction with commodities and their technical characteristics, which cannot be defined a priori. Now we have something more concrete to offer in the way of analyzing the learning process of consumers. Learning is at the basis of innovation in consumption as defined above. It concerns the modes of use and the consumption practices which are part of a mode of consumption.

This notion refers to the combination of commodities and the individually and/or socially engineered practices that concur to define the specific form taken by the satisfaction of needs. Modes of consumption, therefore, rather than being defined by, are shaped in conjunction with, commodities and their technical characteristics. In fact, the very characteristics of innovation in consumption are determined with the definition of the modes of consumption. To emphasize this point we could say that commodities do not attain their final form and characteristics until they are part of a prevailing mode of consumption.

The significance of this change in perspective is illustrated by the consumption theory examined earlier. Duesenberry argues that the urge for quality is the incentive to consume which tends to undermine the desire to save. Marglin explains the conflict between saving and consumption in a similar way. How can this force operate without a constant stimulus coming from technological novelty, product innovation and, more generally, from a system of evolving modes of consumption? In other words, to be sustained over time, emulation and antagonistic behavior need change in the combination of goods and practices designed to satisfy needs. This suggests that innovation may be a necessary component of the 'ratchet effect', but also that emulation and life styles differentiation need to be analyzed in conjunction with the commodities they contribute to creating. New products in particular are not selected on some abstract technological ground, but rather based on the capacity to reflect social values and individuals' desire for social status. Thus product innovation acquires a meaning distinct from both that associated with Schumpeter's long wave or Sweezy's epochs of capitalist development, and the mere 'frost on the cake' of product differentiation. It recreates the conditions for dynamism within the hierarchy of social status and life styles, affecting the process of change of modes of consumption.

The interest of these combinations rests mainly on the fact that they change over time. They change because the identification of individuals and groups through consumption has its roots in the process of development of socially determined needs, which in turn requires the development of commodities and systems of commodities.

Consequently, to understand changes in consumption patterns, beyond technological determinism and social manipulation, requires (1) an analysis of the various dimensions of modes of consumption and the critical aspects related to their social and technical feasibility; and (2) the study of their location within the structure of needs and of potential for their evolution starting from the existing structure of consumption. This implies that change in the modes of consumption, that is in the form of satisfaction of single needs, must be complemented by the analysis of the system of interdependent needs which is at the basis of a mode of life. The development of personality first and then the structure of interdependence, which is typical of structures of needs and of systems of commodities, may lead to the rise of new modes of life, which stimulate and regulate the definition of new consumption alternatives.

The evolution of the consumption sphere is then marked by the process of change of modes of consumption and the emergence and development of new modes of life, a process driven by the identification of individuals and groups through consumption and their interaction with commodities and systems of commodities. Conversely, commodities, modes of use, consumption practices and interdependencies depend on the stage of development of the sphere of consumption. When a mode of consumption becomes the norm for the satisfaction of a particular need and a set of modes of life is fully determined, the consumption sphere is modified.[14] And yet this is not a static, permanent situation, but rather the potential for further change.

2.3   The Theory of Market Creation

Innovation in consumption inserts dynamism in modes of consumption, redefining consumption alternatives. At the same time it redefines the structure of needs and permits its development. In order to clarify how the process of transformation of the consumption sphere is at the basis of market creation it is necessary to further elaborate the relationship between the development of need and the forms of satisfaction of needs.

The key notion is that of interdependence of needs and the mutual determination of needs and systems of commodities. The development of needs and personality is the force driving the evolution and multiplication of life styles, which an evolving system of commodities contributes to structuring in a system of developing modes of life. The dynamic theory of consumption then has at its core need development, which is the potential motivating market development strategies and the development of commodities and systems of commodities. This is the basis for the possibility of new consumption alternatives and the emergence of new modes of life.

Investment is the tool which firms use to structure the market in a way consistent with their self-expansion. From the point of view of the firm, change in consumption is primarily the result of investment aimed at internalizing potential market in the growth process of the firm. From the point of view of the markets, however, change in consumption has a complex relationship with market expansion, via new complementarities, productive interdependence and induced investment. Thus market creation follows from net investment and determines the growth of aggregate circulation.

In the approach presented here, modes of life encompass both the social norm set by a life style, through which differentiation in consumption grows, and the new stimuli coming from (a) the unstable process of determination of personal identity, and (b) a system of commodities which grows larger and more complex through the manifestation of new complementarities and the integration of functions. The crucial point is that the long-term viability of a mode of life depends on investment in these commodities.[15] As the process unfolds, the opportunities for the development of the needy individual and of his identification through consumption are redefined. This creates new possibilities for market development, motivating further rounds of investment.

The transformation of the consumption sphere was associated above with the new specification of modes of consumption and the emergence of new modes of life. What comes to light is the other side of this process of transformation. An evolving set of modes of consumption and system of modes of life fuel the transformation of the consumption sphere in a way consistent with the creation of new markets, therefore sustaining the growth process. Investment is fundamental in determining the process of change but, as we will see shortly, performs a different role according to the phases of market development. It pulls the growth of the market and then it is driven by its expansion. It realizes the underlying growth potential of the economy which then recreates the stimulus for further investment.

At this point we can further clarify also the relationship between new products and market creation. Through new products new needs may indeed emerge and become opportunities for investment. Still they are simply the most evident linkage between firms' strategy of market development and the transformation of the consumption sphere. The opportunities due to technology development and industrial research and, more generally, innovation on the production side are crucial, as we will see shortly, in the early phase of market development. And yet their role depends on the capacity to develop the potential implicit in a system of modes of life. Thus the strength and characteristics of the endogenous process of market creation depend on the intensity and articulation of the strategies of market development, but market creation occurs through the development of new modes of life which as such is the most long lasting cause of transformation of the CSPH.

3.   THE PROCESS OF MARKET DEVELOPMENT[16]

3.1   The Transformation of the Consumption Sphere and Potential Market

Market development governs the form of the market creation process: that is the structural determination of the market. Since it is a net addition to investment spending it affects the size of aggregate circulation, directly and through its induced effects. And yet, as pointed out above, market development acts as the main force of change only through the transformation of the CSPH.

Investment in innovation and the exploitation of the opportunities created by new technology represent the firms' effort to shape the consumption sphere in a way favorable to their expansion. Firms' work on market development is therefore the main force behind the development of commodities and systems of commodities and the link between firms' objectives of self-expansion and market creation. Still, the success of their drive for expansion depends on the capacity for transforming potential market into actual market outlets and creating uncommitted income in the process.

What needs to be stressed is that in a system of production based on market relations the notion of need can be grasped only in conjunction with the notion of potential market. The source of potential market is potential demand, a potential implicit in the latent structure of need and the development of the needy individual; for the firm potential market is the opportunity to grow by exploiting that potential, thereby contributing to market expansion in the aggregate while pursuing its goal of self-expansion. Potential market depends on previous development of the structure of need, manifested in established modes of life and modes of consumption. It emerges as a possibility implicit in the variation of current patterns of consumption and a stimulus to investment aimed at modifying current forms of needs satisfaction. Consequently it has a greater degree of determinacy than potential demand.

Firms' work on market development is primarily directed to exploiting potential market for purposes of self-growth.[17] In their struggle to gain a competitive edge, firms transform that potential into actual market creation, by means of investment in productive technology, organization, material and immaterial resources. Market development is therefore substantiated by a strategy of investment in a variety of different areas, from the acquisition of new technology to market research, from experimentation with new products to policies of image and selling effort. The efforts directed to the translation of potential market into market creation, when successful, sustains the rate of growth of the unit, as well as of the aggregate economy, as can be expected from any form of autonomous investment.

These efforts are exerted in a well defined direction. The structuring and articulation of the consumption sphere is the result of past market development and of the determination of the needy individual which that implies; its evolution recreates the conditions for change. It follows that, at any point in time, the market development effort is not confronting existing demand, but rather identifies and develops the potential implicit in the structure of need, that is potential demand, into a more narrowly defined notion of potential market which then motivates, from the demand side, the size and forms of investment directed to its exploitation.

3.2 The Stages of Market Development

It is precisely the process of definition and then of exploitation of potential market which suggest that the strategy of market development is marked by stages which correspond to the changing role and characteristics of investment.

The precondition of a market development strategy is a market definition stage, in which the potential represented by the latent structure of need must be investigated and expressed to determine the characteristics of potential market. We enter then the first stage, that of market construction in a proper sense. Autonomous investment and innovation are directed to defining consumption alternatives aimed at the most receptive consumers. When a mode of satisfaction of needs is defined as a small market niche, we enter a second phase: the process of diffusion and generalization will be sustained by investment directed mainly to the creation of productive capacity, along with the technical and organizational requirements of the appropriate scale of production. This process of determination of investment, however, ceases and is reversed when the growth of capacity is purely induced by incremental growth of demand. Subsequently the stabilization of the market is the incentive for investment in reorganization aimed at cost cutting and/or at product differentiation. This is the basis for a strategy of market development increasingly focused on pricing and market segmentation. Uncommitted income is throughout the condition for market development. However, it becomes more important in the two last phases, as investment creates new income and the possibility of cost cutting and therefore price decreases.

We can conclude that the process of market development goes through an innovation phase, an intensive and then an extensive growth phase. There is a rather close relationship between these phases and those of the product development, which lead to the establishment of a new product in the consumption structure.[18]

In the introduction phase, the consumers at the cutting edge of innovative consumption are fundamental to establishing a new product as a useful item of consumption and creating a market niche (Shapiro, 1986). This predisposition is the result of their consumption experience and of discretionary income.[19] Similarly, there are firms which, given their technology and position in the industry, are in fact able and motivated to introduce new products. When the final design for the product is reached through market testing and consumers' feedback, its utility is determined; it enters the second phase, that of development, in which it can now be marketed on a large scale. In this phase the novelty of the product can lead the process of market creation only to the extent to which a mode of needs satisfaction becomes established as a new social norm and standard of quality. In the maturity phase, the product is part of a generalized norm of mass consumption; market expansion increasingly depends on falling prices and/or growing income.

As the rate of growth of sales decelerates and the market approaches saturation, we are approaching the limit of a strategy of market development. The effort to recreate the condition of expansion through investment may take different forms. In principle the slowdown in sales should set up the incentive for a new round of innovation, aimed at exploiting the latent structure of need and the potential market implicit in the newly established pattern of consumption. But it may also be that, given the pace and characteristics of the diffusion process, innovation prolongs the maturity phase well beyond the point at which sales would otherwise begin to fall. This is contingent on taste formation and the development of new complementarities, which may revamp the interest in mature products and already established modes of life. It is hard to conceive the latter without some sort of innovation, which, however, can be rather small.[20]

4.   A RESTATEMENT OF DEMAND-LED GROWTH

4.1   Potential Market and Schumpeter's Theory of Economic Development

It is now possible to complete the theoretical scheme centered on the consumption–growth relationship relating the new approach to the question posed in Chapter 1. There it was pointed out that the interest for Schumpeter's theory of economic development was its concern with the mechanism of development in the abstract. This is the same concern of the scheme discussed above. In both cases the focus is on the endogenous mechanism of growth in a market economy, which is now located in the structural dynamics of market creation associated with the evolution of consumption patterns.

In Schumpeter's scheme expansion is instead entrusted to a supply-determined dynamics, resting on the vision of the entrepreneur and on the disruptive character of the new combinations. What is missing, it was argued, is a demand side, identified with the notion of potential demand. Schumpeter was quite explicit on the reasons why he had no analysis of the demand side as such: he considered demand unimportant for growth, since consumers are not initiators of change and taste can be taken as a datum because it changes slowly. Consequently, despite his insights into the relationship between innovation and demand, he focused on the supply side and did not attempt to develop a dynamic counterpart of traditional demand theory.

This problem has not really been discussed by neo-Schumpeterian theory. And yet, though Schumpeter has no theory of market creation, it would not be quite correct to say that he did not see the relevance of the issue, which surfaces in his analysis of the establishment of mass markets, but remains mostly implicit in the notion of creative destruction.[21]

The notion of potential market gives content and economic relevance to the notion of potential demand, which was introduced in Chapter 1 mainly as a negative concept, that is what was missing from Schumpeter's scheme of economic development.[22] The notion of a latent potential implicit in the dynamics of economic development of market economies, that is potential demand, is now specified in a way consistent with the process of growth within a system of market relations.

With respect to Schumpeter's scheme in particular (1) it motivates the action of the entrepreneur and connects the latter to consumption evolution; (2) it endogenizes the mechanism of development, grounding the vision of the entrepreneur and the opportunity created by invention and technical progress in a self-sustaining dynamics. From a more general point of view it is part of a scheme which lays out the foundations for a dynamic theory of consumption and market creation, therefore addressing the two questions raised by Pasinetti's model. Indeed, the response to these questions lies in a theory of demand appropriate for the analysis of growth, which implies the elaboration of the demand side of economic development.

4.2   Endogenous Structural Change and Uneven Industrial Development

The point is that not current demand, but rather a theory of the growth of demand, is crucial for the analysis of development: that is a theory of the change though time of the level and composition of demand. Such a theory is based on the process which sustains the structuring of the consumption sphere and keeps in motion the process of transformation. Potential market, that is the potential for development, is self-generating along the main lines of the consumption sphere evolution.

Such an evolution is intertwined with the structural dynamics of market creation. Market creation implies a structural dynamics, a changing structure of production, due to the direct and indirect effects of market development on the composition of industrial output. In turn, structural dynamics, underwriting the process of market creation, sustains income creation and the growth of aggregate circulation. Indeed the main characteristic of endogenous structural change is that new industries and structural dynamics are not simply the results of, but also active forces in the process of, market creation.[23]

In particular, a group of industries leads the process of structural transformation and fundamentally determines the rate of growth of the aggregate economy. This is what Levine calls the developing sector of the economy. Its strategy of market development is fundamental for the process of market creation and income growth. At the same time the pattern of investment of this sector determines the process of uneven industrial growth. This is magnified by the discovery of new productive complementarities and industrial linkages. Their joint effects reverberate into the structure of production, inducing further structural adjustment.

The structure of production and the structure of consumption are in balance when the mix of old and new industries, those going through experimentation of new products and those experiencing rationalization of the production process, is such that effective demand is adequate, in its size and composition, to absorb current output and propel expansion. In no sense do these circumstances suggest some balanced path of growth, even as a methodological device. They simply illustrate the dynamics of uneven industrial development, which contribute to the determination of the aggregate rate of growth of the economy.

4.3 Structural Dynamics, Demand-led Growth and Effective Demand

In Chapter 1 it was stressed that demand-led growth suffers from the unexplained nature of the demand increase that sets in motion the virtuous circle between growth of output and productivity growth. In particular, Kaldor never really discussed the question of the sources of demand, or a theory of demand growth. It is now possible to suggest a view quite distinct from the previous theoretical elaboration of this notion.

Having defined along general lines the process which transforms potential demand into market creation I have specified the demand side of the development process. Thus it is possible to give a new basis to the analysis of demand growth. In the perspective developed above the core of demand-led growth is the inner process of determination which accounts for the transformation of the consumption sphere and the structural dynamics of market creation.

This helps to respond to the limits of the notion of demand-creating technical change advanced by Yoshikawa (see Chapter 1), which falls short of any analysis of endogenous market creation. More broadly it addresses the weakness of the underconsumptionist view, which could not explain the internal generation of new markets by the very process of economic development, but rather discusses the possibility of overcoming a tendency towards stagnation in the light of exogenous stimuli, such as the geographical extension of markets or the march of technical progress. To distinguish this approach from the notion of demand-led growth found in the literature we can call it the theory of demand-led growth in a structural, long-term perspective. The reformulation of demand-led growth suggests also that the scheme based on the consumption–growth relationship is in fact an articulation of the principle of effective demand in the long run.

To the extent to which the transformation of the consumption sphere is driven by exploitation of the potential market by market development strategies, the notion of demand-led growth advanced above rests on the idea that investment determines change in the consumption structure and the latter creates the conditions for investment. The main consequence is that the distinction between investment and consumption as the opposite, and competing, sides of the income-creation process is misleading when discussing the fundamental dynamics of the growth process.[24]

A theory of demand appropriate to the analysis of growth must contain a theory of the growth of demand and therefore a theory of market creation;

the latter, however, comprehend a consumption component and an investment component, which in turn is divided into an autonomous and an induced component. The consumption component depends on the investment component. However, in a long-run perspective the principle of effective demand operates through the transformation of the consumption sphere and a specific pattern of structural dynamics. Thus the evolution of the consumption sphere suggests a theory of the growth of demand in which consumption is not simply a passive component of aggregate demand, but rather part of the process of structural determination of the market. It follows that the theory of demand appropriate for the analysis of growth is a theory of demand growth where the principle of effective demand operates as the demand side of economic development.

NOTES

1. This may help to overcome also the, at times excessive, complication of Levine's presentation. In the Preface of Vol. II he observes: 'the difficulty associated with the redefinition of the project ... in the direction of a fresh attempt at theorizing, seemed to have relegated the virtue of simplicity to the status of a secondary concern' (Levine, 1981, p.x).
2. This process can be analyzed also from the mirror image of what constrains change in the patterns of consumption. Levine argues that change is limited 'to those patterns of consumption consistent with the reproduction of personalities, and therefore with existing patterns of need identified with those personalities. These patterns of consumption involve specific utilities which come to be associated with the structure of social practices, by which the individual personality asserts itself'. The result is an 'enduring pattern of demand' that constitutes an inertia and 'impedes alteration of the modes of consumption and patterns of demand' (Levine, 1981, vol. II, p.218)
3. 'The set of social practices (that is acts of consumption) by which a person fulfills his needs defines what we have termed a "form of life"' (ibid., p.277).
4. 'For pre-modern society, since the mode of consumption was given, it was also well-known' (ibid., p.139).
5. Indeed: 'An innovation, which redefines a structure of need, is an opportunity for accumulation' (ibid., p.159).
6. 'The determination of the level at which the expanded reproduction of the aggregate market takes place can only be fixed upon the basis of the determinants of the structural development of the market' (ibid., p.216).
7. 'In order to create a new market, the firm must simultaneously pursue three specific goals: (1) the creation, in the sense of defining, both of a new need and of the means to its satisfaction (a new utility); (2) the establishment of the social identification of the utility with its particular product; (3) the integration of the new need and of the new utility into the existing matrix of consumption' (ibid., pp.138–9).
8. 'On the side of consumption, the system of developing commodities defines a system of developing modes of life. It is out of these established, yet still dynamic, modes of life that new social practices emerge, both as further development of current patterns, and as a variation of those patterns' (ibid., p.230).

9. 'The reciprocal determination of the markets for means of production and means of consumption expresses concretely the mutual dependence of the process of ongoing expansion of wealth, and the process of development of a sphere of individual consumption which utilizes wealth for the end of the development of individual need ... This process ... develops products for a range of modes of consumption, and makes those products appropriate in form and price to take their place in a range of modes of life linked to a range of income levels. Rapid internal development of the structure of wealth implies rapid development of modes of consumption. At the same time, the inherent dynamism and the differentiated structure of the modes of consumption create space and opportunity for product development which stimulates the intensive development of the market for means of production' (ibid., p.174).

10. He argues that, to the extent that 'capitalist expansion cannot be understood without explicit consideration of the determinants of consuming patterns, and of aggregate demand' (ibid., p.276), it is necessary to break with the classical tradition, which rests on the exclusion of a theoretical treatment of consumption. On the other hand, traditional consumer theory is an unsatisfactory attempt to fill this vacuum. 'Our investigation of the determinants of capitalist expansion has required the introduction of a degree of specifications of modes of consumption greater than that implied in the traditional "theory of consumer behavior". This greater determinacy derives ultimately from the idea that individual needs are socially determined' (ibid.). While a person's pattern of consumption 'expresses the uniqueness of the individual's personality ... the individual discovers his personal consumption pattern in his relation with others ... Furthermore, the means of consumption ... are provided by other individuals and by society' (ibid., p.277).

11. 'Need and utility are social facts linked to a social practice defined outside the firm. The development of the market for the firm, therefore, presupposes that its product be established in relationship to a social practice which is not determined by the firm' (ibid., p.159).

12. Not only does it make available consumer products with specific characteristics, but also prices them according to firm's strategies of market development and determines consumers' income.

13. Gershuny (1983) has articulated the notion of social innovation, that is changes in the technique of need satisfaction. This involves technology, but also the definition of new modes of use of commodities.

14. Indeed needs are fully determined only when the forms of their satisfaction are determined.

15. In fact, a theory of consumption evolution must also be a theory of output.

16. The notion of market development discussed here goes beyond that of the business literature on marketing. The latter focuses mainly on the relationship between sales and promotion, that is market planning, not on market creation as the key mechanism of expansion. This is not per se the firm's concern, though it enters its strategic planning as one of the main variables of the external market environment.

17. That implies speculation on the direction taken by need development and potential demand and experimentation around the characteristics of potential market.

18. The product cycle is a well known notion. Here it is specified with respect to the process which marks the evolution of the consumption sphere.

19. This is quite consistent with the idea that the previous development of needs makes these consumers most capable of defining the needs-satisfying power of a new product.

20. This possibility is of particular interest because, as we will see, the development of some market during the recovery of the 1980s may have followed this pattern.

21. It appears as a consequence of the diffusion process, which expands the scale, scope and articulation of the market, not of any elaboration of the demand side of economic development and structural dynamics.
22. From this point of view it completes the scheme of economic development.
23. It may be noted here that all of this can be seen in the light of a growing division of labour and of qualitative change which is the source of A. Young's increasing returns.
24. Indeed it seems contradictory to the very notion of expanded reproduction and with income determination in the long run.

6. Empirical analysis and the recovery of the US economy in the 1980s

1.   THE STRUCTURAL DYNAMICS OF MARKET CREATION

The simple scheme presented in Chapter 5 has two main purposes: (1) outline in the abstract the mechanism through which market expansion proceeds and sustains the growth process; (2) constitute the framework for more detailed analysis at the theoretical and the empirical level. To move on in this direction some of its characteristics deserve closer examination.

With respect to Levine's analysis the structural theory of demand-led growth has similarities and differences. In the theoretical framework centered on the consumption–growth relationship sustained growth depends on the self-generation of the potential market and its exploitation by the strategies of market development. Consequently the focus of the theory is on the structural dynamics of market creation associated with the evolution of the consumption sphere, that is, the evolution of the forms of satisfaction of socially determined needs. Thus the fundamental similarity concerns the nature of the scheme and the internal logic of the process which sustains growth in the long run. In both cases we have an abstract description of the self-determination of the growth process.

It may be argued that the scheme shares the lack of definitive predictions of the analysis of the accumulation process presented by Levine.[1] In particular, it does not answer in definitive way the question of the tendencies towards stagnation. This follows indeed from the very nature of the scheme.

At the theoretical level personality development and the development of socially determined needs are the basis of the potential demand. The active strategies of firms realize the potential latent in the notion of the individual as a social entity through investment in market development. To the extent that the potential is recreated by change, the process appears to have no limits. However, while economic development occurs following the process of market creation, the entire process hinges on its integration into the firms' drive to self-expansion.

Levine does explain how placing a new product within the given structure of consumption could imply more than spending for the acquisition of new means of production and scrapping old equipment to create new industries. It affects the underlying structure of needs and, through their interdependence, the systems of commodities. Still the development of needs and the market-based forms of need satisfaction is predicated upon the capacity of firms to exploit that potential for purposes of self-expansion. This can indeed generate expansion, but the size of aggregate circulation it engenders remains unclear.

The satisfaction of needs is subordinated to the purpose of self-expansion, but the neediness of individuals is not completely contingent on the market. This tension is at the basis of the endogenous dynamics of growth; it is the pressure which keeps running the process of development. Thus, on the one hand, any long-run tendency towards stagnation must be analyzed in this perspective, on the other, the actual outcomes will depend on the concrete form taken by the growth process. The tension between the forces inherent to a system of market relations and the circumstances of a specific phase of development shape the actual structural dynamics of the economic system. Only the concrete articulation of the process can give definitive answers.

Furthermore it must be noted that the scheme of sustained growth based on the process of market creation does indicate the limits imposed on personality development, and therefore on the dynamics of change of the social forms of needs satisfaction, by the system of market relations based on firms' drive to expansion and dominated by wage labour. The growth process described along these lines envisages just the opposite of unlimited growth, a strongly constrained path of development.

In a system of market relations the separation of the laborer from his work is fully accomplished; laboring is only a means to so much wealth sustaining a mode of life, consistent with a form of life and a set of modes of consumption. This separation represents an opportunity, since it constitutes a potential for development of personal identity and is the basis for the redefinition of the interdependent systems of needs and commodities. This possibility, however, contrasts with the form of life of the wage earner which has two fundamental characteristics: it is relatively fixed and, as far as the form of needs satisfaction is concerned, limited to a few alternatives. Change may be severely constrained by the fundamental stability and uniformity of consumption patterns imposed on workers by the level of the real wage. In other words, a weak dynamics of the real wage would favor some uniform social standard of consumption where individuals are little more than pure accidents, undermining considerably the possibility of different forms of needs satisfaction that the separation of the laborer from his work creates.

The development of the structure of wealth, which arises from the process of growth, presents a similar two-sides effect. Its increasingly articulated structure magnifies the possibility of realizing the potential contained in individuality and the development of the structure of needs. It has the capacity of fostering neediness and needs satisfaction. At the same time the structure of wealth is the result of and reinforces an uneven distribution of income; it is therefore rooted in inequality and tends to reproduce it. This may constitute a limit to market creation, especially to the extension of the market. From this point of view market creation is constrained by the very social mechanism in which the means to the satisfaction of needs is wealth. Thus it may be argued that inequality is at the same time propelling and limiting the process of need development.

The theoretical framework centered on the consumption–growth relationship, therefore, highlights the crucial importance of the distribution effects generated by the structural dynamics of growth and, in particular, the dynamics of the real wage. A rising real wage is the condition for developing the neediness of a large part of society and contrasting the scarce potential for personality development which is implicit in the forms of life and consumption patterns of wage earners. This makes explicit the limits on neediness and need development imposed on a large proportion of individuals.[2] Many individuals, indeed a very large percentage of the working population, tend to be mostly defined with respect to a form of life which can subsist within a range of wage levels. For these individuals it may be more difficult to break away from established consumption patterns. As a consequence, in the absence of rising wages, the system is deprived of a strong incentive to develop change and variety and in turn its internal dynamism and rate of market creation are constrained. Consequently, despite the fact that wages can indeed be above subsistence level, which in the language of classical political economy represents the lower limit under which the wage cannot go, the level and the dynamics of wages may constitute a barrier to market expansion.

It may still be argued that this is no definitive answer to the question of the indeterminacy of the theory, with particular reference to the tendencies towards stagnation. This is indeed the defining trait of the theoretical framework we are working with. The lack of determinate predictions is not, however, at the expense of, and actually magnifies the importance of, the analysis of the process through which long-term growth may occur. To be sure, the theory of demand-led growth presented here can be further articulated and refined. However it should not be dissatisfying to conclude that the response to this indeterminacy is in the process itself. This is the terrain where theoretical analysis should give space to empirical investigation.

Crisis of accumulation, evidently, may occur. Nevertheless the mechanism of self-expansion is now specified. This specification allows for the analysis of the potential for expansion which expanded reproduction exploits and recreates; that is the potential implicit in the structural dynamics of a determinate period. The theoretical treatment of the consumption–growth relationship is therefore open to the determination based on empirical analysis and actually leads in that direction. This is a fundamental difference with respect to Levine's theoretical work. The approach develops his insights into the nature of the growth process towards a theory of the stages of development of advanced market economies based on the evolution of the CSPH. Such a theory, while contributing to the articulation of the principle of effective demand in the long run, is the theoretical framework against which to define the scope of empirical investigation.

2.   THE EMPIRICAL ANALYSIS OF THE CONSUMPTION–GROWTH RELATIONSHIP

The purpose of the empirical analysis is to establish the specific pattern of economic development and thus clarify the way in which the mechanism of self-expansion is articulated and realized. To this extent the empirical analysis complements the attempt at theorizing. While shedding light on the actual characteristics of the transformation of the consumption sphere and of the market creation process, it also emphasizes the relevance of the theoretical scheme, which makes it possible to discuss the facts of development within an overall view of the structural dynamics of growth.

Owing to the nature of the questions raised in the theoretical chapters and the still general and sketchy character of the approach to the consumption–growth relationship, it is not surprising that there are difficulties in developing a neat empirical analysis. Quite obviously the stage of development of the theory allows only for a first exploration of the problem.

With respect to the inner process of determination of the consumption sphere analyzed above, what we observe on the surface is rather the specific form taken by the satisfaction of needs, that is modes of consumption and the rise and structuring of new modes of life, which together determine the observed evolution of consumption patterns. Changes in consumption patterns are the appearance, what is observable, and therefore an approximation of the changes in the sphere of consumption, though they proceed from its transformation. Similarly the transformation can be analyzed considering changes of output composition, trends of industrial transformation and firms' strategies of market development. Knowledge about these aspects should help us to understand the process of change in the consumption sphere and assess the structural dynamics of market creation combined with it.

The empirical analysis should, first, illustrate the actual structural dynamics of a period and, second, help to discuss its interpretation by providing a factual basis to the analysis of the transformation of the consumption sphere. In fact, there are two reasons why the empirical analysis of a particular period may have relevance for more general purposes. Any attempt at analyzing empirically the questions defined in the theoretical framework is indeed a contribution to a general methodology for the empirical analysis of the consumption–growth relationship. At the same time, discussing the long-run potential of a certain phase of transformation of the consumption sphere may yield some insights on the fundamental questions concerning the development pattern of advanced market economies.

3.   LONG-TERM TRANSFORMATION AND THE 1980s RECOVERY

The empirical analysis in this book focuses on the 1980s. It considers the expansion of the period in the perspective of a long-term pattern of transformation. In particular, it takes as a starting point the main conclusion drawn from transformational growth, that transformation 'draws to an end' because of the exhaustion of the potential for market creation which sustained the development of industrial capitalism for over a century.

In this view the 1960s expansion was the peak and the last instance of a process of market creation which proceeded hand in hand with the main transformation of the post-war period. This process is identified, on the one hand, with the extension and generalization of *large-scale production* and *mass consumption*; on the other, with a more progressive distribution of income, where an important role was played by growing wages and other forms of income support for the poor or the unemployed.

It is hardly disputable that these were indeed the general characteristics of the phase culminating in the 1960s expansion. They bear a close resemblance to the accumulation regime which, in a theoretical account of the French Regulation School, goes under the name of 'Fordism' (Aglietta, 1979; Harvey, 1990). Central to this regime is indeed the role of rising wages and the growth of consumption spending.

What obtained full dominance in production, consumption and distribution was a system of market relations centered on the notion of *mass markets*, driven by industrialized productive technology and scale economies. At the core of it was the virtuous circle in which accumulation sustained income growth, and growth of wages in particular, which in turn sustained market formation, with the latter feeding back on the prospects of accumulation and growth. Consumption patterns' evolution, driven by new modes of consumption and ways of life, emerge as a necessary outcome and a powerful force keeping in motion the process of transformation.

After the robust growth of the 1960s cycle the tendency to low growth rates set in. Strong limiting forces constrain the growth process, though not necessarily 'change'; rather the kind of change which creates new markets. The problem concerns the direction of the pattern of transformation engendered by change. It concerns the mechanism translating change into expansion.

It must be recognized, however, that 'mass market'was a particular 'form' taken by the self-expansion mechanism and by the structural dynamics of growth. From the point of view of the consumption–growth relationship it was indeed a specific phase of transformation of the consumption sphere and form of the market creation process.

What comes to light is therefore the scope of the theoretical scheme elaborated above. Addressing the question of the relationship between change in the consumption sphere and the process of the formation of new markets, it becomes possible to articulate the analysis of consumption, and of the pattern of market creation associated with it, beyond the notion of mass markets. This notion indicates more than the size of the market and its rapid expansion. It contains also a rather simplified notion of consumption innovation and evolution. Variations in the process of market creation associated with the evolution of the consumption sphere would then arise as a response to the exhaustion of this pattern of transformation and should address the reasons why, since the 1960s, change no longer propels growth.

The analytical framework developed so far should help us to understand the new phase of development which comes after the years of rapid growth and the industrial restructuring of the 1970s, which otherwise are largely identified with a lapse into stagnation, and help to explain the structural evolution after the decline of transformational growth. However, if indeed the 1980s represent a break in the pattern of development, it would be misleading to approach the analysis having in mind the process of market creation and structural change which was typical of the mass markets of the 1960s. We may need to consider different and more qualitative dimensions of change and consider the possibility of a development of consumption patterns in the absence of rising wages or of a more progressive income distribution.[3]

The theoretical approach centered on the consumption–growth relationship appears particularly relevant precisely for the characteristics of the recovery of those years, such as the revamping of consumption spending and changes in output composition, which, it is often asserted, sustained the growth cycle of the decade. In particular, the transformation of the CSPH should allow for an account of the period that is more satisfactory than other interpretations, and help to comprehend its long-run prospects.

4.   THE RECOVERY OF THE REAGAN YEARS

There is indeed a large consensus on the fact that the 1980s expansion represents a break with the previous period. While in agreement on this point, the interpretation presented in this book fundamentally differs on some generally accepted notions, specifically on the nature of the break and its long-term implications.

The 1980s are widely considered a period of recovery for the US economy and for most of the industrialized world. They have been hailed as the end of a long phase of instability and sluggish growth. More specifically the decade has come to be regarded as a break with the years of 'stagflation' and a return to the conditions for rapid growth and long-term economic prosperity. A second widespread idea is that the change in business climate and economic perspective was to a large extent related to a boom in technological innovation and consumer spending, accompanied by the rise of new industries and new products.

Indeed, for economists and commentators most sanguine about the virtues of the market economy, the 1980s stand in sharp contrast to the previous decade and represent a turning point in the prospects of the US economy. It is to this view that the term 'recovery' is most congenial, since the expansion proves the vitality of the system of social relations associated with 'free market' capitalism, overcoming the combination of stagnation and inflation which characterized the 1970s. In general, however, economists have been rather prudent on these issues. Except for the most outspoken supporters of the Reagan administration policies, many have stressed that the other side of the recovery was the 'twin deficit' problem, the growth of government deficit and the negative balance of trade. Other criticism has insisted on the ephemeral character of the recovery, pointing out the prominent role played by the fiscal policy of the administration, dominated by military Keynesianism, and the rise of financial speculation.

More critical views insist on the peculiarities of this recovery, stressing its weakness. They point at the growth of debt, accumulated by both households and firms, relatively weak investment, slower than normal productivity growth, even slow growth of output, relatively high unemployment and low level of utilization of productive capacity. Again, in comparison to the robust growth of the 1960s, many of the traditional indicators do not give a comforting picture. Thus we ought to conclude that it is far from clear that the recovery recreated the conditions for long-term prosperity.

A detailed account of these views is not my concern here. It is sufficient to point out that, with respect to the forces sustaining expansion, the views range from the apologetic enthusiasm of those who identify them with the economic and social principles of the 'Reagan Revolution', to a critical assessment which concludes that there has not been much of a recovery at all.[4] Critical assessments, however, seem at times to ignore or diminish the amount of transformation which has occurred in the economy, and not only in the sense of decline. Between highly ideological enthusiasm and almost complete dismissal it is at times difficult to give an account of the specific circumstances of the period.

Fiscal policy in general, and strong military spending in particular, together with the impulse given by financial and real estate speculation, may indeed be very important in explaining the strength and characteristics of the recovery, but do not explain by themselves the pattern of structural adjustment of the growth process. My focus on the transformation of the consumption sphere is meant to address this question and more generally contribute to an understanding of the actual structural dynamics of the recovery beyond the limits of the interpretations mentioned above.

Most of the effort to highlight empirically the characteristics of the 1980s in this book is based on statistical evidence. It concerns macro trends, industrial output composition, the structure of consumption and the relationship between market development and growth. Chapter 7 is an overview of the macro variables which define the contours of the 1980s expansion. They are considered within the growth pattern of the US economy in the post-war period. The focus is on the role of consumption spending and effective demand. The second part of the chapter analyzes the changes in the industrial base which have marked the cyclical pattern of the economy from the 1960s. Chapter 8 examines changes in household consumption expenditure composition. The prediction of the consumption structure based on an income-led model is used to highlight the possibility of processes of market creation autonomous from income levels and address the question of the transformation of the consumption sphere. Chapter 9 presents the results of a test of the correlation between market development and sales growth, assuming a broadly defined notion of market development.

The last two chapters of the book elaborate on the results. The statistical analysis is combined with an analysis of stylized facts and observable trends of transformation to suggest an interpretation of the structural dynamics of the recovery. The change in the pattern of growth which emerges during the expansion is the result of a fundamental change in the market creation process and has long-term implications.

NOTES

1.　'This mutual determination [of firm and market] ... remains indeterminate to the degree that: (1) it can, in principle, be maintained on any of a wide range of levels, and (2) its structure, or form, remains unspecified' (Levine, 1981, vol. II, p.216).
2.　According to Levine the association of wage labor with subsistence negates individual freedom and therefore the very notion of individuality.
3.　Within the scheme of TG this possibility implies a halt to the process of market creation.
4.　'Conservatives have been waging economic revolution since the late Carter years. Have they succeeded? Some argue in the affirmative, pointing to lower rates of inflation and the long expansion since early 1983, insisting that "the fundamentals are sound". However the attempt "to change the rules of the game" of the conservative economic leadership of the 80's has not reversed the course of long-term decline of the US economy (Bowles, Gordon and Weisskopf, 1989).

7. Macroeconomic trends and the evolution of the industrial structure

1. THE EXPANSION OF THE 1980s

1.1 Growth and Cycles in the Post-war Period

Though typical of the more optimistic accounts, at times bordering on the rhetoric of the Reagan years, the notion that the 1980s represent for the US economy a period of recovery and a return to rapid growth is rather widespread (Bartley, 1992). To discuss this view we start by looking at GNP growth rates and consider the expansion of the 1980s within the cyclical pattern of the economy in the post-war period. The entire analysis is then based on four 'peak to peak' cycles: 1958–66, 1966–73, 1973–9, 1979–89. This choice stresses the relevance attributed to the 1960s cycle, the last cycle of strong expansion in comparison with the sluggish growth of the 1970s.

If we examine the growth rates of real GNP (President's Council of Economic Advisors, 1987, p.251, table B-5), it is apparent that the 1958–66 cycle is the only one with no negative growth rates, as opposed to negative growth rates in 1954 and 1958, in 1970 and 1974–5, in 1980 and 1982. Fluctuations were rather small, at least compared to the sharp oscillations of the other three cycles. Therefore it is noticeable as a period of steady growth. The 1980s cycle starts with the most severe recession since 1950, followed by a dramatic rebound and a steady and progressively lower growth rate. After 1983 the growth trend approaches the steadiness of expansion of the first half of the 1960s, with seven years of positive growth rates.

A more precise picture can be drawn from the average annual growth rates. Table 7.1 summarizes the growth rates of GNP, disposable income and personal consumption.

The severe recession of 1982 is in itself a reason for the sharp rebound from 1983. It depresses the average growth rate of GNP over the cycle, which is much lower than in the 1958–66 cycle, lower than that of the 1966–73 cycle and in line with that of the 1973–9 cycle. The growth rate of real disposable income is slightly higher than in the previous cycle, but much lower than in the other two periods. Finally, personal consumption expenditure grows a little more rapidly than disposable income, but this is common to all the four cycles. The picture changes dramatically if we consider the years from 1983, in which case the rate of growth of GNP is close to that of the 1958–66 period.

Table 7.1 Average Annual Growth Rates (in per cent)

	GNP	Income	Consumption
1958–66	4.0	3.76	3.92
1966–73	3.2	3.54	3.84
1973–79	2.7	2.35	2.90
1979–89	2.6	2.55	2.87
(1983–89)	3.8		

Note: 1982 constant dollars.

Source: National Income and Product Accounts, Citibase.

Summing up: the recovery of the 1980s follows two cycles marked by wide oscillations and modest growth rates compared to the 1958–66 cycle. Despite the new ascending trend after 1983, the overall growth rate of GNP remains modest, especially with respect to the 1958–66 cycle, and is in fact the lowest of the post-war period.

1.2   Consumption Spending and Aggregate Demand

Some other general remarks can be made on examining the time profile of the macro variables for the post-war period (Graphs 1 to 19, Appendix A). It may be noticed that the consumption ratio (the ratio of personal consumption expenditure to personal disposable income) has a clear downward trend from 1946 until the mid-1970s, and a clear upward trend from 1975 (Graph 5). Also noticeable is the growth after 1983. As a result the ratio is higher in 1988 than it was in the 1958–66 period, and it is close to the level reached at the end of the 1940s. The changes of the average consumption ratio are summarized in Table 7.2.

Table 7.2   Average Consumption Ratio

1948	0.93
1949	0.94
1950	0.92
1958–66	0.91
1966–73	0.89
1973–9	0.89
1979–89	0.92

Source: National Income and Product Accounts, Citibase.

The ratio of personal savings to disposable income has a symmetrical and apposite trend (Graph 6). Though the saving ratio may be abnormally low in the first part of the 1980s, and is indeed heading upward after 1987, there is evidence of a decreasing trend from the beginning of the 1970s, accelerating after 1979.

These are first indications of a central role played by consumption spending in sustaining aggregate demand. Some additional evidence of a consumption-fueled recovery is the time pattern of the ratio of consumer installment debt to personal income (Graph 7). Though part of a long-term increasing trend, consumer debt reaches a new peak after 1985, well above the relatively stable trend of the previous twenty years. This may be due to financial innovation and consumer credit policy, together with changes in the people's attitude towards debt. Note that the debt ratio does not grow during the recession years at the beginning of the cycle, but only after 1983.

The importance of consumption spending is further highlighted by the pattern of investment (Graphs 12 and 13). Gross private domestic investment grows rapidly after a dramatic collapse in 1982, but by 1985 has already stabilized, with no indication of further growth. Though reaching a higher absolute level, the trend is in line with that of the 1970s. Gross investment in producers' durable equipment (Graph 13) has a similar pattern, though the trend in the 1980s suggests a more vigorous expansion than indicated by total gross investment. Other available measures of investment tend to confirm a relatively weak investment spending. Gross and net investment as a percentage of GNP show a dramatic rebound in 1983 and 1984, declining in 1985 and 1986 and then remaining stable, with net figures weaker than gross figures. Another indicator, business expenditure in new plant and equipment as a percentage of GNP, gives an even bleaker picture: the rebound is modest, it takes place only in one year, 1984, followed by two years of decline and a new modest surge.

We may conclude that investment grows after 1982 and hardly at all after 1985. That is not to say that it was not an important aspect of the recovery, but not its main characteristic. On the other hand, a first desegregation shows that after 1983 business expenditure in new plant and equipment in manufacturing grows very little, while in commerce it continues a long-term expansive trend. The weakness of investment may then be particularly relevant for manufacturing and most likely for some sections of it. Nevertheless, output capacity of total industry (Graph 14) is significantly higher at the end of the 1980s than it was in 1979. Capacity utilization in manufacturing (Graph 15) rebounds from the lows of the 1982 recession, stabilizing around 80 per cent after 1984, and increasing from 1986. It remains well below the peak of 1966 (90 per cent) and 1974 (above 85 per cent). Data on capacity, however, are notoriously not very reliable.

Turning to the other two main components of aggregate demand, net exports have an unequivocal pattern, with a drastic decrease which seems to have bottomed in 1986. Federal purchases instead expand at the beginning of the 1980s, after remaining mostly stable in the previous cycle. This trend is fully accounted for by defense expenditure, confirming 'Keynesian Militarism' as the foundation of fiscal policy. State and local purchases also drift upward, but only in the second part of the 1980s, after growing little in the previous cycles.

1.3   Income Distribution

The examination of macro variables can be concluded by considering the question of income distribution. A first indicator, gross hourly earnings of non-agricultural production workers in 1982 constant dollars (Graph 8), shows that the decline of workers' compensation which occurred at the end of the 1970s was not reversed during the recovery and that it remain through the 1980s at the level it was at at the end of the 1958–66 cycle. Another indicator, the average hourly earning index in constant 1977 dollars (Graph 9) confirms that there has been only a modest improvement and that earnings remained well below the level reached in the 1970s. One can conclude that there is not much to expect in terms of a stimulus to consumption spending coming from real wage growth.

The deterioration of the relative position of lower income earners is confirmed by the percentage of aggregate income going to the top fifth of the population (Consumer Income Series, p-60, Bureau of Census) which increases by almost two points from 1981 to 1987, and by the median annual family income, which grows noticeably only for the top two-fifths and especially for the highest fifth of the population (Bureau of Census).

These data can be contrasted with the those on profitability. Data on profits, however, do not give a clear-cut picture. Corporate profits after taxes peak in 1979, come down sharply and recover after 1983 (Graph 10). The composite index of profitability, a more complex business indicator, grows instead rapidly from 1982 reaching a peak which is well above that of the 1960s and 1970s (Graph 11). It does suggest a clear change in the business environment and is, thus far, the most unambiguous indication of a strong recovery.

2.   INDUSTRIAL GROWTH PATTERNS

2.1   Manufacturing Growth Rates

With all the qualifications suggested by the above analysis, I take the notion of 'recovery' as the premise for an investigation of the structural dynamics underlying the expansion. I discuss here manufacturing growth patterns and deal with consumption expenditure composition in the following chapter.

There are two ways in which the desegregated analysis in this chapter contributes to an understanding of the recovery. First, it clarifies the contribution of manufacturing to the overall growth of output; second, it shows which industries have been the most dynamic during the expansion. If we then consider industrial growth patterns within the cyclical pattern of the economy we can begin to explore some more specific questions: can we associate the recovery with a group of industries which, after experiencing sluggish growth in the 1970s, expanded rapidly in the 1980s? Is output composition and industrial structure very different from that of the high-growth 1958–66 cycle?

In order to discuss these questions it is necessary to analyze industrial structure changes over time. Taking the industrial structure of the mid-1960s as the starting point, I want to isolate a pattern of recovery, defined by high growth rates in the 1958–66 cycle, sluggish growth in the two following cycles, and rebound in the 1980s. Consequently a typical recovering industry has an output growth rate above that of the average of manufacturing in the first cycle, below in the two following cycles, and again above in the 1980s. A typical stagnating industry has the same characteristics, except that in the 1980s its growth rate remains below that of manufacturing. The pattern of recovering and stagnating industries is separated from that of *expanding* and *declining* industries, characterized by persistent growth rates above (below) the manufacturing average in most or all the four cycles.

Such analysis is based on the deviations of output growth rates for the 143 three-digit manufacturing industries of the Standard Industrial Classification. These deviations are calculated by subtracting the growth rate of output of the manufacturing sector from that of each of the 143 industries. These growth rates are averages computed for each of the four 'peak to peak' cycles.[1] This is just another way to analyze changes of industrial output composition, capable of identifying growing and declining industries. I have then used the set of conditions listed below to identify the industrial patterns relevant for my purposes. I first separate *growing* from *shrinking* industries, according to an output growth rate higher (lower) than the average for the cycle of the 1980s. The subgroups are then defined by additional conditions.

Expanding industries have a rate of growth above average for the three cycles before that of the 1980s; in strong expanding industries the rate of growth in the 1980s is also higher than that of the two previous periods. *Recovering* industries are characterized by a rate of growth below average for at least one of the two cycles before that of the 1980s. In addition, strong recovering industries had a rate of growth above average also in the 1958–66 cycle. *Declining* industries have a rate of growth below average in all the three cycles before the 1980s; *stagnating* industries have a rate of growth above average in the 1958–66 cycle and below in the two following cycles. For weak stagnating industries the rate of growth in the 1980s, though below average, is higher than in the two previous cycles.

The list of these conditions and the industries groupings resulting from them are indicated below.

1. Growing industries $\qquad$ $x_{i_4} > 0$

Subgroups:

1a.	$x_{i_{1\text{-}2\text{-}3}} > 0$	Expanding
1b.	$x_{i_{2\text{-}3}} > 0$	Strong expanding
	$x_{i_4} > x_{i_{2\text{-}3}}$	
1c.	$x_{i_{2\text{-}3}} < 0$	Recovering
1d.	$x_{i_{2\text{-}3}} < 0$	Strong recovering
	$x_{i_1} > 0$	

2. Shrinking Industries $x_{i_4} < 0$

Subgroups:

2a. $x_{i_{1\text{-}2\text{-}3}} < 0$ Declining

2b. $x_{i_1} > 0$ Stagnating

$x_{i_{2\text{-}3}} < 0$

2c. $x_{i_1} > 0$ Weak stagnating

$x_{i_{2\text{-}3}} < 0$

$x_{i_4} > x_{i_{2\text{-}3}}*$ (negative values)*

2.2   Summary of Industrial Patterns

There are sixty-six industries with a rate of growth of output above that of manufacturing in the 1979–86 period. Forty-three follow the recovery pattern as defined above. Eighteen of them had a rate of growth higher than that of manufacturing also in the 1958–66 cycle (strong recovering). Seventeen industries have a rate of growth consistently above that of manufacturing (expanding). Seven of them have a growth rate higher in the 1980s than in the two previous cycles (strong expanding). Finally, there are six growing industries which do not fit any of the criteria defined for the subgroups. We can conclude that the growing section of manufacturing includes less than half of the three-digit industries and that the recovering trend is rather widely spread.

The industries with an output growth rate below the average (shrinking industries) number seventy-seven and a large number of them (forty-five) do not fit any of the criteria defined for the subgroups. Thus the analysis is much less successful at isolating any clear pattern. It indicates that of the remaining thirty-two industries nineteen have a rate of growth consistently below that of manufacturing in the three periods before the 1980s (declining industries); thirteen have a growth rate higher than that of manufacturing in the 1958–66 cycle and then a below average rate (stagnating industries). The results point at the large number of industries which during the 1980s had growth rates below the average, indicating that for a large section of manufacturing the 1980s have not been years of expansion. Moreover, the pattern of decline and stagnation which characterizes over thirty-two three-digit industries was not reversed by the expansive trend of the economy.

To further analyze these results let us consider first the twenty two-digit sectors, to return later to the three-digit industries.[2] Using the results above it is possible to identify five '*positive-growth*' two-digit sectors, which are made up predominantly of recovering, expanding or growing industries:

Food and Kindred Products (SIC 20), Lumber and Wood Products (SIC 24), Furniture and Fixtures (SIC 25), Printing and Publishing (SIC 27), Instrument and Related Products (SIC 38). Overall, out of the thirty-six included in these five sectors, only six three-digit industries are stagnating, declining or shrinking. Printing and Publishing especially is noticeable for the presence of expanding and recovering industries only.

At the opposite end, the presence of shrinking, stagnating and declining industries clearly dominates seven '*negative growth*' two-digit sectors: Tobacco Manufacturers (SIC 21), Leather and Leather Products (SIC 31), Stone, Clay, and Glass Products (SIC 32), Primary Metal Industries (SIC 33), Fabricated Metal Products (SIC 34), Machinery, except Electrical (SIC 35), Miscellaneous Manufacturing Industries (SIC 39). However, with the exception of Leather and Leather Products and Miscellaneous Manufacturing Industries, there are recovering or expanding industries even within these sectors.[3] Still there is a fairly clear trend. It is impossible to speak of an overall trend for the other eight two-digit sectors, given the presence of divergent patterns of growth for the three-digit industries. I would call these two-digit sectors, in contrast with 'positive growth' and 'negative growth', '*non-growth*' sectors.[4]

This by itself indicates the limitation of the picture given by the two-digit sectors and the necessity of a finer analysis. Let us then turn to the three-digits industries with a more specific focus: examining which industries have sustained the expansion in the 1980s and distinguishing between the recovering and the expanding patterns.

More than half of the expanding industries (nine out of seventeen) are concentrated in three two-digits sectors: Printing and Publishing (SIC 27), Instruments and Related Products (SIC 38), Electric and Electronic Equipment (SIC 36).[5] On the other hand, such diverse industries as Office Furniture (SIC 252, in Furniture and Fixtures) and Office and Computing machines (SIC 357, in Machinery, except Electrical) can be considered part of a common trend of expansion of office-related equipment; similarly Miscellaneous Plastics Products (SIC 307, in Rubber and Misc. Plastics Products) and Plastics Materials and Synthetics (SIC 282, in Chemicals and Allied Products) indicate another trend of long-term expansion. We can therefore identify five cores of long-term expansion associated with: (i) publishing; (ii) instruments; (iii) electronics; (iv) office-related equipment and computers; (v) plastics.[6] To these we must add Drugs, Paper Mills, Misc. Primary Metal Products and Floor Covering Mills.[7]

The recovery pattern is most evident in 'positive growth' sectors such as Food and Kindred Products, Lumber and Wood Products, Printing and Publishing, where it is characteristic of the industries more clearly connected to printing. It is also present in those 'non-growth' sectors where there is hardly any long-term expanding trend, such as Textile, Apparel, Transportation. Within 'negative growth' sectors it concerns the glass and stone products industry (in Stone, Clay and Glass Products), the most generic metal products industries (in Fabricated Metal Products), chewing and smoking tobacco (in Tobacco Manufacturers) .

We can conclude that the recovery pattern is evident in industries within traditional mass production markets (Food, Textile, Apparel, Transportation, Printing), or associated with the exploitation of natural resources (Lumber, Pulp and Paper Products, Glass, Stone). We can also identify a recovery pattern associated with construction, which includes industries such as Partitions and Fixtures, Public Building & Related Furniture (both in SIC 25, Furniture and Fixtures), Paving and Roofing Materials (in SIC 29, Petroleum and Coal Products), and may help to explain the recovery of at least some of the 'natural resources' industries. The remaining recovering industries are associated with the generic production in the chemical, rubber and metal industry,[8] with the exception of Communication Equipment (SIC 366) and Ophthalmic goods (SIC 385).

To sum up: it is rather obvious that we cannot speak of a recovery sustained by a generalized expansion of manufacturing output. What is noticeable is rather the opposite: the selective nature of expansion focused on the recovery of a good number of industries and the continuing expansion of a limited number of relatively well identified areas of manufacturing.

However, only eighteen of the forty-three industries which have indeed recovered from slow growth in at least one of the two cycles before the 1980s, were top growers also in the 1958–66 cycle. These results suggest little similarity between the industrial expansion of the 1960s and the 1980s recovery, not only in quantitative terms (number of industries which were top growers in both periods), but also in terms of continuity of trends of industrial transformation. This conclusion is strengthened by observing the composition of this subgroup.[9] It includes rather diverse industries. Interesting, for different reasons, is the presence of relatively technologically sophisticated industries, such as communication equipment and ophthalmic goods, or of mature industries, like motor vehicles and transportation equipment. Using the tentative criteria suggested above, we can say that four industries belong to the traditional mass markets group, four to the natural resources group and two to construction.

Thus the recovering trend provides little evidence of a common manufacturing core leading industrial dynamics in the two periods. There is instead evidence of a sustained industrial transformation based on long-term expansionary trends. They concern some of the most technologically dynamic industries, most notably computers and electronics, publishing, instruments and advanced chemicals, including drugs.

NOTES

1. $X_{in} - X_n = x_{in}$, where:
   i = Standard Industrial Classification code;
   n = Periods: 1(1958–66), 2(1966–73), 3(1973–9), 4(1979–86).
2. In the second table of Appendix B three-digit industries are listed under the two-digit sector. They are also attributed to one of the six large groups denoted by Roman numbers:
   I.   Recovering industries: subgroups 1c. and 1d.
   II. Expanding industries: subgroups 1a and 1b.
   III. Growing industries: satisfying only condition $x_{i_4} > 0$.
   IV. Declining industries: subgroup 2a.
   V.   Stagnating industries: subgroups 2b. and 2c.
   VI. Shrinking industries: satisfying only condition $x_{i_4} < 0$.
3. Notice the long-term expansionary trend of Office and Computing Machines (SIC 357) within an otherwise 'negative growth' sector (SIC 35). There is another expanding industry in Primary Metal Industries. Recovering industries are in Stone, Clay, and Glass Products (three), in Fabricated Metal Products (two), in Primary Metal Industries (one) and in Tobacco Manufacturers (one).
4. Chemicals and Allied Products (SIC 28) and Electric and Electronic Equipment (SIC 36) are noticeable for the pattern of expansion of half of the three-digit industries. Textile Mill Products (SIC 22), Apparel and Other Textile Products (SIC 23), Paper and Allied Products (SIC 26) and Rubber and Misc. Plastics Products (SIC 30) have some recovering industries, but only three expanding industries. In the case of Transportation Equipment (SIC 37) there is an almost equal split between recovering and shrinking industries. Petroleum and Coal Products (SIC 29) is a non-growth sector with only one recovering industry connected to construction.
5. *Publishing*: Miscellaneous Publishing (SIC 274), Manifold Business Forms (SIC 276), Greeting Card Publishing (SIC 277); *Instruments and Related Products*: Engineering & Scientific Instruments (SIC 381), Measuring and Controlling Devices (SIC 382), Medical Instruments and Supplies (SIC 384); *Electrical and Electronic Equipment*: Radio and TV Receiving Equipment (SIC 365), Electronic Components and Accessories (SIC 367), Misc. Electrical Equipment and Supplies (SIC 369).
6. The list of 'strong expanding' industries (Subgroup 1b.) may add a further detail to the picture of long-term expanding trends: Office Furniture (SIC 252); Office and Computing Machines (SIC 357); Radio and TV Receiving Equipment (SIC 365); Paper Mills, except Building Paper (SIC 262); Miscellaneous Publishing (SIC 274); Greeting Card Publishing (SIC 277); Engineering & Scientific Instruments (SIC 381).
7. Drugs (SIC 283, in Chemicals and Allied Products); Paper Mills, except Building Paper (SIC 262, in Paper and Allied Products); Misc. Primary Metal Products (SIC 339, in Primary Metal Industries); Floor Covering Mills (SIC 227, in Textile Mill Products).
8. Metal Services, nec (SIC 347); Ordnance and Accessories, nec (SIC 348); Paints and Allied Products (SIC 285); Misc. Chemical Products (SIC 289); Reclaimed Rubber (SIC 303); Fabricated Rubber Products, nec (SIC 306); Secondary Nonferrous Metals (SIC 334).
9. Strong recovering industries (Subgroup 1d.): SIC 239 – Misc. Fabricated Textile Products; SIC 254 – Partitions and Fixtures; SIC 261 – Pulp Mills; SIC 264 – Misc. Converted Paper

Products; SIC 278 – Blankbooks and Bookbinding; SIC 285 – Paints and Allied Products; SIC 289 – Misc. Chemical Products; SIC 295 – Paving and Roofing Materials; SIC 306 – Fabricated Rubber Products, nec; SIC 321 – Flat Glass; SIC 323 – Products of Purchased Glass; SIC 334 – Secondary Nonferrous Metals; SIC 347 – Metal Services, nec; SIC 348 – Ordnance and Accessories, nec; SIC 366 – Communication Equipment; SIC 371 – Motor Vehicles and Equipment; SIC 379 – Miscellaneous Transportation Equipment; SIC 385 – Ophthalmic Goods.

8. Consumption expenditure composition

1. THE EVOLUTION IN THE POST-WAR PERIOD

A fundamental feature of the present analysis is the attention given to the demand side. The second aspect of structural transformation I examine is therefore the evolution of consumption spending in the post-war period.

The first level of desegregation available in National Income and Product Accounts (NIPA) shows the expenditure in durables, non-durables and services, as a share of total personal consumption (Citibase, quarterly data, current dollars, 1946–89). Those shares have changed significantly from 1946 to 1989 (Appendix C, Graphs 20–22). Durables account for almost 18 per cent of total consumption in the early 1950s and for less than 14 per cent in 1989. Non-durables' share accounts for less than 33 per cent of consumption expenditure in 1989, with a sharp decline from almost 60 per cent at the end of the war and around 50 per cent at the beginning of the 1950s. Services' share has an opposite trend, going from above 30 per cent at the beginning of the 1950s to more than 54 per cent in 1989.

Considering the evolution over time it can be observed that the durables' share has the most marked oscillations, following quite closely the cyclical pattern of GNP. With the exception of the 1949–51 peak it nevertheless remains substantially within a range defined by a minimum of 12 per cent in the troughs and above 15 per cent in the peaks. Non-durables and services' shares are in contrast most noticeable for the steadiness of their time trend, of decline and growth, respectively. In particular, non-durables' share declines over the entire period, oscillating more visibly during the 1970s and decreasing sharply in the 1980s; services' share grows rapidly in the 1950s and then at a slow rate, crossing the time path of non-durables at the beginning of the 1970s. It returns to rapid growth from the beginning of the 1980s.

Focusing on the 1980s it can be noted that the durables' share, after collapsing to post-war lows, grows from 1983 to reach a peak in 1987 and then oscillates around a roughly stable trend in the last years, edging downward in 1989. Non-durables's decline becomes more evident from 1980, though it stabilizes in 1987, while the rate of growth of the services' share accelerates, with a pause in 1984–6. It can be concluded that, at a first, very aggregate level, the 1980s are noticeable for the rapid growth of consumption of services, but also for the relatively high expenditure in durables, slowing down as non-durables stabilize.

The second level of desegregation available in National Income and Product Accounts gives data on twelve broad expenditure categories, as shares of total personal consumption. These data are a first indication of the magnitude and direction of change of consumption composition which occurred in the post-war period.

Before attempting any analysis of these trends it should be noted that they mirror the movements of very aggregate spending categories where goods and service-like activities are pulled together on the basis of the type of needs or functions they are meant to satisfy.[1] Not only do they therefore suffer from the problems of statistical manipulation,[2] but they are also affected by the heterogeneity of the industries involved. In particular the accuracy of these shares as a representation of consumption spending structure is affected by different dynamics of prices. It is indeed reasonable to hypothesize that some prices are under a downward pressure, reflecting more efficient production and economies of scale. It is not clear, however, to which expenditure categories it may more fully apply. The question is made more difficult by quality improvements, which can be reflected in higher prices. The crux of the matter is, of course, the relationship between productivity (and quality) and prices (relative prices) and, in general, the relationship between price setting and efficiency gains,[3] which in turn depend on technology, organizational changes and infrastructures development.

On the other hand, it would be scarcely satisfactory to make reference to price indexes, given the composite character of these categories and the problems of reliability of these indicators. In fact to improve the accuracy of the NIPA spending categories would require disentangling their evolution from the specific technological and market dynamics of a very large and complex aggregate of industries, a task which would take the present research away from its main goals.[4]

At the same time it can be argued that there is a bright side to the use of these categories. Precisely because they are large and aggregate they have the advantage of describing an underlying pattern of change which is not systematically distorted by industry-specific factors. Admittedly this is not an answer to the problems raised above. Nevertheless it may be sufficient to highlight the major trends in the evolution of consumption spending and discuss the underlying process of change in the sphere of consumption.

Indeed a quite clear picture of long-term consumption evolution seems to emerge from the analysis of NIPA spending categories. Changes in the relative position of the spending categories are summarized in Table 8.1.

Table 8.1   *Consumption Expenditure Composition (in per cent)*

	1950	1988
Food	30.0	19.0
Housing	11.0	15.5
Medical Care	5.0	12.75
Transportation	13.0	12.6
Household Operation	15.2	12.0
Recreation	5.7	7.6
Personal Business	3.4	7.3
Cloth	12.0	6.5
Welfare&Religious	1.25	2.27
Private Education	0.9	1.75
Personal Care	1.25	1.5
Foreign Travel& Other	0.35	1.00

Source: National Income and Product Accounts, Citibase, annual data.

From 1950 to 1988, food and clothing had the largest decline, medical care and personal business had the largest advance. There is little change in the share of transportation and personal care. Five of the remaining six categories increased and one, household operation, decreased. Consequently it can immediately be seen that the distribution of consumption spending has grown more even, with most categories expanding at the expense of food, clothing and, to a much smaller extent, household operation. On the other hand some categories, though growing dramatically, remain relatively small.[5]

Analyzing the time profiles (Appendix C, Graphs 23–34) we can observe that food, clothing and household operation have a clear long-term trend of decline, while medical care, education, recreation, personal business and religious and welfare activities have an opposite, upward trend.[6] The other four categories do not have a clear-cut pattern of growth or decline. Spending for housing grows until the early 1960s and then stabilizes, to edge upward from 1979. Transportation expenditure oscillates around a fairly stable trend from the early 1950s, edging downward from the end of the 1970s. Therefore they are both noticeable for being, at least for a prolonged period of time, a stable component of consumption spending. Also foreign travel expenditure remains stable for about twenty years, but then it collapses in the 1970s. Finally, personal care expenditure has a peculiar 'one-peak' time profile: it grows until the late 1960s and then it declines sharply until the beginning of the 1980s.

If we consider now more closely the pattern of the spending categories in the 1980s it can be observed that nine of them show noticeable peculiarities which may suggest significant processes of change. We can see a further impulse to the expansion of some of the growing categories, such as medical, education, recreation and personal business, and also an increase, though modest, of housing expenditure. The decade is also characterized by a new declining trend in transportation, a sharp reduction in household operation, the end of the decline of personal care expenditure, and the sudden expansion and contraction of travel expenditure.

2.   THE ENGEL LAW AND THE THEORY OF CONSUMPTION

This overview highlights the existence of two major trends: the decrease in relative importance of the most basic items of households' budgets, such as food, clothing and household operation; and the growing importance of new areas of consumption, mainly services, especially medical expenses and personal business. Less impressive is the growth of education, recreation and religious and welfare activities.

This evidence is consistent with the idea of a progressive saturation of inferior needs associated with the empirical regularity known as the Engel law and therefore suggests that the latter can be a first useful approximation for the study of consumption structure evolution. Any finer analysis, however, also highlights the severe limitations of this approach for developing a theory of consumption.

Pasinetti has shown that the Engel law is almost the only foundation for a theory of demand which goes beyond the static approach of demand theory based on the notion of consumer choice. In his growth model the generalization of the Engel curve notion allows for the treatment of the demand side within the analysis of growth and structural change. However the Engel law is an insufficient foundation for a theory of consumption evolution; by itself it cannot predict which expenditure categories could grow or shrink in relative terms. This kind of generalization is precisely what the law cannot do, because the principle of saturation of inferior needs is too weak to determine which areas of consumption are dominated by an income elasticity higher or lower than one. That is indeed what is implied saying that the law is just an observed empirical regularity. In this respect the empirical examination indicates that some expenditure categories do not have a clear pattern of growth or decline; for those which do it is still difficult to make the association with superior or inferior needs.

The Engel law in reality suffers from two kinds of problems. The first is the ambiguity inherent to a simplified notion of needs and needs hierarchy, specified only with respect to biological, life-sustaining, natural needs as opposed to all the rest. Indeed this is the classical political economy distinction between 'necessities' and 'luxuries'. By definition the working class would consume only necessities; what is not necessary, but rather superfluous, identifies the consumption of the wealthy classes, which represents a departure from the mere level of subsistence. The hierarchy of needs assumed by the Engel law is based on this distinction, which is fundamental to generating the income-led non-proportional growth of demand.

The second problem stems from the implicit identification between needs and goods. It was noticed earlier that hierarchy of wants does not mean hierarchy of goods, the crucial point being the technology connection. This aspect of the problem is clarified by Ironmonger's analysis of the impact of technical change on demand patterns (Ironmonger, 1972).

In the theoretical framework presented earlier the introduction and innovation of consumer durables bears a clear relationship to the process of market development and to the product cycle and is therefore independent of income dynamics. Moreover the determination of the actual composition of the consumption basket depends on the evolution of the modes of consumption, defined as a combination of goods and consumption practices.

Focusing on the changes in the modes of satisfaction of needs, according to the state of the technology and of what has been called 'social innovation' (Gershuny, 1983), we can gain a better perspective of consumption evolution than relying purely on the satiation rule of the Engel law. The latter ignores the modes of satisfaction of needs, and thus bypasses changes of products, technologies, infrastructures and social norms, which affect consumption choices and ultimately consumption composition. In turn the process of change depends on the development of the economic system in general and on that of the consumption sphere in particular.

3.   THE EX-POST FORECAST OF CONSUMPTION SHARES

3.1   The Forecast Model

To discuss on an empirical ground these issues I want to test how closely an income-led model predicts the composition of consumption expenditure in the 1980s. A discrepancy between an ex-post forecast of consumption shares and actual values in the 1980s, using a model estimated from the early 1950s to the end of the 1970s, would be an indication that factors other than income levels have had a significant influence on consumption composition. The inclusion of wealth and income distribution should improve the accuracy of the prediction, and therefore give full significance to these autonomous factors.

I estimate a single equation model with explanatory variables median income (87 dollars), share of income of the highest quintile of income distribution (current dollars) and wealth (eq. 89 in Fair, 1984, 82 dollars) and dependent variables for each of the twelve personal consumption expenditure categories of National Income Accounts.[7] The estimation period goes from 1952, the earliest observation available for wealth, to 1979.

It is a relatively straightforward and uncontroversial theoretical model.[8] It is neither a test of a particular theory of consumption nor a sophisticated estimation of Engel curves. The fit defines how good the model is, and then the income-generated dynamics, to predict consumption shares. Wealth and consumer debt are operating through their positive effect on spending and therefore reinforce the dynamic led by current income. The effect of income distribution should improve our understanding of the shift towards 'luxuries', goods whose income elasticity is high, since we have an increasing polarization of income distribution, with a larger share accounted for by the highest quintile.

A first estimation of this model shows a serious problem of serial correlation. The question arises as to the best correction for auto-correlation.[9] Without such a correction, regression estimated parameters are not reliable, typically showing a better fit. Under these conditions forecasting may be problematic.

Examining the auto-correlation function and the effects of different possible corrections for auto-correlation on the D–W statistics, the level of significance of the parameters and the overall explanatory power of the equations, it seems that one lag Moving Average and Auto-Regressive process corrections, at times combined or with their two lags correspondent, yield acceptable results. I then re-estimate the twelve equations for the 1953–79 period (see equations in Appendix C). Based on the fit, the sign and significance of the coefficients, this seems to be a reliable model to use for an ex-post forecast of consumption expenditure categories for the 1980s.[10]

The ex-post forecast is comprised within the two bands of the confidence interval of the forecast error. This source of error is quite independent of the fact that the model is likely to forecast better for some of the consumption categories than for others, since the estimated parameters depend on the stability of the relationship in the period of estimation.

3.2 The Forecast Results

In Appendix C, Graphs 35–46, the forecast values are plotted against actual values. The forecast is represented by the dotted line, actual values by the solid line. The two error bands are labeled with 'H'(high) and 'L'(low). By inspection it may immediately be noted where actual values diverge from the forecast beyond the confidence bands. These are the most important results for my purposes. They are, however, part of a rather complex picture.

To order the results of the forecasting exercise I have taken into account whether the actual values are substantially above, below or close to the forecast; remain within the confidence interval; are converging or diverging with respect to the trend of the forecast. The combination of these three elements identifies three groups:

1. categories for which there is a good correspondence between forecast and actual values: actual values lie outside the confidence bands interval at the beginning of the 1980s but have a converging trend which brings them substantially close to the forecast (Food, Cloth, Educa, Welfre);
2. categories whose actual values remain clearly above (Medic, Recrea, Persbu) or below (Houseop, Person) the forecast, are consistently outside the confidence bands and show a non-convergent trend;
3. the three remaining expenditure categories (House, Transp, Travel) are noticeable for the marked oscillations and no convergence of actual values towards the forecast. In particular House oscillates around the upper band and diverges upward after the mid-1980s; Transportation remains within the lower band to diverge downward after 1985; Travel has a peculiar pattern, with large oscillations which remain mostly within the confidence interval.

It can be concluded that the model predictions are fairly reliable for some consumption shares, but not accurate for a good number of them. However, while in the second group the forecast misses clearly the actual values, in the last group the bad correspondence is the result of wide oscillations.

Before any further analysis, let us consider the income-driven forecast results with respect to the long-term evolution of consumption composition examined in section 1. The most reliable predictions concern four categories which have a clear long-term pattern of decline (Food and Cloth) and expansion (Educa, Welfre). In this case the pattern of actual values does not seem to be decisively influenced by other determinants outside those considered by the forecast model, though their convergence can be the result of distinct phenomena.[11]

At the opposite end the bad predictions for the second group are a clear indication that other factors exert a significant influence, modifying their long-term trend.[12] Autonomous factors must be at work to explain the upward pattern of medical care, recreation and personal business. Similarly an explanation is needed for the case of expenditure categories (Houseop and Person) which have decreased more than predicted by the forecast. A peculiar problem is posed by Person. There is no trend whatsoever in the long-term evolution of this category. Moreover the downward divergence of actual values from the forecast coincides with a stabilization after almost two decades of sharp decline.

Finally, the third group is made up of three categories (House, Transp, Travel) which do not have a long-term pattern of growth or decline. The forecast exercise therefore confirms their sensitivity to more short-term variables than those considered in the regression model.

The forecast results also confirm the difficulty of an 'a priori' classification of expenditure categories along the lines of a distinction between 'necessities' and 'luxuries'. Good predictions (first group) concern categories with both long-term ascending and declining trends. The same is true of bad predictions (second group). A further effort in that direction is to take into account the sign of the income distribution variable of the forecasting model. The sign is negative for food, clothing, household operation, personal care, education, recreation and travel; positive for house, medical care, personal business, transportation and religious and welfare activities. Once again, the attempt to discriminate between spending categories associated with the satisfaction of inferior and superior needs fails to provide a consistent picture.[13]

To conclude: the ex-post forecast has more clearly identified a number of phenomena of the 1980s whose interpretation is difficult within the income-generated dynamics of the model. Such a prediction can then be used as the backdrop for the study of the structural determinants accounting for the actual pattern of consumption composition. The need of other determinant beyond the influence exerted by income growth is evident for those which diverge from the forecast and for those categories which do not have a clear pattern of growth or decline, highlighting the problems inherent to the Engel law approach to the analysis of consumption evolution.

4. CONSUMPTION COMPOSITION AND NEW MARKETS

Interpreting the overall picture emerging from the analysis of long-term trends and ex-post forecasts raises a number of problems. At the onset of the analysis I mentioned the problem of the effects of price dynamics on the relative size of consumption shares. It may be appropriate at this point to say a few words on how they can influence the results of the analysis.

It can be supposed that downward pressures on prices may have a significant impact on expenditure categories such as Food, Cloth, Houseop, Person, and in general in the most established areas of spending of the household budget, dominated by mass-produced goods. We should recall also the influence of low-priced imports, which have largely replaced domestic production in some markets.[14] At the opposite end an upward price pressure may account for the steep rise of medical care expenditures in the 1980s or for the upward long-term trend of education expenditure. Similarly the boom of real estate values in some of the metropolitan areas, at least up to 1987, may have had a significant influence on the expenditure for housing in the 1980s.

It is also reasonable to assume that other economic variables may be relevant to the explanation of the divergence of consumption shares from the forecast. For instance it is reasonable to assume that the pattern of House is influenced by fluctuations of the interest rate, via the cost of mortgages. The dollar exchange rate can probably help to explain the pattern of Travel, which seems to follow quite closely the cyclical appreciation and depreciation of the US currency. But then other factors may have even more important sector-specific implications. In the case of housing, one may note the importance of phenomena such as growing urbanization and the associated effects on the housing market and real estate sector; in the case of transportation, the growing importance of transportation, connected to a rising demand for mobility, though this may be more than compensated by development of transportation infrastructures and the consolidation of transport technology.[15] Note finally that expenditure for housing and transportation both depend on land use and localization patterns which are part of an evolving spatial structure.

It is evident that this approach almost inevitably leads to a list of 'ad hoc' explanations for the individual areas of spending. Though full of reasonable observations, this approach cannot substitute for a systematic interpretation. Nor can it be rescued by a more detailed analysis, though that would certainly be possible and interesting. In other words, it poses the problem of a theoretical perspective to guide the interpretation.

In this respect it can be noted that 'ad hoc' explanations can be divided into two types of influences: (1) the short-term effects of oscillations of economic variables which originate outside the long-term dynamics of structural change and in some instances impose their importance over structural determinations; (2) social, demographic and, in general, non-economic factors which are part of the dynamics of change. An example of the first type of effects is the case of Travel, where the influence of the dollar exchange rate seems to be more important than any restructuring of the tourism industry. Examples of the second type are the influences of the spatial structure on the expenditure for transportation or housing, but also the overall aging of the population which by itself creates more demand for medical care.

While the effects of economic variables can be assimilated, for the present purposes, to exogenous shocks, non-economic factors are intertwined with the long-term dynamics of structural change. Both can be distinguished by the persistent economic forces which drive the endogenous process of structural transformation identified in the structural dynamics of market creation specific to the particular phase of development of the economic structure.

The above distinction is quite similar to that made by Schumpeter searching for the inner mechanism of economic development. It is well known that Schumpeter locates the mechanism of economic development in the innovation process. However, the interpretation of his views advanced in Chapter 1 suggests that an essential aspect of growth and structural change is the development of new markets. The premise is therefore that the core of the dynamics of change is the process of market creation which is combined with the evolution of the consumption sphere. This is what I refer to when speaking of the economic forces constituting the structural determination of consumption patterns.

Returning to the forecast exercise, it was noted that in some cases the unsatisfactory correspondence between actual and predicted values may depend on sector-specific factors. This problem is more evident for the expenditure categories which have a broken pattern marked by wide oscillations. It then becomes even more difficult to disentangle these effects from structural determinations discussed in the theoretical scheme. For the categories which conform, more or less smoothly, to a trend of expansion or decline the most interesting are those where the actual values are above the forecast, since they suggest a demand expansion which is not captured by the regression model. This group includes Medic, Recrea and Persbu.

In the case of Persbu, whose expenditure more than doubles in the post-war period, but noticeably takes off after 1980, there seems to be solid ground for arguing that growth is a result of product innovation and industry restructuring. In particular it can be explained by the development of financial services, their marketing to consumers, and the increasing awareness and importance of financial investment on the part of the public.

Underneath the expansion of medical care and recreation is the 'quality of life' demand, the exploitation of the potential implicit in changes of life styles and in the 'free time' dimension, phenomena typical of modern industrial societies and therefore connected to the improvement of living standards and working conditions. But there is more. Medical care and recreation represent the development of new large markets which have seen, during the 1980s, many organizational and technological changes, combined with the penetration by business and commodity production. For example, the advances in medical science and therapeutical means have a weight of their own in determining the expansion of this type of expenditure, via enlarged and increasingly sophisticated technologies.

At the opposite end we have the more than proportional decrease of expenditure categories such as Houseop and Person. In the case of Houseop and Person it could be argued that the lack of innovation in the modes of satisfaction of needs and the scarce opportunity for further need development in these well established areas of consumption spending explain the absence of a strong expansionary trend which could counter the effects of market saturation. However, given also the already noticed downward price pressures which may have contributed significantly to the shrinking of these types of expenditures, we should not underestimate the pressures created by product innovation and life style changes, which may have helped to stabilize spending in these areas. In the case of Houseop, which includes appliances, we can recall the introduction of a new generation of consumers' durables and the rise of new complementarities associated with them, which may have sustained the bulk of spending. In the case of Person, there is no ready explanation for the pattern of continuous and sharp decline after 1968. As for its stabilization in the 1980s, one may notice that this category includes health clubs, which is certainly one area of expansion during the 1980s and could be seen as part of the already mentioned 'quality of life–free time' dimension, an aspect of need development which may have sustained demand expansion.

NOTES

1. For instance: food includes both the purchase of food and that of meals, therefore lumping together expenditures associated with distinct consumption technologies and practices and different impacts on the industrial structure.

2. National income statistics rely often on imputation procedures, with the problems which may arise from that, the most well known being that of the imputed rents for those who own their homes.
3. The problem is well illustrated by Pasinetti, especially in his 1993 essay.
4. Research on productivity and price indexes and industries' relative weights measurement could indeed be useful for a more focused empirical analysis.
5. For instance: education's share, which refers only to private education, almost doubles, but remains a small portion of total expenditure. The same applies to religious and welfare activities and to foreign travel.
6. Within this overall pattern there are differences. Among declining categories, clothing is noticeable for the sharp decline in the 1950s; household operation expenditure shows a broken pattern, with a sharp decline in the second part of the 1960s and again in the 1980s. Among growing categories, the rate of growth of personal business expenditure accelerates markedly after 1981. In contrast for education and recreation the rapid growth of the 1960s gives way to almost flat rates during the 1970s and to renewed growth in the 1980s.
7. A second specification adding consumer debt – Business Conditions Digest, Ratio Consumer Credit Outstanding to Personal Income – as an independent variable does not add to the explanatory power of the model. A measure of consumer debt is contained in the variable wealth in Fair (1984).
8. I depart from the literature and Fair specification in so far as I do not take into account the effect of the interest rate. The rate of interest does not add very much to the explanatory power of the relationship. It may be important to stress a particular theory of consumption. It should be noted that prices are not included either.
9. The D–W statistic improves using 1954–66 as sample estimation period, but a 1953–79 sample seems more appropriate for forecasting into the 1980s. The problem of course is that of correct specification. In this respect it should be noted that 'this statistic [the Durbin–Watson statistic] was actually first developed as a test for autocorrelated disturbances … However, it is more suitably regarded nowadays as a test statistic for possible mis-specification' (Thomas, 1997, p.158).
10. It must be stressed that the purpose of the exercise is solely to highlight by means of a rough approximation the main tendencies of the consumption structure evolution. More 'ad hoc' econometric techniques are indeed discussed in the literature (Deaton and Muellbauer, 1980). Furthermore the short period of estimation and the fact that we are dealing with shares makes largely irrelevant the study of the stationary properties of the time series used for the forecast.
11. The convergence from below of 'necessities' such as Food and Cloth after 1984 could be attributed to the slow income growth of the early 1980s and the shift of income distribution that may have forced these categories to weigh more on low-income households, whereas the predictions for Educa and Welfre are overall the best generated by the model.
12. It must be noted though that the pattern of actual values does not contradict the tendencies signaled by long-term trends, but only magnifies them.
13. Whereas the sign is what you would expect for some categories, given the long-term trends, it is puzzling for recreation, private education and foreign travel. At the same time, could we conclude that the expenditure for housing, medical care and transportation could be treated as 'luxuries'? In any event we certainly do not get a clear-cut answer.
14. The loss of competitive edge of some areas of US manufacturing was a main theme of the debate about the industrial restructuring of the 1980s. A look at the imports–output ratio between 1972 and 1982, however, shows some unexpected results. Though the largest increase is for the Shoes and Leather industry, large increases concern Office Equipment, except Computers, Machinery and Motor Vehicles. The ratio had actually decreased, not

only for computers, but also for Textiles, Knitting, TV, Radios and Phonographs (Report of the President's Commission on Industrial Competitiveness).

15. Transportation expenditure is such a composite category that it is hard to speculate on any set of more specific explanations.

9. Market development and output composition

1. MARKET DEVELOPMENT AND OUTPUT GROWTH

To pursue the analysis of the evolution of the consumption sphere in the 1980s we can also take a different point of view. Changes in the composition of consumption expenditure, especially when they suggests a rate of market formation exceeding that implied by income growth, point in the direction of 'autonomous' factors determining market creation. In general, the specific characteristics of the development of the needy individual and the form taken by the satisfaction of needs within a system of modes of life depend on the strategy of market development pursued by firms in their effort to shape the consumption sphere in a way consistent with their expansion.

In this chapter the focus is on this fundamental aspect of the market creation process, though the approach is that of macro analysis, rather than that of sector or even product analysis. More specifically, the analysis concerns the relationship between the market development effort and a measure of its success, the rate of growth of sales. The first is defined by a set of independent variables which should capture the active role of firms in the market creation process; industry sales, on the other hand, can be treated as very crude first approximation of the changes in the consumption sphere and of market creation.

What is obviously missing is a measure of the extent to which market development has indeed translated potential market into market creation and how much of the expansion of sales signals changes in modes of life and modes of satisfaction of needs leading to an overall expansion of the market. Despite this limitation,[1] this way of proceeding gives factual basis grounding to the interpretation of the recovery and also to the discussion of more general concerns raised by the theory of the consumption–growth relationship. In particular, this type of testing addresses the question of the relationship between technology, investment and market growth as a key issue for interpreting the 1980s and for the long-term path of advanced market economies.

Before the econometric testing, the variables which 'measure' the market development effort require two general remarks. Market development is a central notion in the effort to analyze the relationship between technical change, innovation and investment, on the one hand, and the consumption sphere, on the other. This set of variables should therefore be capable of quantifying the many dimensions contained in the notion of market development, but at the same time they cannot but reflect the limitations imposed by the available data sources. The result is a set of independent variables which, though containing a fairly general and largely accepted hypothesis about the factors which affect sales growth, is still original with respect to the literature on innovation and technical change, particularly in so far as it attempts to measure the impact of new products and some aspects of the marketing effort.

2.   ECONOMETRIC TESTING

2.1   Variables and Data Series

Contrary to the complexity of the questions it should help to analyze stands the straightforwardness of the model used for the econometric testing. Output growth is the dependent variable, taken as the measure of the success of investment in market development. Four indicators are used as explanatory variables: number of new products, expenditure in advertising, expenditure in R&D, net investment in plant and equipment. Patents have been excluded. A measure of the level of 'industrialization' of the industry, to be defined by means of a sort of concentration ratio or other measure of financial control, is a possible fifth indicator, which however is not considered here.

Ideally the test would involve a time series multivariate regression. Not only could we test the correlation of the above indicators with the dependent variable for all the industries of the sample, but we could also examine changes through time for selected industries. In particular we could observe in which industries this correlation is strongest and whether it increased in the 1980s. The result would be even more significant if a strong correlation were found for expanding and recovering industries. This type of testing is impossible, given data availability. The counting of new products is available only for 1982. Also data on advertising are not readily available and have to be manipulated to become usable. The only testing possible is a cross-section analysis. Also the lag structure is pretty much determined by considerations around data availability. The size of the sample will depend on the completeness of the information for each of the variables.[2]

A brief overview of the conceptual problems raised by each of the independent variables is necessary to complete the description of the testing and may help to evaluate its results. The investment data come from the same source as the output data. Net investment at the three-digit level in 1982 dollars is available from the data base of the Office of Business Analysis of the Department of Commerce. These should be fairly reliable data and there is no issue of comparability and completeness, since they come from the same domain, that of statistical sources. It is not clear, however, to what extent new plant and equipment can be associated with restructuring and innovation. Restructuring may take place with relatively small outlays in plant and equipment. Presumably new technology is embodied in new machinery, and that is some indication of the intensity of innovation. Most important, net investment implies expansion of capacity and therefore of output.

The question of comparability of data arises with two variables, new products and advertising, which come from business sources. It is hard to assess their reliability, but it is reasonable to suppose that the advertising data can be a guide to short-term decisions, within certain industries and product groups, rather than an indication of a more general effort of market development. Moreover manipulation of these data is necessary to match them with three-digit industries, adding to the problem of their reliability (see Appendix D). The survey of new products seems more reliable; since the methodology for the collection of the data is clearly spelled out and the amount of data manipulation considerably less (see Appendix D).

The R&D data raise three kinds of problems. The ambiguity of the relationship between innovation and R&D expenditure and the difficulty of establishing the productivity of R&D expenditure, and therefore the impact on output, are well documented in the literature. We should mention also the sensitivity of this kind of investment to the technological characteristics of the industry. As a proxy for market development, R&D expenditure has another problem. It seems entirely possible that research and development expenditure in one industry may not create much market, that is sales growth, for itself, but rather do so for other industries, depending on the inter-industry structure. Finally the data set has only fourteen industries listed and the data had to be applied to 143 three-digit industries, a procedure which, though unavoidable, is likely to make the information much less interesting.

In addition to these explanatory variables a trend variable, taking into account the rate of change of sales over a ten-year period, is added to give full relevance to the regression analysis.

2.2 Model Specification and Results

The cross-section regression equation used for the test has the following form:

Dsales=b_1+b_2Dinvest+b_3Salestrn+b_4Newprd+b_5DR&D+b_6RDSales+b_7 Adver

where

Dsales = average rate of change of output, 1983–6,
Dinvest = average rate of change, net investment, 1980–83,
Salestrn = average rate of change of output, 1973–83,
Newprd = new products, 1982,
DR&D = rate of change R&D expenditure, 1980–81 (constant 82 dollars),
RDsales = R&D–sales ratio, 1981,
Adver = per cent rate of change of the advertising expenditure–sales ratio, 1983–4.

Despite the relatively high R^2, the independent variables chosen as measures for market development and available for an eighty industries sample have all, with the exception of net investment, coefficients which cannot statistically be distinguished from 0. This overshadows the fact that they actually turn out to be small and negative. The only significant coefficient, which is also positive and high, is that of the sales trend variable. The overall significance of the relationship is confirmed by the F statistic which is significant at the 1 per cent level of confidence. In contrast, the test for the existence of serial correlation is indeterminate.

Before discussing these results a few observations are in order. Some experimentation with the regression model with different samples shows that the R^2 improves slightly when adding independent variables. The first regression has as independent variable, besides the sales trend and investment, new products, available for 117 industries. The second and third add the rate of change of R&D expenditure, and the ratio of R&D to sales, available for 101 and 92 industries, respectively. The last sample, when advertisement is included, is of eighty industries. The coefficients remain statistically non-significant. Dropping the trend variable, one of the independent variables, new products, becomes significant with all samples, with a positive coefficient around 0.02. Dropping the sales trend variable, the Durbin–Watson statistics indicate no autocorrelation and the F statistics indicate that the relationship remains statistically significant.

Excluding the trend variable, the R^2 drops to about 0.2. This is the explanatory power of a bivariate regression involving sales growth and new products. Regressing the sales trend on the latter, the R^2 is 0.45. It could be inferred that the two variables are correlated. Using them together causes the variable new products to lose its importance.

There seems therefore to be some ground rescuing the variable new products, at least to the extent that its behavior is quite distinct from that of the other four independent variables, which, as noted above, are never significant and add little to the R^2 of the regression.

3.   MARKET DEVELOPMENT AND GROWTH IN THE 1980s

The results of the cross-sectional analysis suggest that there is no correlation between investment in market development and sales in the period considered. Most disturbing in this respect is the fact that the trend variable accounts by itself for most of the explanatory power of the relationship, denying precisely the role of independent determination of sales growth based on market development strategies.

Quite independently of the theoretical hypothesis about the relationship between market development, market creation and changes of consumption patterns that it is intended to explore, this is a somewhat unexpected result. Given the rather plausible specification of the regression equation one would expect that at least some of the independent variables would have an impact on sales. There is indeed a broad agreement on the importance of investment in technology to foster innovation and of advertising in improving sales performance. The most controversial aspect may be that of new products, which is the only one finding some support in the test.

It seems reasonable to draw two general conclusions from these results. With respect to the notion of market development discussed in the previous chapters, the model specification is far from being satisfactory. Consequently the possibility that the relationship involves other variables expressing independent determinants and that a better specification of the model could improve the results cannot be discarded. Thus the analysis of the relationship between market creation and consumption sphere evolution can be only very partially illuminated by the simple model used for the econometric exercise. On the other hand, the complexity of the notion of a consumption sphere and the difficulties of quantification imply that many aspects of the theoretical argument remain outside the reach of the modeling required by econometric testing.

Despite the specification and data reliability problems, the testing adds new elements to our knowledge on the evolution of the consumption sphere and the process of market creation in the 1980s. Nor should its value be underestimated as a systematic effort to explore the relationship between investment in market development and market creation. In particular, it reaches a quite clear, though somewhat unexpected, result: that the hypothesis of a strong dependence between investment, R&D, advertising and sales is unwarranted for the central years of the 1980s expansion. Thus, the test suggests that the movements of sales during the recovery of the 1980s cannot be correlated with investment in market development and innovation in any simple, straightforward manner. This clears the way to the search for the mechanisms accounting for the considerable amount of change observed in the sphere of consumption in the period.

The model used for the testing suggests a more general conclusion. Indeed, the relationship between trend and target variable discussed here can be considered a discrimination test for innovation. Only when the sales trend is not dominating can we expect a phase of 'creative destruction'. This could be a first condition for a set of criteria identifying a Schumpeterian expansion, though doing so is beyond the scope of the present investigation.

NOTES

1. It is hard to see how these limits could be overcome, unless moving to a more qualitative type of analysis.
2. For a description of the data sources and of the other aspects of the testing, see Appendix D.

10. The structural dynamics of the 1980s: recovery and the transformation of the consumption sphere

1. THE RESULTS OF THE EMPIRICAL ANALYSIS

As pointed out earlier, the empirical analysis has a limited and self-contained goal, to illustrate the structural dynamics of the 1980s, with particular attention to consumption evolution, and highlight some 'facts' about the recovery. This chapter summarizes its results and puts them in the broader perspective of the industrial transformation. The observed pattern of change is then used to discuss the transformation of the consumption sphere and the process of market creation. This is the basis for the interpretation of the recovery presented in the concluding chapter.

1.1 The Macroeconomic Profile

The analysis at the aggregate level in the first part of Chapter 7 casts considerable doubt on an unqualified use of the term 'recovery' for the expansion of the 1980s. Based on GNP growth rates, it is hard to maintain that it was a strong cyclical upturn, at least in comparison with the 1958–66 cycle. Indeed the data suggest a rather weak expansion by post-war standards. It seems questionable to conclude that the recovery led to a return to prosperity.[1]

Overall the statistical evidence gives a fairly clear picture of the peculiarities of the recovery. Together with the rapid growth of GNP and per capita disposable income after 1983, what is mostly noticeable is the role of consumption spending in sustaining aggregate demand, though draining savings and pushing consumers into debt, while investment is weaker than could have been expected. A second peculiarity is the standstill of workers' compensation. After the decline in the 1970s, there has been little improvement. But even profits are not at record highs. Still the profitability index suggests a major change with respect to the previous cycles. Finally, what seems certainly to have changed is income distribution, as the recovery benefits higher-income recipients.

1.2   Manufacturing Growth Patterns

The aggregate analysis poses even more cogently the question of what has really changed in these years. The desegregated analysis therefore becomes even more relevant.

Though certainly not complete, the picture of manufacturing growth patterns highlights three main facts: (1) the large number of shrinking industries (seventy-seven, more than half), some of which follow a pattern of long-term decline (nineteen) or stagnation (thirteen), and therefore a widespread declining pattern in manufacturing in the central years of the recovery; (2) a recovering pattern which concerns less than one-third of industries (forty-three) which indeed returned to growth rates above the average, though only eighteen had growth rates above average also in the 1960s cycle; (3) the expansion of a relatively small number of industries (seventeen), which represents the continuation of long-term trends already present in the 1960s.

Thus the recovery was not centered on a generalized growth of manufacturing and the cyclical upturn can only very partially be associated with the recovery of the manufacturing industries which were top growers in the 1958–66 cycle. Based on the remarks made in Chapter 7 it seems fair to conclude that the recovering industries, rather than pushing the process of structural change, benefited from improved market conditions. In other words their recovery was the result of a structural dynamics mostly originating elsewhere in the economic structure.

More relevant processes of structural change seem rather associated with the industries which expanded steadily at growth rates higher than the average since the 1960s, some at increasing rates in the 1980s (strong expanding). Their growth suggests some fairly clear trends of industrial transformation.

1.3   Consumption and Output Composition

The evolution of the structure of consumption in the post-war period shows indeed a pattern of non-proportional growth, consistent along general lines with the Engel curve, but it is also marked by movements which are hard to explain in that framework. Therefore, though confirming the validity of the Engel curve as a general guideline for long-term evolution of consumption spending, the empirical analysis confirms also its weaknesses as a theory of consumption evolution. This conclusion is strengthened by the ex-post forecast into the 1980s.

The observed evolution of the consumption structure suggests that structural determinants, distinct from the effects of sector-specific economic variables and non-economic variables, affect consumption independently from the income-driven non-proportional growth of demand. This calls attention to the *causes of long-term shifts in consumption expenditure, which can add to the ordering of the Engel curve.*

On the other hand, the cross-section regression analysis in Chapter 9 shows that the expansion of sales of US manufacturing in the 1983–6 period cannot be associated with outlays in capital, technology and marketing investment, though the test tentatively confirms the importance of new products. It must be concluded that there is no support for the idea that investment in market development, at least as measured by the variables included in the regression equation, led manufacturing output growth during the recovery.

The test suggests that the main force behind the expansion was not an *investment push driven by innovation*, directing the attention to other determinations that may have had a decisive influence in shaping the expansion of the economy. It also raises the question of the role and characteristics of investment, which is fundamental to understanding the process of change.

2. RECOVERY AND STRUCTURAL TRANSFORMATION

The statistical evidence indicates that indeed economic growth did not return in the 1980s to the vigorous pace of the 1960s and that, considering the macroperformance of the US economy in previous cycles, even the very notion of the recovery is questionable. And yet the process of change is quite evident both in the industrial structure and in the consumption structure.

2.1 Process of Change and Industrial Patterns

From the point of view of the manufacturing industry structure, assessing the process of change is first of all a matter of recognizing the unevenness in the process of industrial development. Separating decline from growth, it is then possible to qualify the expansion of some areas of manufacturing. In this respect we noted that the expansion of the 1980s was marked by the return to growth of a number of industries, including a limited number of top growers in the 1958–66 cycle, and the continuation of some long-term trends of expansion.

These two results suggest that there is little continuity with the industrial structure of the 1958–66 cycle and the recovery of the economy had a substantially different industrial dynamics, where a prominent role may be played by expanding industries. At the same time, the statistical evidence, while confirming that major changes are taking place with respect to the 1960s, does not suggest a *clear structural break* with respect to the 1970s.[2]

However, neither the large amount of change observed, nor the characteristics of industrial growth of the period should be underestimated. In particular, what comes to light is a process of selective expansion within the manufacturing industry. While only some sections of manufacturing had a strong impact on output expansion, the trend centered on the expanding industries suggests a process of industrial transformation led by some pivotal industries which are the dynamic core of an otherwise slow growing manufacturing sector.

2.2 Consumption Spending

Some clearer conclusions can be drawn from the analysis of consumption evolution. There is evidence that the recovery was sustained by consumption spending. What is most noticeable, however, is the deep change in the consumption structure.

The analysis confirms the sensitivity of the consumption structure to factors specific to the single expenditure categories and, more importantly, highlights the fact that other determinations magnify or contradict in the 1980s the income-generated dynamic of demand expansion. The forecast values show noticeable divergence from the pattern of consumption spending predicted by an income-led model. This is the clearest indication that factors autonomous from the spending propensities of consumers, guided by the principle of saturation in a hierarchical ordering of needs, have an important role in determining the consumption structure.

In the 1980s the bulk of the 'autonomous' expansion of consumption spending was in some areas of superior needs, which are satisfied by what we can broadly call 'service industries' (Health Care, Entertainment, Finance, Education). Some interesting remarks concern also the pattern of spending in other areas (Nutrition, Personal Care) affected by technical change and consumption innovation.

These are the areas where one would reasonably expect the most intense process of market creation and structural change. The analysis of the consumption structure then poses the question of the kind of transformation underneath the rise of new industries and new products, which have changed the structure of final demand.

2.3   Growth Patterns and Market Creation

The analysis of manufacturing growth patterns indicates that there is little
evidence of a manufacturing-driven expansion. The results of the test in
Chapter 9 confirm that and warn against an unqualified reference to a
recovery driven by innovation and market development. Thus, even with
the caution imposed by the limitation of the test, there is no evidence of a
clear break associated with an investment boom and/or a radical innovation-
driven expansion.

The regression equation includes a counting of new products and a
measure of advertisement expenditure, and yet it is based on largely
accepted notions on the relationship between innovation, investment and
market creation. Though it can hardly be taken to be a test of a neo-
Schumpeterian hypothesis based on technology-driven investment, it seems
sufficient to indicate that an attempt to explain the recovery along those
lines encounters serious difficulties. In other words, while it may not be
damaging to the general views maintained by neo-Schumpeterian theory, it
warns against any recourse to Schumpeterian arguments, such as
innovation, technology, new products and/or entrepreneurship, as key
factors in explaining the expansion and the market creation process of the
1980s. Most damaging to any interpretation in this direction is the poor
sensitivity of desegregated manufacturing output to variables other than the
sales trend.

3.   TRENDS OF TRANSFORMATION

3.1   Industrial Transformation Reconsidered

We have therefore reached three main conclusions about the structural
dynamics of the period. Neither the pace of aggregate growth nor the
manufacturing dynamics indicates a decisive break with the 1970s.
Furthermore it seems fair to conclude that any Schumpeterian explanation
of the expansion is not quite appropriate. These negative conclusions
contrast with the evidence of a deep change of consumption spending
composition. Thus, while less than impressive growth rates suggest that
there was no reversal of the tendency to a low growth rates regime, there
are indications of a change in the mechanism of growth and market creation
which remains to be explained.

In order to discuss the problem posed by these results we have to
consider the process of industrial transformation from a broader
perspective: we ought to consider the dynamics of services and then

develop a comprehensive view of the process of industrial transformation. Indeed industrial transformation must be seen in the light of two phenomena: (1) the decline in the production of goods versus services and (2) the role played by services in the restructuring of production processes and in the overall changes of output composition.

In Chapter 7 we have seen that the growth of the service sector output stands in sharp contrast with the decline of industry output throughout the post-war period. The growth of the service sector continues unabated through the recovery, confirming and reinforcing such a long-term trend. As a result, during the 1980s, output expansion is mostly driven by the growth of service-like industries and only by some sections of manufacturing.

These phenomena must be seen in a light of a change in the role played by services. In a very interesting analysis of the 'service economy' (Stanback et al., 1981) it is stressed that changes in the composition of output between products and services are not the result of some change in the preference structure, but rather of changes in the organization of the productive process. The growth of services is sustained by their increasing importance as intermediate input rather than as items of final consumption. But this implies that products and consumption activities have changed as well. While changes in the input structure respond to technology, they determine qualitative change in consumption.

The search for quality, the differentiation of products and the structuring of new life styles is just the other side of a reorganization of the productive system driven by large-scale production and the potential for economies of scale it entails. The very process of industrialization of production processes and homogenization of consumption models sustains the creation of permanent market niches and therefore market complexity and segmentation. In fact, 'Larger markets provide demand sufficient to support a larger number of differentiated models' (Stanback et al., 1981, p.28).[3] The process is reinforced by specialization in the information channels and cultural media, which in turn takes the form of product differentiation from the point of view of the industries involved.[4]

We can conclude that the role played by the service sector, coupled with its constant growth, is the main factor linking industrial transformation and consumption evolution. This has strong implications for the process of transformation of the consumption sphere.

3.2 Industrial Transformation and the Consumption Sphere

While the rise of producers' services is one of the most important characteristics of the industrial restructuring of the 1970s, the changes of the consumption structure indicate that in the 1980s not only industrial transformation but also output expansion depends largely on the growth of services. Thus the 1980s are dominated by the unfolding effects of the tendencies of industrial transformation emerging in the 1970s, but also by new phenomena. such as the emergence of new industries, which profoundly change the structure of consumption and the household consumption basket. Thus the evolution of the consumption structure must be comprehended in a larger transformation which redefines consumption possibilities and routines.

This is fundamental to understanding *the nature of the structural break* with the previous period and addressing the question of the recovery. Rather than interpreting the bulk of the transformation along the lines of a Schumpeterian expansion, driven by new products and a surge of industrial investment, it seems more appropriate to think of a transformation which reshapes the consumption sphere and drives the process of market creation. An essential aspect of it is the change in the composition and characteristics of investment, directed to the restructuring of productive processes particularly in the rapidly growing service-like industries. The pattern of industrial investment determines innovation and affects consumption spending. In turn, the particular form taken by market development shapes the process of market creation and ultimately the characteristics of income creation and distribution.

3.3   New Products, New Industries, New Markets

To highlight the characteristics of the new phase of development emerging in the 1980s it is possible to identify three directions of transformation of the consumption sphere. The first is the restructuring of consumers' good markets based on the definition of high standards of quality. For consumer durables, such as automobiles, appliances and consumer electronics, but also for non-durables, like apparel and food, the effort to compete by means of 'technological obsolescence' translates into a strategy of introduction of new lines of products with higher standards of performance, which define the up-to date level of quality for specific areas of consumption spending. This implies both technological and markets research and, often, the creation of specialized services closely linked to the growth and restructuring of entire industries. A good example may be the fashion industry.

New lines of products embody most recent technologies. Typically these take the form of replacement of mechanical and electrical devices with electronics components in durables, the increasing sophistication of the technology of materials, components and ingredients mix for non-durables, and the diffusion of computer-based design and manufacturing for both. As a result of the new technology, desirable characteristics of the product are more fully realized and new ones are made possible.

Product innovation aimed at high quality and elevated standards of performance is combined with product differentiation, distinguishing between highly priced, high-quality, 'new' (up-to-date) products and low-priced, standardized 'old' products. The marketing effort is directed to present new high-quality products as distinct from their old counterparts and from standardized, imitation products, directed to less affluent consumers. Rapid industrialization is quite successful in creating market expansion, due to rapid price decreases and rationalization in the commercial channels. 'Volume' markets develop alongside innovation. This process is quite consistent with a polarized pattern of consumption, distinguishing between high-quality, luxurious, status-creating goods and 'standardized', cheaper counterparts.

A second general trend is that of the 'industrialization' of consumer services, their transformation into what we properly call 'industries', with increased fixed capital, productive rationalization, financial concentration and dramatic changes in their cost structure. Industrialization implies a transition to mass production for products that were produced previously on a smaller scale. Large, complex organizations take over highly fragmented, low capital intensity activities. This is really the kind of transformation in which product innovation goes hand in hand with the restructuring of the production process. The empirical analysis of the demand structure suggests that this type of process involves in the first place the areas of rapid expansion of spending such as health and recreation. More generally, examples of this kind of restructuring are the entertainment, travel and tourism industries, as well as the evolution in the production and delivery of food.

There is a third direction of transformation of the consumption sphere that deserves mention. Product differentiation and the parallel development of differentiated life styles and social practices increase the complexity of the consumption sphere. This requires the growth of a composite sector of activities giving stability and coherence to the new pattern of consumption. These activities include primarily services inputs which have increased tremendously their commercial relevance[5] and activities such as training and communication, which have some collective character and the quality of social interaction and expertise, combined with delivery of services and presence of equipment.

Admittedly, it is not clear how to define this growing sector, except for noting that many of the new activities depend heavily on the development of information and telecommunication technologies and often on the skills of a social class of professionals and small entrepreneurs.[6]

3.4   Need Development and the Culture of Consumption

An important aspect of the transformation of the consumption sphere during the 1980s is the particular relationship between need development, the social environment of consumption and what can be more narrowly considered the culture of consumption.

To the extent that the pattern of consumption emerging in the 1980s is centered on the revamping of the interest in a new generation of consumer goods and the provision of services on a large scale, it may seem that the discussion on the recovery hinges fundamentally on a rejuvenation of consumerism, with a strong bias towards luxurious consumption. The transformation of the consumption sphere in the 1980s, however, seems considerably more complex.

The image creation function of media and advertising, combined with the search for high levels of quality by means of a new structure of inputs, is part of an effort to redefine taste hierarchies and life styles. This is not only the marketing of waste, that is the effort to promote new commodities within the domestic and public life which have dubious 'utility', but rather the planning of differentiated markets for different income and cultural groups. On the other hand, a finer stratification increases market complexity. It requires a culture of consumption developing in step with the market, overcoming local and cultural differences or capable, in some instances, of exploiting them. More than before, market development requires the culture of consumption to operate as a potential for change and variety, rather than purely extension on a larger scale of a mode of consumption or a mode of life. Accordingly the sectors and activities where new ideas are created, defined and marketed are growing in size, importance and sophistication.

A more carefully planned and differentiated culture of consumption serves the purpose of enlarging the market through increasing complexity and a continuous, pervasive effort to redefine commodities, modes of life, consumption alternatives and consumption practices. At the same time the new culture of consumption reasserts consumption as a sign of social status. Affluent consumption of the 1960s is now redefined as the glamorous life style and status symbols of the new wealthy classes. There is therefore a *cultural and ideological element* of the economic process, which helps to appreciate the character of consumption evolution and consumer goods innovation, which is specific to different phases of development. During the 1980s recovery this change went hand in hand with the desire for newness, the desire to forget about the gloomy days, the tiredness with the myths and aspirations of collective endeavors and socially directed goals, in the name of a return to more private pleasures and to conspicuous consumption.[7]

This motivation, though not economic in content, is important for renewing the incentive to spend on consumption and for the social dynamics, which is part of the evolution of the consumption sphere. It creates the conditions for change on which market forces can operate. It seems to have been capable of communicating the feeling that prosperity had been restored. In a similar vein, it can be argued that 'Reaganism', with its emphasis on entrepreneurship, free initiative and individual freedom, was an aspect of the recovery, though hardly an economic variable.

3.5   Income Distribution, Consumption Patterns and Social Polarization

The macro implications of the transformation emerging in the 1980s concern both the income creation process, which is the main focus of the analysis, but also income distribution. On the basis of the statistical evidence, we have assumed throughout that income distribution has grown more uneven. This is confirmed and reinforced by structural change trends and the tendencies within the labour market.

Income distribution must be seen in the light of dramatic redistribution of employment and output between services and manufacturing and within each of these two sectors. It is sufficient here to stress that they benefited some and penalized other social strata, skills and professional profiles, thereby contributing to a redefinition of the social hierarchy and of opportunities and strategies of behavior of a large part of society.

On the other hand, labor markets are dominated by the disappearance of the well-paid jobs of traditional manufacturing, a phenomenon often discussed in the literature on industrial restructuring and labor markets (Bluestone and Harrison, 1982; Gordon, Reich and Edwards, 1982). In the 1980s this tendency was redefined along the lines of a tripartition of the labor markets identified by Reich (1992). The dynamism of certain industries, and within them of the segment of employment paid high wages, results in an increasingly uneven income distribution.

An increasingly differentiated pattern of consumption is therefore consistent with a segmented labor market where the phenomenon of the 'shrinking middle', constituted by blue-collar manufacturing jobs, is combined with the establishment of a clear distinction between well-paid high skills and low-paid low skills in the new industries, mainly services, which expand during the recovery. Labor market segmentation determines very distinct wage and social status and, most importantly, prospects and opportunities for different groups of workers and professionals. It feeds social polarization. This, however, is a severe limitation to the prospect of need development and market creation. It is made worse by the constraints imposed on public sector spending, which affect negatively the standard of living and prospects of lower-income social classes.

In face of these social trends, the stress laid on consumption spending as a key factor fueling the recovery may appear peculiar. It may appear even more questionable considering the wage dynamics. In fact, it is precisely the social dimension of the transformation that indicates the complexity of the issue. It is not that the average household has spent more or too much. Some households have consumed more; others may have barely kept up with previous levels of consumption, or even lost ground. I am not, therefore, arguing any 'consumption binge' thesis.[8] But all have consumed differently, and they would not have consumed as much had the consumption pattern not been reshaped. Though wage earners may have had to work longer hours because of lower wages, as suggested by labor market studies, they nevertheless ought to rely more on consumption of marketed goods to satisfy their needs. In these circumstances consumption demand, even though wages are stagnating, may grow and give the impression of a consumption boom.

A second aspect of this argument is that a more uneven income distribution, and even an increasing social polarization, can be favorable, in particular circumstances, to 'innovating' consumption. In particular, a redistribution of income in favor of property and salary income, without a drastic fall in the wage rate and in employment, can turn into a support for consumption spending, if combined with a sustained transformation of the consumption sphere and of the forms of needs satisfaction. What remains open to question is the possibility of sustaining this kind of transformation and its impact on the long-run growth potential of the economic system.

NOTES

1. This is the main conclusion of Bartley (1992) in one of the most optimistic accounts of the Reagan years.
2. Christy and Mohr (1986) reach this conclusion after focusing on changes of industries' proportions in the period up to 1984. Their theoretical perspective, however, squarely rests on the distinction between microlevel, which is where the explanation ultimately lies, and macroperformance, which is just the result of agents' decisions in the aggregate.
3. Small batch production responds precisely, especially in light manufacturing, to the need of flexible production and differentiated markets. Piore and Sabel (1984) have maintained that this is the new logic driving modern industrial development.
4. Stanbarck and his co-authors note that this long-term process of industrial transformation implies that innovation may not be so much a matter of 'new products', as the automobile and electric appliances have been. 'We do not argue that there are no new products with similar broad appeal just over the horizon ... But it is probable that factors other than new products are now playing a more important role in changing the way in which the consumer

spends his money. Such factors are to be found in the areas of urbanization, work, family structure, and social organization' (1981, p.39).

5. Examples may range from communications to media and advertising and in general 'image-creating industries', from the services available at home through telematics to the personal services industries. They may also include delivery services and the packaging and merchandising industry.

6. A distinct problem is that of the development of 'social services'. This is a complex issue, which cannot be discussed here. The complexity is the result of the juncture of several phenomena, which are part of the problem. In the theoretical framework centered on market creation, their growth signals two facts: a sector of growing demand which can be exploited by private, semi-private or collective forms of business organizations (see the growing debate on non-profit organization or the so-called 'third sector'); but also the magnitude of the negative effects on society of the changes in the production process and in the consumption sphere: that is the by-products of the process of structural transformation, which require a growing investment in people and society in general.

7. Albert Hirschman has discussed this aspect with reference to a 'private–public cycle' and the experience of 'disappointment' in consumption (Hirschman, 1982).

8. In this respect most of my argument is not contradictory to Robert Blecker's interpretation of 'excess consumption' in the 1980s. (The Consumption Binge Is a Myth, *Challenge*, May/June 1990.)

11. Consumption deepening and intensive growth: a new hypothesis

1. THE CONSUMPTION–GROWTH REGIME OF MASS CONSUMPTION

The empirical evidence and the trends of transformation discussed above suggest an interpretation of the structural dynamics of the 1980s based on a change in the consumption–growth relationship. The break with the previous decade is marked by the emergence of a regime of consumption deepening and intensive growth of the market. In order to discuss this point we need to take a step backward to reconsider the characteristics of the consumption–growth regime which matures during the expansion phase of the 1960s and represents the peak of the transformation of the post-war period.

From the point of view of the consumption sphere, evolution the 1960s boom was indeed the result of a dramatic change in the forms of need satisfaction. The establishment of a set of new modes of consumption and new modes of life was mainly driven by the diffusion of consumer durables. The peak of the transformation was consequently the result of the industrialized methods of large-scale production translating into standardized mass consumption markets. The rapid growth of the latter further improved productivity gains, with a share going to workers in the form of rising real wages and to the general public in the form of lower prices. Thus, in this phase, the consumption sphere becomes dominated by the forms and rules of mass consumption, resulting in a specific pattern of consumption and in a 'regime' of *consumption widening*.

The rise of real wages is a central element of this process of transformation centered on mass consumption. Consumption widening, however, rests on an even more fundamental phenomenon: the capacity of modern industrial production technology to create new modes of consumption and a system of brand new modes of life with respect to both the luxury life style of wealthy classes and the relatively small urban élites, and the traditional consumption patterns of the agricultural population and of the working class.[1] Thus the distinguishing features of consumption widening are the establishment of new modes of life organized around industrially mass-produced consumers' products and the capacity to extend innovation in consumption to new social strata, enlarging the social basis of the process of transformation.[2]

In this perspective the high growth cycle of the 1960s appears to be the peak of the transformation of the consumption sphere in the post-war period, dominated by the formation of mass markets and fueled by the diffusion of new products and new modes of life. The striking feature of the evolution of the consumption sphere was the rising standard of consumption, the 'opulence' of the middle and middle-lower classes, now incorporating a large proportion of industrial workers.

Within the pattern of consumption centered on mass consumption innovation proceeds together with the standardization of consumption options. The possibility of new modes of consumption rapidly resulted in a set of standardized norms for need satisfaction and in their differentiation with respect to a limited number of new ways of living. Combined with the rise of real wages it led to a rapid diffusion of the novelty of mass consumption, with the latter further sustained by employment growth. Indeed, in this phase of transformation, not only real wages rise, but also the number of wage earners and of wage-based ways of life and forms of needs satisfaction.

In this phase the market creation process relied mainly on the quantitative extension of the market along the lines defined by consumption innovation. *Extensive growth of the market* is the form of market creation associated with this specific phase of consumption evolution. On the one hand, it is sustained by consumption innovation in the forms of need satisfaction, which replace the old ones and the need structures associated with them; on the other, by an income redistribution driven by real wages growth. The latter stimulates both the search for new consumption options and the rapid diffusion of new modes of life through the social structure. As a result the market was the social mechanism increasingly providing for needs satisfaction, therefore ensuring the enlargement of the size of aggregate circulation.

2.   LIMITS OF CONSUMPTION WIDENING AND EXTENSIVE GROWTH OF THE MARKET

2.1   Change and Standardization

Though well studied from many points of view, the specificity of this consumption regime, and of the process of market creation associated with it, has not been analyzed with respect to a general view of the consumption–growth relationship. In other words, consumption widening and extensive market growth have become the benchmark of modern consumption and, we might say, of the development of advanced market economies. It has gone almost unnoticed that they implied a specific bias in the social and technological form taken by needs satisfaction. *What has raised little discussion is the link between the forms of need satisfaction and the limits they imposed on the structural dynamics of market creation.*

Consumption widening is associated with the standardization of the forms of needs satisfaction and the growing homogeneity of the modes of life which achieve rapid diffusion and social acceptance. The need structures defined by this limited number of modes of life provide sufficient scope for product differentiation and market segmentation. Differentiation establishes and reinforces the existence of a few, increasingly well defined, modes of life and consumption options. Consequently market expansion is driven by the diffusion of the norms of modern consumption and inclusion of new social classes. Change, in production and consumption, is directed to this purpose and widens the social basis of the process of market creation.

This process of change implied no doubt a larger number of consumption alternatives and new possibilities for need development, but it ran its course rather quickly. Indeed the emergence of the critics of consumerism signals precisely the fact that the limits had become evident while the process was still unfolding. The other side of the process is the progressive inertia rooted in the standardization of modes of consumption and modes of life. From the point of view of the consumption sphere, evolution custom and habit tend to enhance routines. They act to maintain both the established forms of satisfaction of needs and the personality structures associated with them. This inertia is a burden on the process of change. That of itself is a limit to the development of personality. We can conclude that within routinized patterns of consumption there is not much room for the development of individuality.

This must be all the more true at the lower levels of income. Uncommitted income can indeed be created, but it implies more standardized products rather than novelty capable of redesigning modes of consumption and modes of life. Standardized products are by definition designed and distributed when a new mode of consumption has become the social and technological norm, indeed a standard in the satisfaction of a particular need and an element of what becomes an established mode of life. If we consider also the limits imposed by profitability on the creation of uncommitted income, the pressure to remain stuck in routinized patterns of consumption must be rather strong for wage earners.[3]

The theoretical perspective discussed in Chapters 4 and 5 indicated the scarce potential for personality development which is implicit in the forms of life and consumption patterns of wage-earners and the obstacle to change constituted by their relative stability and uniformity. *Now what comes to light is that these limits are reproduced by routinized patterns of consumption.* Though exerting a strong pressure towards transformation and market expansion in the phase of rapid diffusion of consumption innovation, firmly established routinized patterns of consumption become an obstacle to change. They typically contrast variety and differentiation and constrain the evolution of the consumption structure. Thus they are associated with a weak potential for market creation.

Market growth is then limited and the low growth rates of the economy parallel the slow growth rates of consumers' durables markets governed by an overall tendency to market saturation. The second element reinforcing this tendency is of course the standstill of wages and a regressive income distribution. In an economic structure increasingly dominated by wage labor, when a regime of rising wages and income redistribution is replaced by a contrary and persistent tendency, there can be no incentive to change coming from the spending side. This is true in two senses: there is no possibility of improving living conditions and exploring new dimensions of need. Consequently the extension to new consumers of consumption innovation is severely constrained and the social basis of the process of market growth cannot expand.

2.2   Novelty and Norm

Both these points need qualification. Consumption widening pulled by rising wages has brought new consumers into the norms of modern consumption and generalized the modes of consumption and modes of life made possible by large-scale productive technology. Novelty and drastic change in the forms of need satisfaction certainly determined the possibility of exploring new dimensions of need and personality development. However it must be recognized that the most powerful part of the mechanism of market expansion, that is the dramatic changes of the consumption sphere associated with the rules and forms of mass consumption, *cannot sustain expanded reproduction indefinitely.* Indeed their generalization, that is their diffusion and established dominance, is predicated upon standardization and homogenization of consumption alternatives and consumers' behavior. From the point of view of the *forms of consumption* this does not enhance *novelty*, but rather a *norm*. The process then becomes increasingly sensitive to income distribution. When wages do not grow, the possibility of expansion ceases and the system is stuck in a low-growth regime which may be close to stagnation.

This is not inconsistent with a modest improvement of consumption standards while wages grow at a slow pace and the wage structure evolves. However a very large portion of the consumption structure remains fixed and income is spent to support this structure. The point is that in these circumstances the rise of the real wage, in order to stimulate the exploration of new dimensions of neediness, should be very significant. Uncommitted income generated by falling prices can create new possibilities to improve or modify modes of life identified with standardized products and consumption routines. It can hardly disrupt the established pattern of consumption.

The question then is: in the absence of a massive growth of wages or redistribution of wealth, what kind of change can stimulate new expansion? Change should create new dynamism with respect to the stability and relative uniformity of routinized patterns of consumption. It needs to disrupt established forms of life largely identified with standardized modes of consumption. Novelty can indeed break these established forms but, in order to become market creation, it must be capable of undermining the old modes of life, developing needs and the capacity to satisfy needs. It must recreate potential market, overcoming the limitations of the regime of consumption widening and extensive growth of the market.

3.   A NEW CONSUMPTION–GROWTH REGIME

3.1   Consumption Deepening

The limits on the process of market creation engendered by the pattern of consumption described above cause a transition to a new consumption–growth regime which emerges during the 1980s recovery.

In the phase of extensive growth, the development process was based on the enormous potential for market creation created by the possibility and then the diffusion of a set of new modes of consumption and modes of life. The norms of modern consumption and the associated social status sustained investment, employment and wages. However, when the limits of the development potential implicit in routinized consumption patterns become more binding, the slowing down of growth rates implies a structural dynamics unfavorable to employment and wages. This may exert strong pressures on income distribution.

To get out of this circle, product innovation and market development should develop needs at the frontier of the current patterns of consumption. In order to do so, innovation in consumption must constitute an alternative to the current established modes of consumption and modes of life in two senses: (1) improving the standards, the social norm of needs satisfaction; (2) propelling needs development further, in new areas of market growth left open by the current structure of consumption, therefore affecting the same structure. Novelty should develop along these lines and motivate the work of market development of new and established firms. As a result, needs are satisfied differently and new needs develop out of the established structure, sustaining the growth of the potential market.

However this cannot be based on a generalized extension of novelty to a larger social basis. On the one hand, the wage dynamics and the resulting more uneven income distribution are not favorable to such a pattern; on the other, need development must be the distinctive feature of innovative, leading edge consumption and, at the same time, a sign of status, restricted to the wealthy. It must be an attribute of new modes of life to be restricted to a relatively small set of consumers. In other words, novelty is there to establish social differentiation with respect to established and standardized consumption.

Novelty and improved standards of needs satisfaction, often achieved by means of new technologies and sophisticated product development, become the benchmark of a phase in which need development follows a qualitatively finer and more exclusive direction. The second condition for this type of need development is a structure of wealth growing more uneven, thus capable of sustaining need development at the edge of consumption innovation possibilities. This is the basis of the new consumption–growth regime emerging in the 1980s. Indeed *consumption deepening* is not only the other side of a more uneven income distribution, it represents a change in the pattern of transformation of the consumption sphere and in the process of market creation.

The meaning of the transition is clarified by considering its implications for the lower end of the market creation process. The more uneven income distribution must be considered together with the effects of falling prices in the areas of market expansion where new products undergo a rapid process of industrialization. Falling prices ensure that some expenditure items, typically those of rapid growth industries, become part of the basket of consumption of low and medium income households. This highlights the particular pattern imposed by consumption deepening on those households which experience at best modest rises in their real income. On the one hand, innovation in consumption takes up an increasing part of income, squeezing their savings; on the other, it is restricted to the products which are redefined by the process of industrialization and marked by a rapid fall in prices.

Thus, despite the rise of new consumption possibilities and the expansion of spending in selected areas of consumption, the process of change can only enhance to some extent individuals' development and the potential for market creation. The result is a more polarized pattern of consumption evolution which, while contributing to the growing complexity of the consumption sphere, highlights the limits of consumption deepening for need development. In other words: *polarization of consumption patterns* sustains variety and change, but ultimately at the expense of market extension, limiting the effects of consumption innovation on the growth of the market. Whether or not this may be the cause of stagnation tendencies may remain unclear. What seems questionable is its capacity to ensure rapid growth of the market, overcoming the tendency to a regime of modest growth rates.

3.2   Intensive Growth of the Market

The point is that consumption deepening sustains the process of market creation along a pattern which can be called *intensive growth*. Intensive growth is an alternative to the quantitative extension of the market. Its fundamental characteristic is that the growth process works *because* it is limited, that is, *directed to selected specific groups of consumers and selected markets and/or areas of needs satisfaction.*

In the 1980s the fundamental characteristic of intensive growth is a *divergent pattern of product innovation and market development strategies.* On the one hand, we have novelty and high-quality standards of need satisfaction, associated with the new modes of consumption and the modes of life of the wealthy and emerging social strata; on the other, a process of imitation, based on the industrialization of the same novelty at the lower end of the market, exploiting large-scale economies, cheap inputs and standardized design. *Thus market development propels on the one hand novelty, on the other imitation.*

These opposite, but mutually consistent, processes of product innovation and market development can keep running the transformation of consumption along a highly complex pattern. This complexity is organized around the polarization of consumption patterns mentioned above and reinforced by a differentiation developing within the social structure, between the losers and the winners in the changing competitive environment.[4]

Intensive growth rests on this overall strategy of *macro segmentation of consumption markets* which determines the specifics of market development and consumption innovation. This segmentation corresponds to distinct pricing policies. Market development typically determines high prices for new, cutting edge products and low prices for old, standardized products.

Leading edge market development and innovation in consumption shape the modes of life of the wealthy and new emerging social strata, creating the economic space and the potential which drives, through net investment, the growth of aggregate circulation. At the same time innovation and technology-driven investment transform old industries and create new ones. This is fundamental to the enlargement of the market following the imitation process, since it affects the general spectrum of consumption possibilities and changes the composition of spending towards new areas of consumption. In particular the latter is associated with the rise of new industries where technological innovation and the industrialization of production processes determine new products' characteristics.

In sum: intensive growth typically addresses the need structures at the frontier of the current patterns of consumption, defined by the modes of life of the new wealthy classes, and in the areas of consumption which are more likely to attract the purchasing power of consumers, mainly because of the opportunities linked to industrialization and low-cost production. The impetus in that direction is ensured by the imitation process, which is driven by the emerging need structures revealed and exploited by leading edge consumption. The process of market creation is then based on the combination of the effects of leading edge and quality-enhancing consumption with the imitation–industrialization of consumption options. *Indeed they represents two routes to market creation.*

The intensity of the development process, however, ultimately rests on the capacity to develop and exploit need structures. New products may imply, together with changes in the modes of consumption and modes of life, the emergence of new need structures, that is the possibility of altogether new modes of life. That may expand potential demand.

In the 1980s, however, the development fostered by new products seems more directed to upgrading current routines of consumption and expanding consumption possibilities. Indeed the list of what we can call 'a second generation' of consumer durables, which dominated innovation in the decade, is rather long: it includes the VCR, the microwave oven, the cellular phone and the new TV sets. They were hardly innovation breakthroughs, rather a further step in an evolving path. They resulted in a more or less dramatic redefinition of the combination of products and practices and of variations within the structure of modes of life. In fact the consumption pattern was not fundamentally disrupted, but rather reshaped by them. In this case, new products, and in general consumption innovation, determine only a partial displacement of needs structures. To that extent need development, even within leading edge consumption, may be limited.

This must be all the more true for the imitation process. The displacement of needs structures, which may be limited within cutting edge consumption, is even more constrained at the other end of the market. Industrialization here plays the double role of sustaining the spread of innovation in consumption while constraining need development within narrow forms dictated by imitation and low cost. Were the development of need to take a different direction it would encounter the limitation imposed by income distribution. It must be noted however that, while the potential for need development of the imitation process may be limited, the contribution to market expansion may be significant because of its large social basis.

Overall intensive growth appears to be a pattern of market growth constrained both from the spending side and from the innovation side. The burden of leading the transformation is restricted to the high-quality standards and status-enhancing characteristics of the new modes of consumption and modes of life of the wealthy. The kind of consumption evolution strongly associated with market creation, that is with the investigation of new possibilities of consumption, is restricted to a large minority identified with those social strata which, because of skills, productive functions and social location, are reaping the benefits of the process of industrial transformation. They have both the capacity and the means to invent new consumption practices. And at the same time they are that part of the workforce which sees income and opportunities rising.[5] Thus the operation of the process of market creation depends more fundamentally than before on the new wealthy classes. Innovation propels change in the consumption patterns, but market creation appears constrained by this limited, though highly dynamic, social basis.

3.3   Technology, Innovation and Market Development

Intensive growth must be seen in the context of an increasing sophistication of productive technology and growing industrialization of productive processes, with specialization of marketing strategies and channels. It represents an advance in the pattern of development of industrial economies, not a jump back into some sort of 'élite' consumption.

Indeed the macro segmentation of the market implies the industrialization of consumption options and in general of small-scale production, including quality-based production. The characteristics, the novelty and the price of products are determined by the technical specification of the inputs, the marketing strategy and the quality of the modes of consumption and modes of life they enhance, not by any attribute of the old-fashioned luxury goods or of craftsmanship per se. Thus consumption deepening and intensive growth mean a specific, but no less intense, process of consumption innovation and transformation of the consumption sphere than in the phase of extensive growth. The point is not the intensity, but rather the direction, of the process of transformation.

Novelty is pervasive, but structured around distinct patterns of change reflecting new social rules and values. In particular, it assumes a central relevance of the innovation-based imitation effect, which ensures a stimulus to consumption spending.[6] Similarly product innovation is intense and determines increasing product complexity and differentiation. Though following divergent patterns, as described above, it may have the same technological basis.[7]

This of course implies market development and, in particular, significant investment to redetermine the pattern of consumption. Expenditure may be particularly intense in certain areas, following a growth pattern more concentrated than before in a few sectors; it may move further and further forward the technology frontier, pushing ahead the sophistication and diffusion of productive technology. However it cannot easily match the rapid growth that sustained the establishment of mass markets. In fact, the vast effort of market development and reorganization of the productive structure may have results which, in the aggregate, are less impressive than the deep process of change would suggest and more modest than in the extensive growth phase. This depends also on the changing role of investment and technology.

What is typical of intensive growth is the effort to identify and exploit new possibilities of expansion by means of new technology and innovation in a slowly growing market. This contrasts with the notion of investment as capacity building, typical of extensive growth, mainly directed to existing lines of production, which stresses the association of technology changes with productivity growth. Intensive growth emphasizes instead the strategic role of technology and investment, and in particular the role of advanced services and research-intensive industries, in the identification of new product development options and consumption possibilities.

4.   THE 1980s IN A LONG-TERM PERSPECTIVE

4.1   Recovery and Structural Transformation

The hypothesis presented above of a transition to a new consumption–growth regime helps to interpret the 1980s expansion. It also suggests a redefinition of the growth process which has implications for the long-term growth pattern of the US economy. Indeed the structural dynamics of the 1980s recovery raises a number of questions that are better understood in the perspective of the following cycle of expansion.

The recovery was not a strong upturn. Nor did it resemble a phase of extensive growth, where market expansion is driven by massive investment in manufacturing and/or dramatic changes due to new products. Investment and innovation are mainly aimed at industrial transformation and indeed a reshaping of the sphere of consumption, rather than at expansion in the traditional sense of capacity building and standardization of consumption patterns. Moreover the transition to intensive growth magnifies the process of uneven development of the industrial structure.[8] Investment in market development propels the selective expansion of certain industries and markets, more than sustaining the process of market creation in general. This is not contradictory to the existence of a strong innovative sector. Quite the opposite: it rather poses, even more sharply than before, the question of its role and impact on the process of market creation.[9]

The technological breakthroughs of the period, located in information technologies, telecommunications, biotechnology and a few other areas of scientific and technological research, represent indeed new long-term technological trends. During the 1980s, they reach a degree of maturity that establishes them as the benchmarks of a new epoch. And yet, in retrospect, they appear still to be at an early stage of development. Though central to the process of industrial transformation, they were not able to sustain a generalized new investment wave and/or a new age in need development.[10] In particular, technological development and innovation, though proceeding at a fast pace, did not lead, at least during the 1980s recovery, to a drastic displacement of need structures and therefore to a strong rise in potential demand. *The point is not so much the lack of effects of the new technologies, but rather the characteristics and selective path of intensive growth, which leave a high degree of uncertainty on the market creation prospects.*[11]

In the 1980s, technology and product innovation exploited especially their potential for differentiation and commodification of life styles, and operated mainly through the redefinition, with respect to those prevailing in mass consumption, of the modes of consumption and the modes of life within an increasing complexity of the consumption sphere. Thus, as opposed to the claim that technology and new products were the foundation of a new boom, the transformation rests on a subtle and pervasive mechanism of transformation driven by the stress on consumption spending as identification with the new standards of consumption and emerging modes of life. It was consistent with and supported by a new hierarchy of wealth. This appears to be the fundamental dynamic of change which sustained the expansion. Whether or not it generated a consumption boom is an open question. Certainly there was a considerable amount of change in the sphere of consumption.[12]

The recovery of the 1980s was a successful example of redefinition of needs in a way consistent with private consumption and personal wealth. The transformation of the modes of life and the consumption cultures mirrors and validates the new income and social hierarchy. This is why market creation relies so much on consumption as a sign of status and on the leading role of the 'glamorous' consumption of the new wealthy classes. However, as pointed out before, this works also as a severe constraint. In fact, though responding to the limits of the consumption–growth regime of mass consumption, the transformation could not reverse the tendency to modest growth rates, or, at least, it was not able to do so during the 1980s. Thus it raises the question of *whether such transformation could sustain itself into a long-term expansive trend.*

This is indeed the most problematic and difficult question posed by the analysis of the decade and it should be answered in the negative. Indeed we have found evidence of a deep process of transformation, but also of the difficulties of this becoming market creation.

4.2 Self-limiting Forces

An analysis of the long-term prospects of the structural dynamics of the 1980s should take into account two kinds of problems. The new consumption–growth regime, as articulated in the 1980s, encounters a strong barrier in the self-limiting forces originating precisely in the process of industrialization and commodification of social life and in the income distribution associated with it. As pointed out by Marglin (1984, p.364), our society is quite successful at devising commodity-based solutions to the problems of social life. New markets have indeed emerged from the commodification of new needs, which were not, or were only partially, satisfied through the market only a few years ago. Examples are those of health, personal and even spiritual needs.

The question posed by this kind of development is whether market-based solutions foster individualism, rather than the individual identity. In the first case they must rely on a culture of consumption and on forms of satisfaction that tend to define needs in a way consistent with the market; this may, at some point, conflict with or constrain the potential dynamism inherent in the development of individual personality. According to Levine, the system of market relations has an inherent potential for expansion resting on the social nature of needs, the development of the needy individual and the transformation/multiplication of modes of life which that entails. That potential is, however, constrained by the structure of wealth, which, in a system of market relations, is the means to the satisfaction of needs.

In the absence of other alternatives for investment, the process described above may exacerbate the conflict between market forms of need satisfaction and need development. In principle this can undermine the capacity of the system to recreate the condition for potential demand and therefore the incentive to market development. In other words, the development of needs is constrained by the very process of differentiation and commodification of modes of life, which represents the market response to the desire to assert individual personality. In particular, it can be argued that the focus on private consumption is conflicting with the development of individuals, at least to the extent that it requires some kind of collective consumption. It is important to stress that, in the absence of correcting mechanisms, the limitations to the process of market creation engendered by the transformation of the consumption sphere in the 1980s are therefore self-generated.

A second problem arises with respect to the specific limits of each of the three main directions of transformation discussed in Chapter 10. We can observe that the new market created around the revamping of the market of consumer durables and non-durables is indeed limited by income distribution. In fact it implies a strong bias towards luxury consumption and cheap, imitation goods. This pattern can be sustained only by pushing forward product and market polarization, which may soon encounter severe social and effective demand limits.

The process of industrialization of certain services is an instance of evolution of commodity production and, in some cases, systematic penetration of market relations into new areas of social production. Some trends emerging in the 1970s came to maturity in the 1980s, favored by the transformation of the life styles and expectations, but also by the lower cost, of the services provided. These processes are likely to continue and, strictly speaking, there is no clear limit to them, except the extension of the areas of social production in which market relations can evolve.

Finally the expansion of the composite economic sector which sustains the innovation in the modes of life and the modes of consumption, and therefore ensures the reproduction of the consumption sphere along lines of constant evolution, is also subject to a severe constraint. Some of the activities included in this admittedly loosely defined sector have one characteristic in common: they are useful because of their collective character. The output of activities such as training and communication cannot be consumed in isolation and require some collective action, combined with delivery of services and presence of equipment. They have therefore the characteristics of a public good, as is often the case of services which satisfy superior, life style types of need (Scitovsky, 1976). Or, as in the case of the environment, the satisfaction of the kind of needs involved cannot be addressed purely in terms of efficiency, because of their collective nature.

The problem is particularly relevant because these could be large areas of need development, therefore a potentially powerful force for expansion. However market forces may not be capable of exploiting it, to the extent they are typically directed to satisfying needs in the form of private consumption. It is doubtful that they can develop the potential for enhancement of individual personality, while remaining strictly functions of support of private consumption practices. Considering that neither is income distribution favorable, nor is there an explicit effort to structure the functions of the public sector in this direction, need development may be restricted and a powerful source of dynamism subtracted from the system.

To the extent that the process of change did not recreate the conditions for long-term growth, it seems misleading to speak of a return to economic prosperity. Even leaving aside consideration of the negative social consequences of growing inequality, the main problem may be that social change, as well as structural dynamics, is constrained. This may stabilize the economy at a low level of recreation of potential demand and opportunities for market development. It can be concluded that the long-run potential of the recovery is questionable.

4.3   The 1980s and Beyond: Structural Change and Market Creation

The long expansion of the 1990s
In light of the questions raised by the 1980s transformation, the theoretical approach suggested in this book seems quite helpful to understanding the stylized facts of economic development, labor markets and society at large in the 1990s. Without embarking on an analysis of the structural dynamics of the decade, it is relatively simple to outline some of the main lines of transformation. During the 1990s, the pace of the transformation accelerated because (1) some phenomena which were at an early stage in the 1980s more fully displayed their potential for transformation and (2) some of the limitations implicit in the macro segmentation of the market were overcome.

The expansion cycle of the 1990s set in after a brief downturn in 1990 and 1991.[13] We can observe a rapid growth of investment, which was the most dynamic component of domestic demand. That suggests that the expansion was sustained more than in the 1980s by investment spending. It is also consistent with a phase of accumulation of plant and equipment, driven by technical progress and more intense strategies of market development. Gross fixed investment composition indicates that the bulk of the spending is concentrated in construction, with wide annual fluctuations, and industrial equipment. By far the highest growth rates are those of the information processing and related equipment industry. Thus it is not far fetched to say that in the 1990s the information technologies reached a new level of dominance in the way the economy produces and is organized. In turn this suggest a fairly clear hypothesis of the pattern of the expansion.

Accordingly, we can say, that the 1990s cycle was in a first phase driven by an investment push that sustained growth in the aggregate and at the same time created the conditions for further market creation. The realization of that potential consolidated the growth process and explains the length of the expansion. This is consistent with a process by which significant and steady investment flows in the information and communication technologies (ICT), and in particular in the software industry, determined both a steady process of innovation of industrial equipment and a boom of new technical possibilities embodied in new products. Thus an intense and highly focused process of market development incubates a second phase.

Following the new technical possibilities there was the delivery of new products with larger and improved capabilities. The new level of development of computer networks and cellular phones enlarged the access of firms and the general public to communication and information. That made possible the emergence of new needs and new forms of satisfaction, setting in place a self-sustaining process of market creation based on the positive feedback between technical and social feasibility of new modes of consumption and the recreation of potential demand and potential market.

Indeed the second phase really began when the highly concentrated phenomena of market development caused a further round of potential demand expansion. The disruption of the established modes of consumption, thus of the specific forms of need satisfaction, activated a surge of new needs and the consequent enlargement and modification of the need structure. An evolving system of new modes of consumption then contributed to the spread of innovation into modes of life. When the latter were permanently modified, that created the space for the rapid diffusion of innovation.

It must be observed, however, that the transformation described above focuses on certain areas of need satisfaction. It is therefore another instance of selective expansion, which also concerns here the need structures. The new aspect is that market creation was sustained not only by the displacement of certain portions of the need structure, but also by the rapid diffusion of consumption innovation. That is why the macro segmentation of the market appears less binding.[14] From this point of view, really the glamorous consumption of 1980s appears a sort of market preparation for the mass character of certain new products.

The Internet scenario: a basic innovation?

The brief analysis of the 1990s elucidates how the pattern of growth centered on consumption deepening and intensive growth of the market can be articulated in a different technological and social scenario. With a very important difference: there is an inherent potential of transformation in the information and communication technologies such that Schumpeter would probably class them a basic innovation. Information and communication are basic inputs for any productive process, but also for any social process and, even more fundamentally, for any human interaction.

Indeed, at the end of the 1990s, investment in ICT and the evolution of the consumption sphere brought the transformation to a new technological and social frontier: the Internet and the New Economy. These terms have become very common in the technological and economic jargon, but also in everyday life. The underlying question is whether the importance of the phenomenon was blown out of proportion by the impressive rise of stock exchange values at the end of the 1990s, or whether we are indeed at the beginning of an Internet Economy revolution.

Here again the conceptual framework centered on the evolution of the consumption sphere and the process of market creation helps to put the problem into perspective. It does so by overcoming the technological determinism of the analysis of cyclical expansion based on the Schumpeterian notion of innovation. The question is: in which circumstances can new technologies become a source of market creation on a scale capable of sustaining long-term expansion? What kind of technological developments and economic restructuring are needed to enter a new phase of development? This is indeed the meaning of the Internet economy, the Web, as a basic innovation.

While it seems rather plausible to assume that the impetus of the US economy largely depends on the advancement of the technological frontier of ICT, it is unclear what that really implies, especially with respect to the notion of a new long wave of development. The Internet in itself is the culmination of a long technological trend originating in the 1970s, the concluding step in the development of computer networks and the advances of telecommunication technologies. It might indeed work as a basic innovation capable of massive creation of new opportunities for economic development and restructuring of production and consumption activities. This is what is really new about the New Economy.

On the one hand, the surge of the stock market and the boom of the Internet companies can be dealt with as a speculative bubble which also found its cure; stock prices, inflated by the expectations around the consequences of the new phenomenon, came to a rapid fall. On the other hand, the stock market has indeed been shown to believe in the possibilities of this new frontier. Of course it has done so in a way consistent with its nature and mode of operation; the betting on the prospects of Internet companies was overshadowed by the speculative motive. The result is a highly volatile market.

Yet, in the perspective of the market creation process, the Internet Economy appears a much more serious affair than the stock market volatility would suggest. Though it remains to be seen whether we have entered a phase of revolutionary change,[15] the striking feature of the last years is the amount of change it induced in personal and collective behavior. Communication and information have really become the core of the expansion because, to an extent never seen before, they have transformed the modes of life and created new ones. Moreover the restructuring of modes of life appears a phenomenon which is only just beginning.[16]

Thus, in a typically contradictory fashion, while the speculative bubble may have been a vast overreaction with respect to the reality of the current trend of transformation, it signals the diffuse understanding that we may be at the beginning of a new phase of structural transformation.

4.4   Conclusions: Unlimited Growth?

Long-term growth

The main thrust of the theoretical perspective presented in this book suggests that the endogenous mechanism of development rests on the structural dynamics of market creation. Structural change and the process of market creation are ultimately rooted in the exploitation of the potential implicit in the development of socially determined needs. For this reason the focus is on the transformation of the sphere of consumption, that is the sphere of social life that realizes the construction of need and of the needy individual. The transformation of the consumption sphere depends on the structural determinations arising from changes in modes of satisfaction of social needs and the structuring of modes of life, what could be called in a broader sense *innovation in the consumption sphere*. In fact the social construction of need is a matter of output composition and quality, but also of new consumption practices and culture.

The evolution of the consumption sphere determines the self-sustaining character of the process of market creation, and thus the possibility of long-term growth through the process of structural transformation. The direction of structural change determines the specific characteristics of distinct phases of economic development.

The consumption pattern centered on consumer durables and the creation of the mass markets of modern consumption were at the center of the structural dynamics that sustained the 1960s expansion. The slowdown of growth rates can be interpreted as a sign of the exhaustion of the market creation potential of that cycle of expansion and the decline, accompanied by a profound process of industrial restructuring, of a well determined pattern of growth. Thus, precisely because of the stage of development reached by advanced market economies, the approach centered on market creation becomes particularly relevant. Indeed it is harder to maintain high growth rates in the face of the increasing complexity of the growth process.

The interpretation advanced in the book suggests that the 1980s recovery was a turning point in the pattern of growth and a break with respect to the consumption–growth regime of the US economy in the post-war period. The empirical analysis confirms that any comparison with the structural dynamics of the rapid growth 1960s cycle is misleading, because of both strength and sectoral composition of the market creation process.

More specifically, the book characterizes the 1980s as a cyclical expansion sustained by a selective and uneven pattern of investment and consumption. The process of market creation derives its specific characteristics from the focus on certain areas of consumption and the macro segmentation of the market, as described above. It is largely incapable of a generalized expansion. Thus it was not a period of rapid growth in the traditional sense of fast accumulation; nor does it seem appropriate to think of a technology-driven displacement of the previous economic structure. But it is a good example of the form taken by economic expansion with a low aggregate growth rate combined with industrial transformation, intense change and an increasingly polarized social structure.

In these particular circumstances the process of market creation rested on the reassertion of status as a an essential aspect of consumption innovation, within an increasing market complexity, and a further penetration of the market into some spheres of social life, typically consumer services. It only partially created the conditions for long-term growth, except for the new maturity reached by some technological trends. The fairly stringent limits of consumption deepening and intensive growth of the market as articulated in the 1980s then raise the question of whether this pattern of transformation can ensure long-term economic growth.

In retrospect, the transformation that sustained the recovery of the 1980s appears a first step on a path which has become clearer. Given the main forces of change, located in the new technologies and in the social reproduction of the consumption sphere, the long expansion of the 1990s is a sign that the development process overcame some of its limits. In particular (1) the investment in new technologies has begun 'to deliver' in terms of market expansion; (2) investment in ICT, and the new products to whose creation it contributed, exerted a strong influence on productive processes and industrial transformation, but also on need structures and the restructuring of modes of life. The rapid diffusion of some new products, despite the income distribution problems, confirms the appeal of the new modes of life.

The pattern of selective and highly concentrated expansion creates, however, a further imbalance in the consumption structure and new problems, linked to the narrow basis of the new modes of life and the obstacles to a deployment of novelty to the rest of the need structure. Thus some of the limits emerging in the 1980s remained and new ones may become binding.

Market creation and the coming of age of information technologies

In his 1988 book, Nell argues that the alternative to industrial mass production, which entered its stagnation phase in the 1970s, that is 'the setting up of the information economy', had hardly begun (p.171). Consequently the sources of growth were largely exhausted and new ones are not in place yet. New information technologies, after their first appearance in the 1970s, had still to demonstrate the capacity to create the conditions for new markets. But they have moved decisively ahead. The articulation of a development phase truly centered on the market creation effects of new information technologies has become increasingly clear.

From the recovery of the 1980s into the 1990s of the two Clinton administrations, the diffusion of information technologies reached a new critical threshold, achieving a remarkable capacity to redefine need structures and new market formation. Economic development in the 1990s thus seems to indicate that the next step in the process of 'transformational growth' is beginning to be clearly articulated.

Though much of the enthusiasm which accompanied the boom of the stock exchange and the astonishing performance of some of the Internet companies melted down, the Internet does suggest a scenario of drastic redeployment of need structure and productive capacity in a profound reorganization of the consumption sphere. The potential for transformation it implies is an open question which needs to be investigated for any analysis of the prospects of advanced industrial economies.

The problem of course is the change in the process of market creation suggested by such a scenario and in particular its consequences for the limits (highlighted above) to the growth process. The empirical investigation of the structural dynamics of the 1980s and some of the main trends of the 1990s suggest a growing complexity of the market creation process and the rise of self-generated difficulties.

The persistent weakness of wages and the dramatic change in working conditions, which combines with the new problems raised by the changes in life styles and in the patterns of consumption, suggest that some of the self-limiting forces set in place during the 1980s could be tamed, but not overcome. This and the new limits which may arise from the current trends of transformation cast considerable doubts on the prospects of the new consumption–growth regime to ensure rapid growth for market economies. One can say that they are indeed part of a new social scenario still hard to define, let alone to interpret.

NOTES

1. 'Since extensive growth of the market implies the incorporation of new consumers, extensive growth creates a condition for the incorporation of developing commodities into consumption bundles' (Levine, 1981, vol. II, p.219).
2. An example of consumption widening is the transformation and homogenization of consumption patterns which accompanies the transition from rural to urban life in an earlier phase of 'transformational growth'.
3. The classical notion of subsistence would then suggest the necessity for wage labor to conform to a well-defined 'form of life', rather than the means for developing the needs of the worker or expressing individuality.
4. The reference here is to the tripartition of the labor market indicated by Reich (1992).
5. Here again the reference is to Reich (1992) and his identification of winners and losers in the new competitive environment. The profile of the 'symbolic analyst' is typical of that part of the labor force whose opportunities, and thus neediness, grow and therefore is the backbone of the new consumption regime.
6. The specific pattern of transformation of the sphere of consumption suggests a 'ratchet effect', rooted in the divergent patterns of consumption innovation.
7. For instance, information technologies, generating distinct productive capacities and products specifications.
8. There is indeed evidence of a dynamic industrial core both in manufacturing and in services which is leading the process of industrial transformation.
9. This raises the question of the diffusion path of new technologies, an issue investigated by scholars such as Rosenberg.
10. The secular pattern of transformational growth was based on the replacement of domestic production and household functions by industrial production. That was the source of market creation sufficient to sustain the long-term expansion culminating in the boom of the 1960s. A new development phase may require a long and complex technological and productive transition.
11. It is now widely recognized that social and institutional constraints play an important role. The question, however, is not to assign 'weights' to social and institutional factors, but rather to discuss the central tendency of structural transformation.
12. Gershuny argues that a wave of social innovation characterized the 1950s and there is evidence of a second wave in the 1980s.
13. Though labeled the longest expansion in post-war history (in January 2000 the expansion of the US economy entered its 107th month, therefore lasting longer than the February 1961 to

December 1969 expansion, 106 months), it can be observed that the annual growth rates remained pretty much in line with the average of the 1980s cycle, at least from 1990 to 1997.

14. Computer networks and cellular phones were a novelty which went through a rapid process of diffusion and, we can say, of massification. Indeed they less and less represent an item of 'status', but more and more a necessity to conform to a certain life style. This makes even clearer the selective nature of the process of market expansion and the fact that it concerns only a portion of the need structure.

15. The examples which come to mind are the setting in place of the railways system or the introduction of the internal combustion engine.

16. At the same time it might face obstacles that begin now to be dimly perceived.

Appendix A: macro variables trends in the post-war period

Graph 1   Gross National Product in 1982 constant dollars

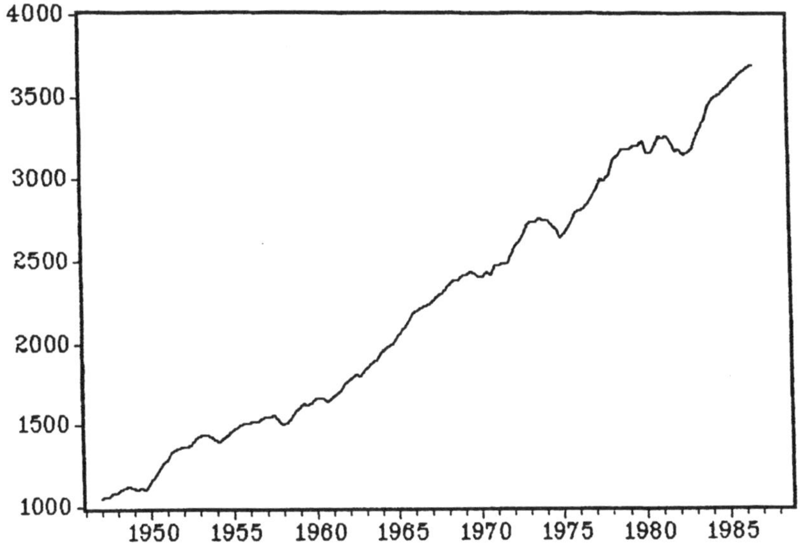

Graph 2   Personal Disposable Income

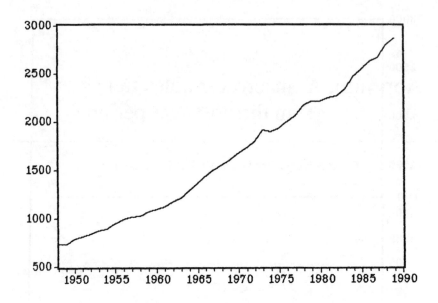

Graph 3   Per Capita Personal Disposable Income

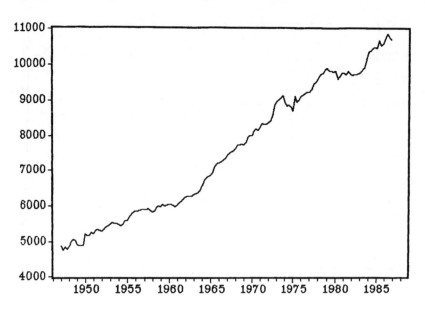

Graph 4   Personal Consumption

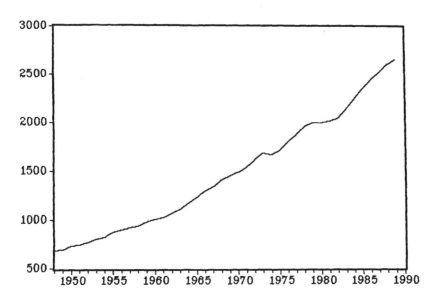

Graph 5   Consumption Ratio

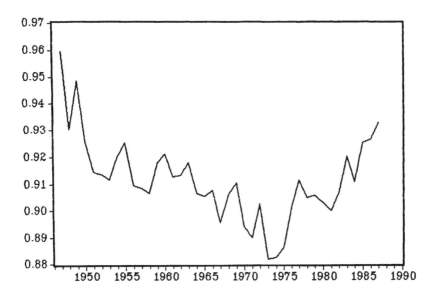

Graph 6   Personal Saving as a Percentage of Personal Income

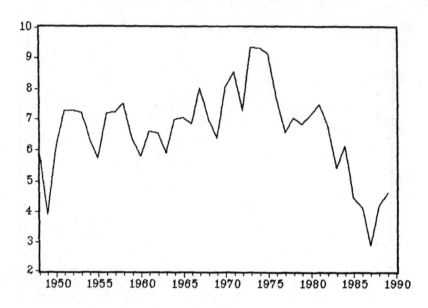

Graph 7   Ratio of Consumer Installment Debt to Personal Income

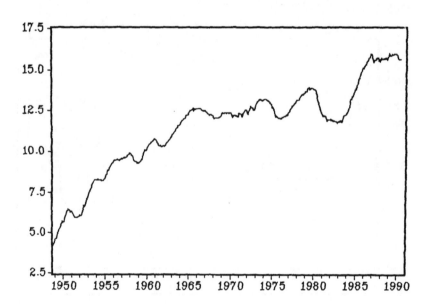

Graph 8   Gross Hourly Earnings of Non-Agricultural Production Workers

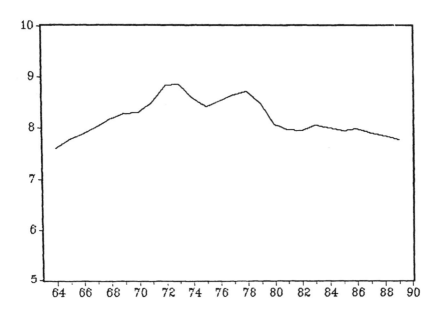

Graph 9   Average Hourly Earnings Index, 1977 constant dollars

Graph 10   Corporate Profits after Taxes, 1982 constant dollars

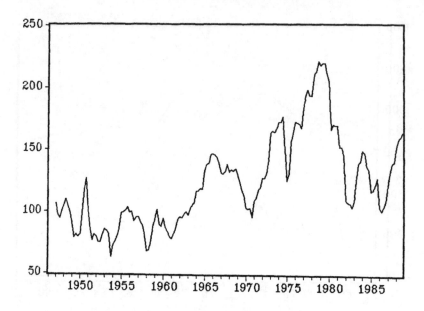

Graph 11   Composite Index of Profitability (1967 = 100)

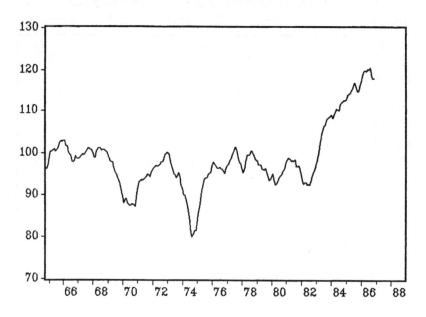

Graph 12   Gross Private Domestic Investment, 1982 constant dollars

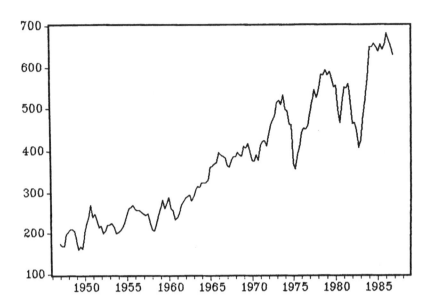

Graph 13   Gross Investment Producer's Durable Equipment, 1982 dollars

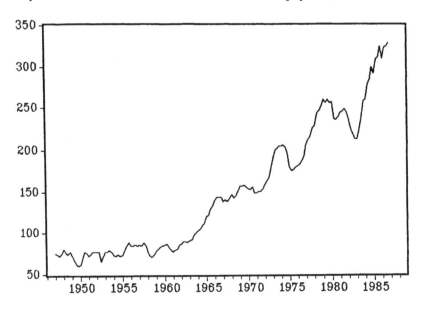

Graph 14 Output Capacity: Total Industry

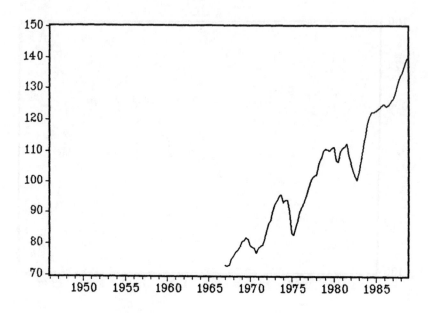

Graph 15 Capacity Utilization Rate: Manufacturing

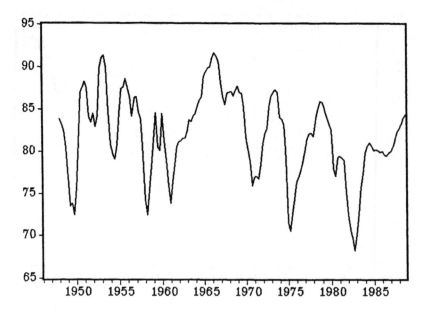

Graph 16   Net Exports, 1982 dollars

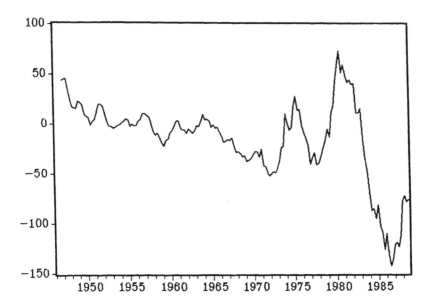

Graph 17   Government Purchases: Federal, 1982 dollars

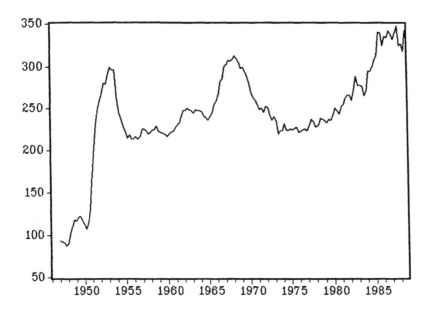

Graph 18   Government Purchases: Federal, National Defense, 1982 dollars

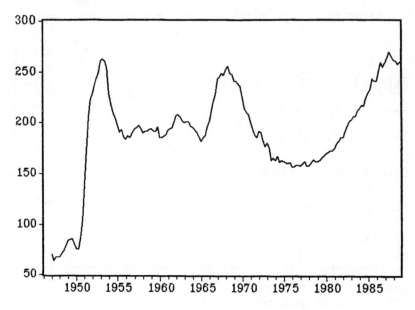

Graph 19   Government Purchases: State and Local, 1982 dollars

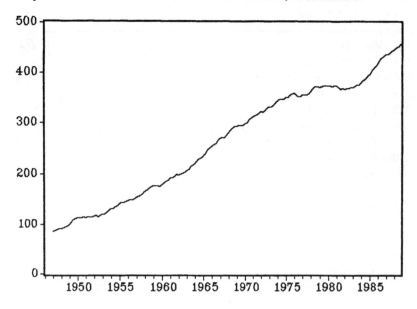

Appendix B: industries grouping

THREE-DIGIT INDUSTRIES GROUPS

Group I - Recovering Industries

Subgroup 1d - Strong recovering

239 - Misc. Fabricated Textile Products
254 - Partitions and Fixtures
261 - Pulp Mills
264 - Misc. Converted Paper Products
278 - Blankbooks and Bookbinding
285 - Paints and Allied Products
289 - Misc. Chemical Products
295 - Paving and Roofing Materials
306 - Fabricated Rubber Producs, nec
321 - Flat Glass
323 - Products of Purchased Glass
334 - Secondary Nonferrous Metals
347 - Metal Services, nec
348 - Ordnance and Accessories, nec
366 - Communication Equipment
371 - Motor Vehicles and Equipment
379 - Miscellaneous Transportation Equipment
385 - Ophthalmic Goods   (18)

Subgroup 1c - Recovering

201 - Meat Products
202 - Dairy Products
203 - Preserved Fruits and Vegetables
204 - Grain Mill Products
207 - Fats and Oils
209 - Misc. Foods and Kindred Products
213 - Chewing and Smoking Tobacco

223 - Weaving and Finishing Mills, Wool
224 - Narrow Fabric Mills
226 - Textile Finishing, except Wool
235 - Hats, Caps, except Millinery
236 - Children Outwear
242 - Sawmills and Planing Mills
243 - Millwork, Plywood & Structural Member
244 - Wood Containers
253 - Public Building & Related Furniture
271 - Newspapers
272 - Periodicals
273 - Books
275 - Commercial Printing
279 - Printing Trade Services
303 - Reclaimed Rubber
328 - Cut Stone and Stone Products
372 - Aircraft and Parts
376 - Guided Missiles and Space Vehicles   (25)

Group II - Expanding Industries

Subgroup 1a - Expanding industries

227 - Floor Covering Mills
276 - Manifold Business Forms
282 - Plastics Materials and Synthetics
283 - Drugs
307 - Miscellaneous Plastics Products
339 - Miscellaneous Primary Metal Products
367 - Electronic Components and Accessories
369 - Misc. Electrical Equipment & Supplies
382 - Measuring and Controlling Devices
384 - Medical Instruments and Supplies   (10)

Subgroup 1b - Strong expanding

252 - *Office Furniture*
357 - *Office and Computing Machines*
365 - *Radio and TV Receiving Equipment*
262 - Paper Mills, except Building Paper
274 - Miscellaneous Publishing
277 - Greeting Card Publishing

381 - Engineering & Scientific Instruments   (7)
(Industries in italics above belong to both 1a and 1b)

Group III - Growing Industries

208 - Beverages
233 - Women's and Misses' Outwear
241 - Logging Camps & Logging Contractors
249 - Miscellaneous Wood Products
259 - Miscellaneous Furniture & Fixtures
383 - Optical Instruments and Lenses   (6)

                                                            [66]

Group IV - Declining Industries

Subgroup 2a - Declining industries

205 - Bakery Products
206 - Sugar and Confectionery Products
211 - Cigarettes
212 - Cigars
214 - Tobacco Stemming and Re-drying
221 - Weaving Mills, Cotton
231 - Men's and Boys' Suits and Coats
234 - Women's and Children's Undergarments
238 - Miscellaneous Apparel and Accessories
266 - Building Paper and Board Mills
311 - Leather Tanning and Finishing
313 - Boot and Shoe Cut Stock and Findings
314 - Footwear, except Rubber
315 - Leather Gloves and Mittens
319 - Leather Goods, nec
324 - Cement, Hydraulic
325 - Structural Clay Products
326 - Pottery and Related Products
396 - Costume Jewelry and Notions   (19)

Group V - Stagnating Industries (Subgroups 2b and 2c in italics)

302 - Rubber and Plastics Footwear

331 - Blast Furnace and Basic Steel Products
332 - Iron and Steel Foundries
335 - Nonferrous Rolling and Drawing
336 - Nonferrous Foundries
342 - Cutlery, Hand Tools, and Hardware
345 - Screw Machine Products, Bolts, etc
346 - Metal Forgings and Stamping
354 - Metalworking Machinery
355 - Special Industry Machinery
362 - Electrical Industrial Apparatus
387 - Watches, Clocks, and Watchcases
391 - Jewelry, Silverware, and Plated Ware   (13)

Group VI - Shrinking Industries

222 - Weaving Mills, Synthetics
225 - Knitting Mills
228 - Yarn and Thread Mills
229 - Miscellaneous Textile Goods
232 - Men's and Boys' Furnishings
237 - Fur Goods
245 - Wood Buildings and Mobile Homes
251 - Household Furniture
263 - Paperboard Mills
265 - Paperboard Containers and Boxes
281 - Industrial Inorganic Chemicals
284 - Soaps, Cleaners and Toilet Goods
286 - Industrial Organic Chemicals
287 - Agricultural Chemicals
291 - Petroleum Refining
299 - Misc. Petroleum and Coal Products
301 - Tires and Inner Tubes
304 - Rubber and Plastic Hose and Belting
316 - Luggage
317 - Handbags and Personal Leather Goods
322 - Glass and Glassware, Pressed and Blown
327 - Concrete, Gypsum, and Plaster Products
329 - Misc. Nonmetallic Mineral Products
333 - Primary Nonferrous Metals
341 - Metal Cans and Shipping Containers
343 - Plumbing and Heating, except Electric
344 - Fabricated Structural Metal Products

349 - Misc. Fabricated Metal Products
351 - Engines and Turbines
352 - Farm and Garden Machinery
353 - Construction and Related Machinery
356 - General Industrial Machinery
358 - Refrigeration and Service Machinery
359 - Misc. Machinery, except Electrical
361 - Electric Distributing Equipment
363 - Household Appliances
364 - Electric Lighting and Wiring Equipment
373 - Ship and Boat Building and Repairing
374 - Railroad Equipment
375 - Motorcycles, Bicycles, and Parts
386 - Photographic Equipment and Supplies
393 - Musical Instruments
394 - Toys and Sporting Goods
395 - Pens, Pencils, Office and Art Supplies
399 - Miscellaneous Manufactures   (45)

                                                                    [143]

TWO-DIGIT INDUSTRIES GROUPS

20. Food and Kindred Products
201 - Meat Products   I
202 - Dairy Products
203 - Preserved Fruits and Vegetables
204 - Grain Mill Products
207 - Fats and Oils
209 - Misc. Foods and Kindred Products

208 - Beverages   III

205 - Bakery products   IV
206 - Sugar and Confectionery Products

21. Tobacco Manufacturers
213. Chewing and Smoking Tobacco   II

211 - Cigarettes   IV

212 - Cigars
214 - Tobacco Stemming and Re-drying

22. Textile Mill Products
223 - Weaving and Finishing Mills, Wool   I
224 - Narrow Fabric Mills
226 - Textile Finishing, except Wool

227 - Floor Covering Mills   II

221 - Weaving Mills, Cotton   IV

222 - Weaving Mills, Synthetics   VI
225 - Knitting Mills
228 - Yarn and Thread Mills
229 - Miscellaneous Textile Goods

23. Apparel and Other Textile Products
239 - Misc. Fabricated Textile Products   I
235 - Hats, Caps, except Millinery
236 - Children Outwear

233 - Women's and Misses' Outwear   III

231 - Men's and Boys' Suits and Coats   V
234 - Women's and Children's Undergarments
238 - Miscellaneous Apparel and Accessories

232 - Men's and Boys' Furnishings   VI
237 - Fur Goods

24. Lumber and Wood Products
242 - Sawmills and Planing Mills   I
243 - Millwork, Plywood & Structural Member
244 - Wood Containers

241 - Logging Camps & Logging Contractors   III
249 - Miscellaneous Wood Products

245 - Wood Buildings and Mobile Homes   VI

25. Furniture and Fixtures
254 - Partitions and Fixtures   I
253 - Public Building & Related Furniture

252 - Office Furniture   II

259 - Miscellaneous Furniture & Fixtures   III

251 - Household Furniture   VI

26. Paper and Allied Products
261 - Pulp Mills   I
264 - Misc. Converted Paper Products

262 - Paper Mills, except Building Paper   III

266 - Building Paper and Board Mills   IV

263 - Paperboard Mills   VI
265 - Paperboard Containers and Boxes

27. Printing and Publishing
278 - Blankbooks and Bookbinding   I
271 - Newspapers
272 - Periodicals
273 - Books
275 - Commercial Printing
279 - Printing Trade Services

276 - Manifold Business Forms   II
274 - Miscellaneous Publishing
277 - Greeting Card Publishing

28. Chemicals and Allied Products
285 - Paints and Allied Products   I
289 - Misc. Chemical Products

282 - Plastics Materials and Synthetics   II
283 - Drugs

281 - Industrial Inorganic Chemicals   VI
284 - Soaps, Cleaners and Toilet Goods
286 - Industrial Organic Chemicals
287 - Agricultural Chemicals

29. Petroleum and Coal Products
295 - Paving and Roofing Materials   I

291 - Petroleum Refining   VI
299 - Misc. Petroleum and Coal Products

30. Rubber and Misc. Plastics Products
306 - Fabricated Rubber Products, nec   I
303 - Reclaimed Rubber

307 - Miscellaneous Plastics Products   II

302 - Rubber and Plastics Footwear   V

301 - Tires and Inner Tubes   VI
304 - Rubber and Plastic Hose and Belting

31. Leather and Leather Products
311 - Leather Tanning and Finishing   IV
313 - Boot and Shoe Cut Stock and Findings
314 - Footwear, except Rubber
315 - Leather Gloves and Mittens
319 - Leather Goods, nec

316 - Luggage   VI
317 - Handbags and Personal Leather Goods

32. Stone, Clay, and Glass Products
321 - Flat Glass   I
323 - Products of Purchased Glass

328 - Cut Stone and Stone Products

324 - Cement, Hydraulic   IV
325 - Structural Clay Products
326 - Pottery and Related Products

322 - Glass and Glassware, Pressed and Blown   VI
327 - Concrete, Gypsum, and Plaster Products
329 - Misc. Nonmetallic Mineral Products

33. Primary Metal Industries
334 - Secondary Nonferrous Metals   I

339 - Miscellaneous Primary Metal Products   II

331 - Blast Furnace and Basic Steel Products   V
332 - Iron and Steel Foundries
335 - Nonferrous Rolling and Drawing
336 - Nonferrous Foundries

333 - Primary Nonferrous Metals   VI

34. Fabricated Metal Products
347 - Metal Services, nec   I
348 - Ordnance and Accessories, nec

342 - Cutlery, Hand Tools, and Hardware   V
345 - Screw Machine Products, Bolts, etc
346 - Metal Forgings and Stamping

341 - Metal Cans and Shipping Containers   VI
343 - Plumbing and Heating, except Electric
344 - Fabricated Structural Metal Products
349 - Misc.Fabricated Metal Products

35. Machinery, except Electrical
357 - Office and Computing Machines   II

354 - Metalworking Machinery   V

355 - Special Industry Machinery

351 - Engines and Turbines   VI
352 - Farm and Garden Machinery
353 - Construction and Related Machinery
356 - General Industrial Machinery
358 - Refrigeration and Service Machinery
359 - Misc. Machinery, except Electrical

36. Electric and Electronic Equipment
366 - Communication Equipment   I

367 - Electronic Components and Accessories   II
369 - Misc. Electrical Equipment and Supplies
365 - Radio and TV Receiving Equipment

362 - Electrical Industrial Apparatus   V

361 - Electric Distributing Equipment   VI
363 - Household Appliances
364 - Electric Lighting and Wiring Equipment

37. Transportation Equipment
371 - Motor Vehicles and Equipment   I
379 - Miscellaneous Transportation Equipment
372 - Aircraft and Parts
376 - Guided Missiles and Space Vehicles

373 - Ship and Boat Building and Repairing   VI
374 - Railroad Equipment
375 - Motorcycles, Bicycles, and Parts

38. Instrument and Related Products
385 - Ophthalmic goods   I

381 - Engineering & Scientific Instruments   II
382 - Measuring and Controlling Devices
384 - Medical Instruments and Supplies

383 - Optical Instruments and Lenses   III

387 - Watches, Clocks, and Watchcases   V

386 - Photographic Equipment and Supplies   VI

39. Miscellaneous Manufacturing Industries
396 - Costume Jewelry and Notions   IV

391 - Jewelry, Silverware, and Plated Ware   V

393 - Musical Instruments   VI
394 - Toys and Sporting Goods
395 - Pens, Pencils, Office and Art Supplies
399 - Miscellaneous Manufactures

Appendix C: expenditure categories, trends and ex-post forecast

Graph 20   Durable Expenditure

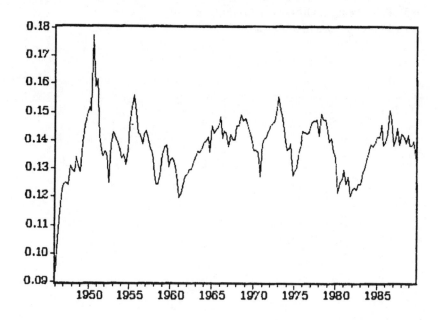

Graph 21   Non-durable Expenditure

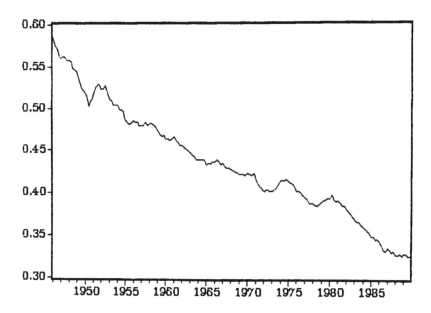

Graph 22   Services Expenditure

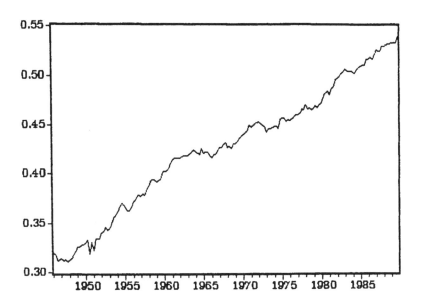

Graph 23   Food and Tobacco Expenditure

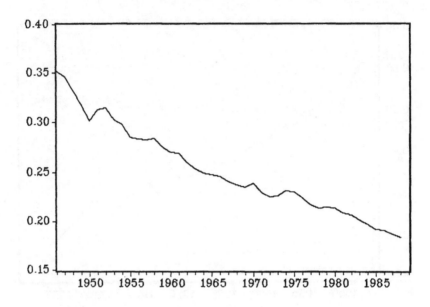

Graph 24   Clothing, Accessories and Jewelry Expenditure

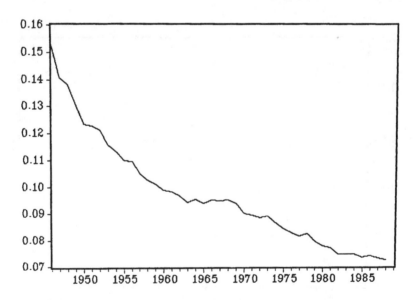

Graph 25   Housing Expenditure

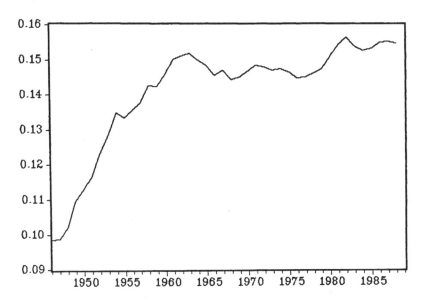

Graph 26   Household Operation Expenditure

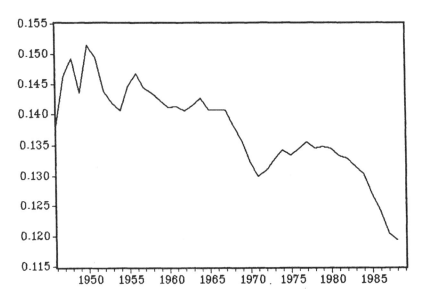

Graph 27   Personal Care Expenditure

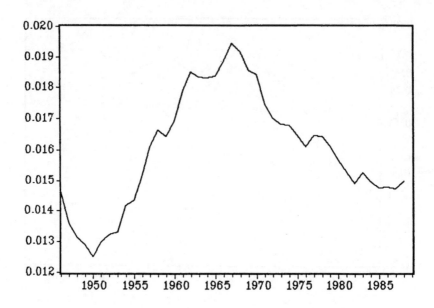

Graph 28   Medical Care Expenditure

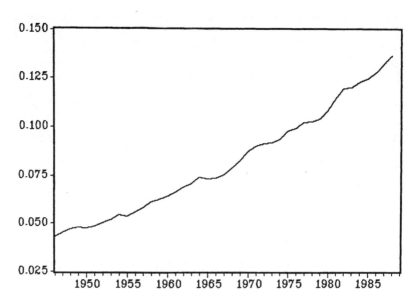

Graph 29   Private Education and Research Expenditure

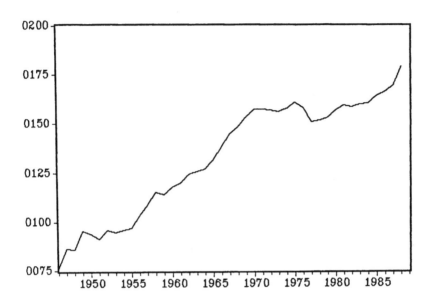

Graph 30   Recreation Expenditure

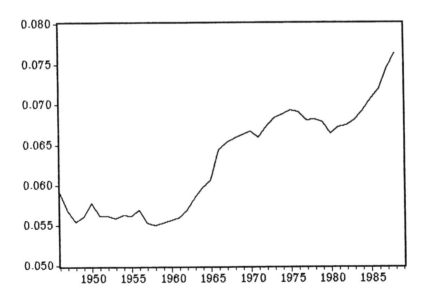

Graph 31 . Personal Business Expenditure

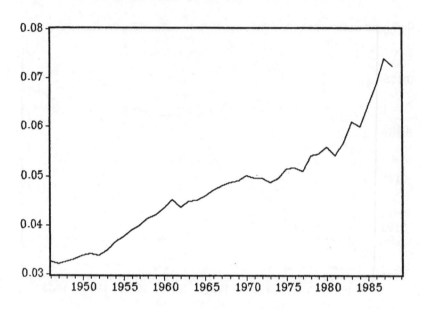

Graph 32   Transportation Expenditure

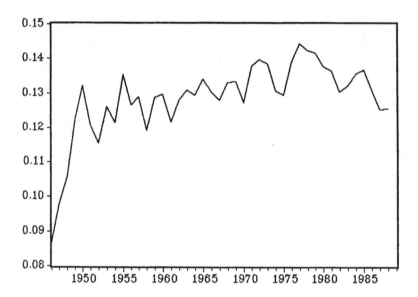

Graph 33   Foreign Travel and Other, Net, Expenditure

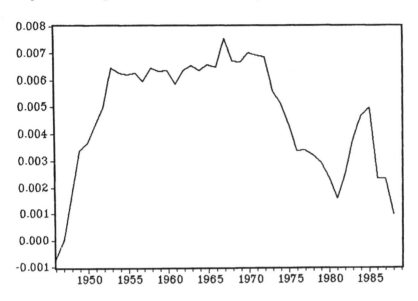

Graph 34   Religious and Welfare Activities Expenditure

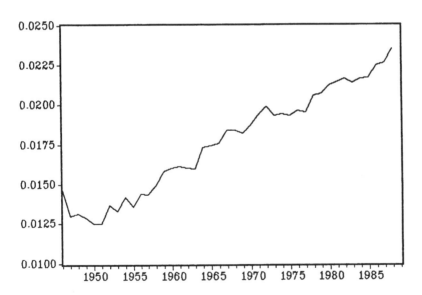

SUMMARY OF REGRESSION RESULTS

Dependent Variable is FOOD
SMPL range: 1952–1979
Number of observations: 28
Convergence achieved after 11 iterations

VARIABLE	COEFFICIENT	STD. ERROR	T-STAT.	2-TAIL SIG.
C	0.3949317	0.0681671	5.7935842	0.0000
MEDIAN	–2.796E-06	7.809E-07	–3.5807845	0.0016
HIFIF	–0.0001182	0.0016446	–0.0718812	0.9433
WEALTH	–1.669E-05	4.186E-06	–3.9878624	0.0006
MA(1)	0.9519535	0.0188319	50.550038	0.0000

R-squared	0.985358	Mean of dependent var	0.253302
Adj R-squared	0.982811	S.D. of dependent var	0.028970
S.E. of regression	0.003798	Sum of squared resid	0.000332
Log likelihood	119.0747	F-statistic	386.9534
Durbin–Watson stat	2.215853	Prob(F-statistic)	0.000000

Dependent Variable is CLOTH
SMPL range: 1952–1979
Number of observations: 28
Convergence achieved after 6 iterations

VARIABLE	COEFFICIENT	STD. ERROR	T-STAT.	2-TAIL SIG.
C	0.1613638	0.0448849	3.5950552	0.0015
MEDIAN	–1.162E-06	5.171E-07	–2.2481915	0.0344
HIFIF	–0.0004383	0.0010829	–0.4047086	0.6894
WEALTH	–4.590E-06	2.773E-06	–1.6552295	0.1115
MA(1)	0.9527791	0.0203959	46.714341	0.0000

R-squared	0.953795	Mean of dependent var	0.096147
Adj R-squared	0.945759	S.D. of dependent var	0.010790
S.E. of regression	0.002513	Sum of squared resid	0.000145
Log likelihood	130.6390	F-statistic	118.6950
Durbin–Watson stat	1.415015	Prob(F-statistic)	0.000000

Dependent Variable is HOUSE
SMPL range: 1953–1979
Number of observations: 27
Convergence achieved after 4 iterations

VARIABLE	COEFFICIENT	STD. ERROR	T-STAT.	2-TAIL SIG.
C	0.1236233	0.0441021	2.8031173	0.0104
MEDIAN	−1.127E-06	6.198E-07	−1.8189498	0.0826
HIFIF	0.0014594	0.0008930	1.6343208	0.1164
WEALTH	−4.737E-07	2.408E-06	−0.1967082	0.8459
AR (1)	0.8478546	0.0369918	22.920090	0.0000

R-squared	0.935295	Mean of dependent var	0.144528
Adj R-squared	0.923530	S.D. of dependent var	0.005748
S.E. of regression	0.001590	Sum of squared resid	5.56E-05
Log likelihood	138.4486	F-statistic	79.50054
Durbin–Watson stat	1.931437	Prob(F-statistic)	0.000000

Dependent Variable is HOUSEOP
SMPL range: 1953–1979
Number of observations: 27
Convergence achieved after 9 iterations

VARIABLE	COEFFICIENT	STD. ERROR	T-STAT.	2-TAIL SIG.
C	0.1767192	0.0397205	4.4490666	0.0002
MEDIAN	−8.460E-07	4.266E-07	−1.9832314	0.0606
HIFIF	−0.0004366	0.0009543	−0.4574435	0.6520
WEALTH	2.875E-07	2.340E-06	0.1228445	0.9034
MA(1)	0.8558135	0.1400579	6.1104267	0.0000
AR (1)	0.3745075	0.1535968	2.4382499	0.0237

R-squared	0.908223	Mean of dependent var	0.138536
Adj R-squared	0.886371	S.D. of dependent var	0.004655
S.E. of regression	0.001569	Sum of squared resid	5.17E-05
Log likelihood	139.4276	F-statistic	41.56294
Durbin–Watson stat	1.915144	Prob(F-statistic)	0.000000

Dependent Variable is PERSON
SMPL range: 1952–1979
Number of observations: 28
Convergence achieved after 4 iterations

VARIABLE	COEFFICIENT	STD. ERROR	T-STAT.	2-TAIL SIG.
C	0.0296836	0.0143956	2.0619866	0.0507
MEDIAN	–3.418E-07	1.739E-07	–1.9650771	0.0616
HIFIF	–0.0003772	0.0003474	–1.0859148	0.2888
WEALTH	2.781E-06	9.345E-07	2.9763024	0.0068
MA(1)	0.6984347	0.1619075	4.3137880	0.0003

R-squared	0.804252	Mean of dependent var	0.016863
Adj R-squared	0.770209	S.D. of dependent var	0.001686
S.E. of regression	0.000808	Sum of squared resid	1.50E-05
Log likelihood	162.4060	F-statistic	23.62453
Durbin–Watson stat	1.069826	Prob(F-statistic)	0.000000

Dependent Variable is MEDIC
SMPL range: 1953–1979
Number of observations: 27
Convergence not achieved after 20 iterations

VARIABLE	COEFFICIENT	STD. ERROR	T-STAT.	2-TAIL SIG.
C	–0.4672866	7.0695087	–0.0660989	0.9479
MEDIAN	1.042E-06	7.375E-07	1.4127661	0.1724
HIFIF	0.0020248	0.0010017	2.0213786	0.0562
WEALTH	–3.243E-06	2.917E-06	–1.1117737	0.2788
MA(1)	0.2847121	0.2615192	1.0886852	0.2886
AR (1)	1.0017337	0.0273736	36.594821	0.0000

R-squared	0.989836	Mean of dependent var	0.077157
Adj R-squared	0.987417	S.D. of dependent var	0.016961
S.E. of regression	0.001903	Sum of squared resid	7.60E-05
Log likelihood	134.2242	F-statistic	409.0434
Durbin–Watson stat	1.668787	Prob(F-statistic)	0.000000

Dependent Variable is EDUCA
SMPL range: 1952–1979
Number of observations: 28
Convergence achieved after 6 iterations

VARIABLE	COEFFICIENT	STD. ERROR	T-STAT.	2-TAIL SIG.
C	0.0083236	0.0073748	1.1286549	0.2707
MEDIAN	3.291E-07	8.258E-08	3.9853154	0.0006
HIFIF	–0.0001565	0.0001782	–0.8783970	0.3888
WEALTH	7.825E-07	4.421E-07	1.7700231	0.0900
MA(1)	0.6144354	0.1366991	4.4948018	0.0002

R-squared	0.974461	Mean of dependent var	0.013285
Adj R-squared	0.970020	S.D. of dependent var	0.002324
S.E. of regression	0.000402	Sum of squared resid	3.72E-06
Log likelihood	181.9327	F-statistic	219.3980
Durbin–Watson stat	2.052219	Prob(F-statistic)	0.000000

Dependent Variable is RECREA
SMPL range: 1952–1979
Number of observations: 28
Convergence achieved after 13 iterations

VARIABLE	COEFFICIENT	STD. ERROR	T-STAT.	2-TAIL SIG.
C	0.0433619	0.0186149	2.3294192	0.0294
MEDIAN	1.445E-06	2.078E-07	6.9550213	0.0000
HIFIF	–0.0002708	0.0004500	–0.6017992	0.5535
WEALTH	–1.619E-06	1.114E-06	–1.4536898	0.1601
MA(1)	0.8267500	0.0853360	9.6881708	0.0000
MA (2)	0.4194643	0.1451247	2.8903717	0.0085

R-squared	0.973042	Mean of dependent var	0.061982
Adj R-squared	0.966915	S.D. of dependent var	0.005564
S.E. of regression	0.001012	Sum of squared resid	2.25E-05
Log likelihood	156.7276	F-statistic	158.8173
Durbin–Watson stat	1.906998	Prob(F-statistic)	0.000000

Dependent Variable is PERSBU
SMPL range: 1952–1979
Number of observations: 28
Convergence achieved after 11 iterations

VARIABLE	COEFFICIENT	STD. ERROR	T-STAT.	2-TAIL SIG.
C	0.0151416	0.0233225	0.6492289	0.5226
MEDIAN	7.532E-07	2.526E-07	2.9822237	0.0067
HIFIF	7.195E-05	0.0005647	0.1274232	0.8997
WEALTH	2.154E-06	1.356E-06	1.5882318	0.1259
MA(1)	0.7693765	0.1527066	5.0382646	0.0000

R-squared	0.961853	Mean of dependent var	0.045599
Adj R-squared	0.955219	S.D. of dependent var	0.005683
S.E. of regression	0.001203	Sum of squared resid	3.33E-05
Log likelihood	151.2745	F-statistic	144.9839
Durbin–Watson stat	1.701110	Prob(F-statistic)	0.000000

Dependent Variable is TRANSP
SMPL range: 1952–1979
Number of observations: 28

VARIABLE	COEFFICIENT	STD. ERROR	T-STAT.	2-TAIL SIG.
C	0.0413083	0.0866840	0.4765386	0.6380
MEDIAN	8.673E-07	9.974E-07	0.8695237	0.3932
HIFIF	0.0015055	0.0020912	0.7199488	0.4785
WEALTH	1.538E-06	5.341E-06	0.2879121	0.7759

R-squared	0.582141	Mean of dependent var	0.131106
Adj R-squared	0.529908	S.D. of dependent var	0.007100
S.E. of regression	0.004868	Sum of squared resid	0.000569
Log likelihood	111.5313	F-statistic	11.14519
Durbin–Watson stat	1.898714	Prob(F-statistic)	0.000089

Dependent Variable is TRAVEL
SMPL range: 1954–1979
Number of observations: 26
Convergence achieved after 4 iterations

VARIABLE	COEFFICIENT	STD. ERROR	T-STAT.	2-TAIL SIG.
C	0.0181310	0.0186803	0.9705932	0.3433
MEDIAN	–1.381E-07	2.064E-07	–0.6692480	0.5110
HIFIF	–0.0003360	0.0003167	–1.0609994	0.3013
WEALTH	5.487E-07	8.150E-07	0.6732767	0.5085
AR (1)	0.9910354	0.2191784	4.5215923	0.0002
AR (2)	–0.0243219	0.2511903	–0.0968264	0.9238

R-squared	0.857461	Mean of dependent var		0.005838
Adj R-squared	0.821826	S.D. of dependent var		0.001290
S.E. of regression	0.000544	Sum of squared resid		5.93E-06
Log likelihood	161.9316	F-statistic		24.06248
Durbin–Watson stat	2.024278	Prob(F-statistic)		0.000000

Dependent Variable is WELFRE
SMPL range: 1954–1979
Number of observations: 26
Convergence achieved after 5 iterations

VARIABLE	COEFFICIENT	STD. ERROR	T-STAT.	2-TAIL SIG.
C	–0.0180584	0.0075495	–2.3919984	0.0267
MEDIAN	3.776E-07	9.721E-08	3.8843262	0.0009
HIFIF	0.0005696	0.0001828	3.1167805	0.0054
WEALTH	6.019E-07	5.468E-07	1.1008410	0.2840
AR (1)	0.1121298	0.2369058	0.4733097	0.6411
AR (2)	–0.2449576	0.2278976	–1.0748579	0.2952

R-squared	0.971500	Mean of dependent var		0.017526
Adj R-squared	0.964375	S.D. of dependent var		0.002157
S.E. of regression	0.000407	Sum of squared resid		3.32E-06
Log likelihood	169.4845	F-statistic		136.3518
Durbin–Watson stat	2.011643	Prob(F-statistic)		0.000000

Graph 35

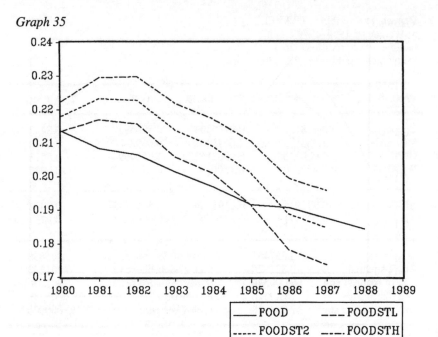

Graph 36

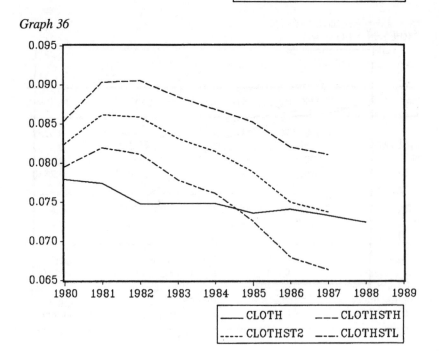

Graph 37

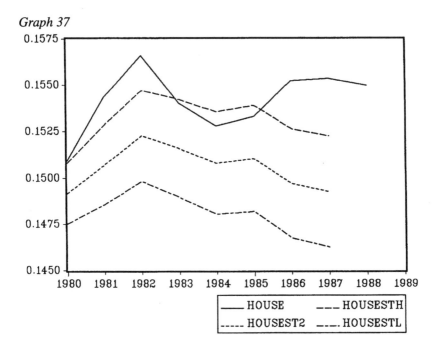

Graph 38

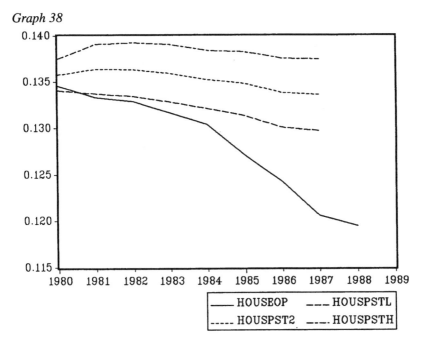

Graph 39

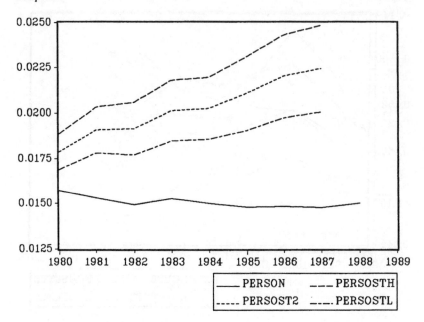

Graph 40

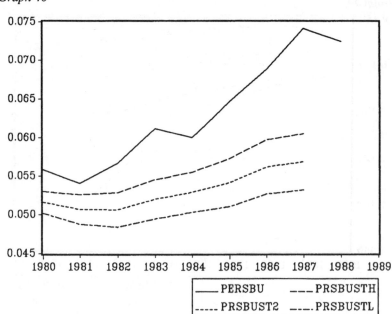

Graph 41

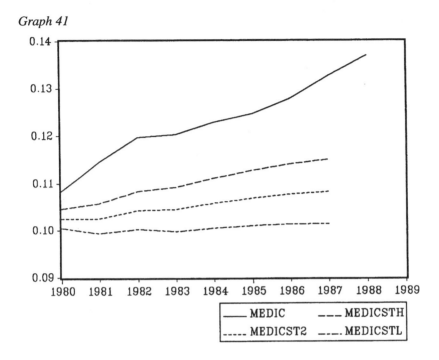

Graph 42

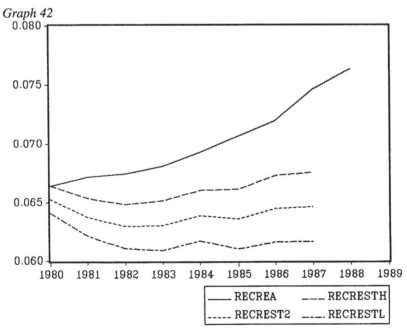

Graph 43

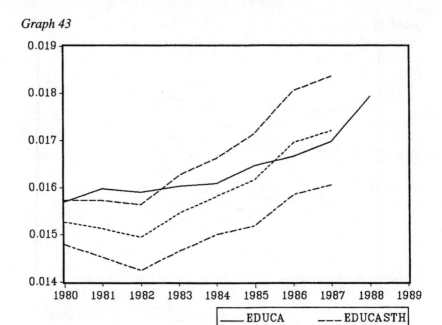

Graph 44

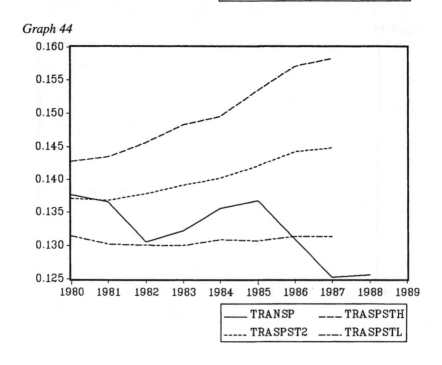

Graph 45

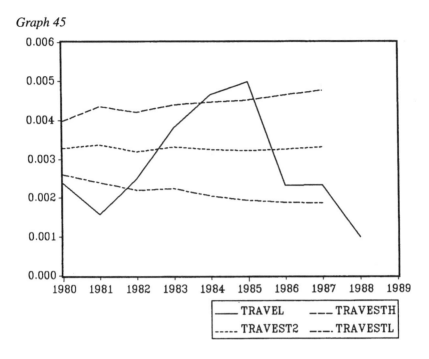

Graph 46

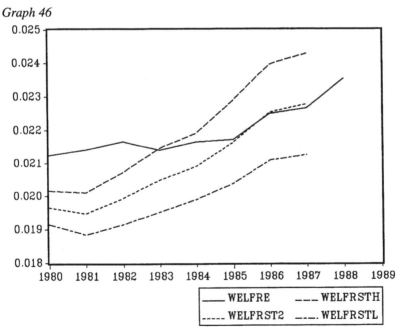

Appendix D: data sources and data series

DATA SOURCES

Output and Investment

Output and Investment data are available at the three-digit level (143 industries), 1982 dollars, in the Production Data Base and the Capital Stock Data Base of the Office of Business Analysis (OBA), Under Secretary for Economic Affairs, US Department of Commerce.

Research & Development

Data on Research & Development Expenditure are from the McGraw-Hill Annual Survey of business plans for research and development. It is a relatively consistent quantitative source of information, at least for the 1980s. The survey was published under a slightly different name 'Annual survey of research and development expenditure' for the 1987–9 period and then discontinued. A consistent series of tables is available from the 24th Survey, May 1979 (1979–82) to the 30th, May 1985 (1985–8). The year of the survey contains planned figures, the year before estimates and the year before that the revised actual figures. The regression covers the period 1953–83. For the years before 1980, the source of the historical data is the National Science Foundation. They are contained in the 30th McGraw Hill Survey, Table V, R&D expenditures in millions of current dollars (converted to 1982 dollars, using the implicit Citibase GNP deflator), and in Table VII, R&D expenditures as a percentage of sales. The problem is that the data are far too aggregated than is desirable.

Each survey has additional information as to the general trend and composition of R&D expenditure, and remarks on each industry. The tone of the remarks is that of a short-run analysis tailored to business users and focused on broadly defined industries (auto, electronics, oil). Of some interest is the breakdown of expenditure in new products and new processes versus improvements (table III) and new product sales (table II).

New Products and Advertisement

The expenditure in advertisement and the number of new products are not available and must be constructed from business sources. The question of new products is the aspect I have investigated more. In the SRI Index, new products are listed under marketing. A limited search on trade journals led to fragmented information, unlikely to provide any data set for a quantitative test.

The data set used in the analysis is in the final report of a Baltimore consulting firm, under contract for the US Small Business Administration.[1] It is a counting of new products based on a survey of 108 trade journals.[2] The definition of 'new product' reflects the judgment of the journals' editors. It is in principle not a bad definition, though obviously influenced by the marketing strategy of the industry. The report was designed 'to determine whether any systematic differences in innovating activities exist between large and small firms; in addition, the study was intended to broaden the industrial coverage used in prior research in the field'. Innovation is defined as 'a process that begins with an invention, proceeds with the development of the invention, and results in introduction of a new product, process or service to the market place'. The definition includes also 'the implementation of a new management practice'. Such a definition fits my purposes well. Unfortunately the data collection concerns a single year, 1982, which was considered sufficient for the purposes of the study.[3]

Expenditure in advertising is available annually in *Advertising Age*, a weekly publication. The magazine reports the results of annual study of advertising and promotion expenditures of Schonfeld & Associates, Evaston, Ill. The study covers more than 5000 individual companies, in 285 SIC industries. The raw data for the study are compiled from the reports filed by publicly owned companies with the Securities and Exchange Commission. For that reason the expenditure includes media and non-media spending such as 'collateral literature, production, etc'. This is why the figures are higher than in media auditing services. For this and other reasons, caution must be used in interpreting the data. The level of desegregation is that of the two, three, or four digits of the SIC. The test uses the annual rate of change of the 'Ad Dollar as a per cent of sales'. There are other studies similar to the Schonfeld & Associates annual report. The AD $ Forecast, by Pansophic Sytems, Inc. has exactly the same characteristics, but is more aggregate coverage.

DATA SERIES

Compiling the series is laborious. New products and advertising are listed according to SIC codes, but there is a good amount of manipulation and estimation to be done to make them consistent with the output and investment data. Two-digit values or averages of four-digit industries were applied to several three-digit industries. In this second case not all the four-digit industries of the corresponding three-digit sector may be included. In short, there are many elements of possible distortion.

Similarly R&D data come in a very aggregated form (fourteen and fifteen industries). In one of the series considered, current expenditure, there are some subdivisions of these major industries. The problem is that the classification does not correspond to SIC codes, though it is rather close.

Sample

The sample was changed four times, since the number of industries for which data are available for all the independent variables decreases as we add new independent variables. Starting from the 143 SIC three-digit industries, for which data on output and investment are available in the OBA database, and adding new products, the sample includes 117 industries. Adding the rate of change of R&D expenditure and then the R&D expenditure to sales ratio, the sample size goes down to 101 and to 92 industries. The fourth sample adds the rate of change of the advertisement to sales ratio, available for 80 industries. The final results are based on the smallest sample, but some experimentation has been done with other samples as well.

NOTES

1. The Futures Group, 1984, *Characterization of Innovation Introduced in the US Market in 1982.*
2. The study considered sources on New Technology (nine, including The Official Gazette of the US Patents and Trademark Office), eight on-line data bases, with information about innovation, and 108 industry sources, that is trade journals. The sources under the first head were discarded because they 'tended to concentrate on highly significant innovations and, in most cases, were international in scope'. The sources under the second heading were discarded because 'Data derived from the on-line data bases were prohibitively expensive in the quantities we hoped to accumulate.' Patent abstracts were viewed as 'poor indicators'. The 108 trade journals were selected for their sections on new products, after a screening of a larger number of publications.
3. 'A collection of data for a ten-year period, which would have allowed "the luxury of time-series analysis and detection of trends" was made impossible by the time and budget

constraints' (The Futures Group, 1984, *Characterization of Innovation Introduced in the US Market in 1982*). This is an indication of the difficulties of building a database on innovation.

Bibliography

AER – The American Economic Review
EJ – Economic Journal
JPKE – Journal of Post Keynesian Economics
JPE – Journal of Political Economy
RES – Review of Economic Studies
RE&S – The Review of Economics and Statistics

Aglietta, M., 1979, *A Theory of Capitalist Regulation*. London, NLB.

Ando, A. and F. Modigliani, 1963, 'The life-cycle hypothesis of saving', *AER*, March.

Appelbaum, E., 1992, 'The integration of household structure and industrial structure: an extension of the input–output model', in W. Millberg (ed.), *The Megacorp & Macrodynamics*. Armonk, New York, M.E. Sharpe.

Arrow, K., 1986, 'Rationality of self and others in an economic system', Stanford University, mimeo.

Baran, P.A. and P.M. Sweezy, 1966, *Monopoly Capital*. New York, Monthly Review Press.

Baranzini, M. and R. Scazzieri (eds), 1990, *The Economic Theory of Structure and Change*. Cambridge, Cambridge University Press.

Bartley, R.L., 1992, *The Seven Fat Years*. New York, The Free Press.

Becker, G., 1965, 'A theory of the allocation of time', *EJ*, vol. 75.

— 1976, *The Economic Approach to Human Behavior*. Chicago, University of Chicago Press.

— and G. Stigler, 1977, 'De gustibus non est disputandum', *AER*, March, vol. 67.

Bleaney, M.F., 1976, *Underconsumption Theories: A History and Critical Analysis*. New York, International Publishers.

Bluestone, B. and B. Harrison, 1982, *The Deindustrialization of America*. New York, Basic Books.

Bowles, S., Gordon D.M. and Weisskopf T.E, 1989. 'Business ascendancy and economic impasse: a structural retrospective on conservative economics, 1979–87', *Journal of Economic Perspectives*, no. 1, Winter.

— 1990, *After the Waste Land*. Armonk, NewYork, Sharpe.

Chenery, H.B., 1960, 'Patterns of industrial growth', *AER*, vol. 50, September.

— and M. Syrquin, 1975, *Patterns of Development, 1950–1970*. London, Oxford University Press.

— and L. Taylor, 1968, 'Development patterns: among countries and over time', *RE&S*, November.

Chipman, J.S., 1960, 'The foundations of utility', *Econometrica*, vol. 28.

Cody J., H. Hughes and D. Wall (eds), 1980, *Policies for Industrial Progress in Developing Countries*. Unido/World Bank, Oxford University Press.

Christy, P.T and M.F. Mohr, 1986, *Changes in the Structure of the U.S. Economy since 1960: A Primer*. U.S. Department of Commerce, Working Paper, January.

Cross, J.C., 1983, *A Theory of Adaptive Economic Behaviour*. Cambridge, Cambridge University Press.

Cyert, R.M. and M.H. De Groot, 1975, 'Adaptive utility', in R. Day and T. Groves (eds), *Adaptive Economic Models*. New York, Academic Press.

Deaton, A. and J. Muellbauer, 1980, *Economic Theory and Consumer Behaviour*. Cambridge, Cambridge University Press.

Debreu, G., 1974, 'Excess demand functions', *Journal of Mathematical Economics*, vol. 1.

Dosi, G., 1984, *Technical Change and Industrial Transformation*. New York, St Martin's Press.

— (ed.), 1988, *Technical Change and Economic Theory*. London, Pinter Publ.

Duesenberry, J.S., 1949, *Income, Saving and the Theory of Consumer Behavior*. Cambridge, Mass., Harvard University Press.

Earl, P.E., 1983, *The Economic Imagination. Towards a Behavioral Analysis of Choice.* New York, Sharpe.

— 1986, *Lifestyle Economics.* New York, St Martin's Press.

Elster, J., 1979, *Ulysses and the Sirens.* Cambridge, Cambridge University Press.

Eichner, A.S., 1987, *The Macrodynamics of Advanced Market Economies.* Armonk, New York, M.E. Sharpe.

Fair, R.C., 1984, *Specification, Estimation, and Analysis of Macroeconometric Models.* Cambridge, Mass., Harvard University Press.

Fishburn, P.C., 1974, 'Lexicographic orders, utilities and decisions rules: a survey', *Management Science*, vol. 20.

Fortune, 1990, 'Turning R&D into real products', 2 June.

Freeman, C., 1974, *The Economics of Industrial Innovation.* Harmondsworth, Penguin. (Reprinted 1982, MIT Press.)

— (ed.), 1986, *Design, Innovation and Long Cycles in Economic Development.* New York, St Martin's Press.

— J. Clark and L. Soete, 1982, *Unemployment and Technical Innovation.* Westport, Connecticut, Greenwood Press.

Friedman, M., 1957, *A Theory of the Consumption Function.* Princeton, Mass., Princeton University Press.

Galbraith, K., 1967, *The New Industrial State.* Boston, Houghton Mifflin (4th ed. 1985).

Gay, A., 1983, 'Comportamento economico ed incompletezza: oltre i limiti delle ipotesi tradizionali', Dipartimento di Scienze Economiche, Università di Firenze, mimeo.

Gershuny, J., 1983, *Social Innovation and the Division of Labour.* New York, Oxford University Press.

Gibbard, A., 1986, 'Interpersonal comparisons: preference, good, and the intrinsic reward of a life', in J. Elster and A. Hylland (eds), *Foundations of Social Choice Theory.* Cambridge, Cambridge University Press.

Gordon, D.M., 1987, *What Makes Epochs? A Comparative Analysis of Technological and Social Explanations of Long Range Swings.* New York, Dept. of Economics, New School for Social Research.

— 1998, *Economics and Social Justice: Essays on Power, Labor and Institutional Change,* Cheltenham, Edward Elgar.

— M. Reich and R. Edwards, 1982, *Segmented Work, Divided Workers.* Cambridge, Cambridge University Press.

Gronau, R., 1977, 'Leisure, home production and work. The theory of allocation of time revisited', *JEP,* vol. 85.

Gualerzi, D., 1994, 'Schumpeter's theory of economic development and potential demand', *Review of Radical Political Economics,* vol. 26, no. 3, September.

— 1996, 'Natural dynamics, endogenous structural change and the theory of demand: a comment on Pasinetti', *Structural Change and Economic Dynamics,* vol. 7, no. 2, June.

— 1998, 'Economic change, choice and innovation in consumption', in M. Bianchi (ed.), *The Active Consumer: Novelty and Surprise in Consumer Choice.* London, Routledge.

Halevi, J. and J.M. Fontaine (eds), 1998, *Restoring Demand in the World Economy.* Cheltenham, Edward Elgar.

Harris, D., 1982, 'Structural change and economic growth: a review article', *Contribution to Political Economy,* vol. 1, March.

Harvey, D., 1992, *The Condition of Post-Modernity.* Cambridge, Mass. and Oxford, UK, Blackwell.

Hirschman, A.O., 1982, *Shifting Involvements.* Princeton, Princeton University Press.

Ironmonger, D.S., 1972, *New Commodities and Consumer Behaviour.* Cambridge, Cambridge University Press.

Kaldor, N., 1966, *Causes of the Slow Rate of Economic Growth of the United Kingdom.* Cambridge, Cambridge University Press.

Kornai, J., 1971, *Anti-Equilibrium: On Economic Systems Theory and the Tasks of Research.* Amsterdam, North-Holland.

Kurz, H. and N. Salvadori, 1998, 'The "new" growth theory: old wine in new goatskins', in F. Coricelli, M. Di Matteo and F. Hahn (eds), *New Theories in Growth and Development.* London, Macmillan.

Kuznets, S.S., 1956/1967, 'Quantitative aspects of the economic growth of nations', *EDCC,* vols. 5 and 15.

Lancaster, K.J., 1971, *Consumer Demand: A New Approach*. New York, Columbia University Press.

Lavoie, M., 1994, 'A post-Keynesian approach to consumer choice', *JPKE*, vol. 16, no. 4, Summer.

Levine, D.P., 1981, *Economic Theory*, vols I and II. London, Routledge & Kegan Paul.

— 1998, *Subjectivity in Political Economy. Essays on wanting and choosing*. London, Routledge & Kegan Paul.

Lowe, A., 1976, *The Path of Economic Growth*. Cambridge, Cambridge University Press.

Mankiw, N.G. and D. Romer, 1991, *New Keynesian Theory*. Cambridge, Mass., MIT Press.

Marglin, S.A., 1984, *Growth, Distribution, and Prices*. Cambridge, Mass., Harvard University Press.

Marschak, T.A., 1978, 'On the study of taste changing policies', *AER*, vol. 68.

Maslow, A., 1954, *Motivation and Personality*. New York, Harper.

Modigliani, F., 1949, 'Fluctuations in the saving–income ratio: a problem in economic forecasting', in *Studies in Income and Wealth*, Vol. 11, New York, National Bureau of Economic Research.

— 1966, 'The life-cycle hypothesis of saving, the demand for wealth and the supply of capital', *Social Research*, June.

Nell, E.J., 1982, 'Growth, distribution and inflation', *JPKE*, vol. V, no. 1, Fall.

— 1988, *Prosperity and Public Spending*. London, Allen & Unwin.

— 1991, *Transformational Growth and Effective Demand*. New York, New York University Press.

— 1998, *The General Theory of Transformational Growth*. Cambridge, Cambridge University Press.

Nelson, R. and S.G. Winter, 1977, 'In search of a useful theory of innovation', *Research Policy*, vol. 6.

— 1982, *An Evolutionary Theory of Economic Change*. Cambridge, Belknap.

Neumann, J. von, 1945–46, 'A model of general equilibrium', trans. G. Morgenstern, *RES*, vol. 13.

Packard, V., 1960, *The Waste Makers*. New York, David McKay Co.

Parker, W.N., 1972, 'Technology, resources, and economic change in the West', in A.J. Youngson (ed.), *Economic Development in the Long Run*, London, Allen & Unwin.

Parrinello, S., 1984, 'Adaptive preferences and theory of demand', *JPKE*, Summer.

Pasinetti, L.L., 1981, *Structural Change and Economic Growth*. Cambridge, Cambridge University Press.

— 1993, *Structural Economic Dynamics*. Cambridge, Cambridge University Press.

Piore, M.J. and C.F. Sabel, 1984, *The Second Industrial Divide: Possibilities for Prosperity*. New York, Basic Books.

Pollak, R.A., 1969, 'Conditional demand functions and consumption theory', *QJE*, vol. 83.

— 1970, 'Habit formation and dynamic demand functions', *JPE*, vol. 78.

— 1978, 'Endogenous taste in demand and welfare analysis', *AER*, *Papers and Proceedings*, vol. 68.

— and H. Wachter, 1975, 'The relevance of the household production function and its implications for the allocation of time', *JPE*, vol. 83.

President's Council of Economic Advisors, 1987, *Economic Report of the President*. Washington, D.C.

Reich, R., 1992, *The Work of Nations*. New York, Vintage Books.

Rosenberg, N., 1982, *Inside the Black Box: Technology and Economics*. Cambridge, Cambridge University Press.

Salter, W.E.G., 1966, *Productivity and Technical Change*. Cambridge, Cambridge University Press.

Schefold, B., 1985, 'On changes in the composition of output', *Political Economy*, vol. 1.

Schelling,T.C., 1984, 'Self-command in practice, in policy and in a theory of rational choice', *AER, Papers and Proceedings*, vol. 74.

Schumpeter, J.A., 1934, *The Theory of Economic Development*. Cambridge, Mass., Harvard University Press.

— 1935, 'The analysis of economic change', *RE&S*, vol. XVII, no. 4, May (reprinted in *Readings in Business Cycle Theory*. Philadelphia, The Blakiston Company, 1944).

— 1942, *Capitalism, Socialism and Democracy*. New York, Harper & Row Publishers.

Scitovsky, T., 1976, *The Joyless Economy*. New York, Oxford University Press.

Sen, A., 1977, *Rational Fool: A Critique of the Behavioral Foundations of Economic Theory*, Italian trans., *Scelta, benessere, equità*. Bologna, Il Mulino, 1986.

— 1985, *Commodities and Capabilities*. Amsterdam, North-Holland.

Shapiro, N., 1984–85, 'Involuntary unemployment in the long run: Pasinetti's formulation of the Keynesian argument. A Review Note', *JPKE*, vol. VII, no.2.

— 1986, 'Innovation, new industries and new firms', *Eastern Economic Journal*, March.

Solow, R., 1956, 'A contribution to the theory of economic growth', *Quarterly Journal of Economics*, vol. 70, reprinted in A. Sen, (ed.), *Growth Economics*. London, Penguin.

Stanback, T.M. Jr., P.J. Bearse, T.J. Noyelle and R.A. Karasek, 1981, *Services: The New Economy*. Totowa, NJ, Allanheld Osmun & Co.

Steedman, J. and U. Krause, 1985, 'Goethe's Faust, Arrow's possibility theorem and the individual decision taker', in J. Elster (ed.), *The Multiple Self*. Cambridge, Cambridge University Press.

Steindl, J., 1952, *Maturity and Stagnation in American Capitalism*, New York, Monthly Review Press.

Stigler, G. and G. Becker, 1977, 'De gustibus non est disputandum', *AER*, March.

Strozt, R.H., 1957, 'The empirical implications of a utility tree', *Econometrica*, vol. 25.

Sweezy, P.M., 1942, *The Theory of Capitalist Development*. New York, Monthly Review Press.

Thomas, R.L., 1997, *Modern Econometrics*, Reading, Mass., Addison-Wesley.

Van Duijn, J.J., 1983, *The Long Wave in Economic Life*. London, George Allen & Unwin.

Veblen, T., 1899, *The Theory of the Leisure Class*. Reprinted New York, B.W. Huebsch, 1918.

Winston, G.C., 1982, *The Timing in Economic Activities*, Cambridge, Cambridge University Press.

Yoshikawa, H., 1995, *Macroeconomics and the Japanese Economy*. Oxford, Oxford University Press.

Young, A.A., 1928, 'Increasing returns and economic progress', *EJ*, vol. 38, December.

Zamagni, S., 1986, 'La teoria del consumatore nell'ultimo quarto di secolo: risultati, problemi, linee di tendenza', *Economia Politica*, vol. III, no. 3, December.

Index

Absolute Income Hypothesis 37–8
accumulation 3–4
  social structures of xx, 10
adaptive consumption 35
advertising expenditure 121–5, 201, 202
aggregate demand 97–9
Aglietta, M. xx, 91
Ando, A. 37
'animal spirits' 8
apparel and other textile products 103–4,
  174
automobiles 7, 42–3
autonomous demand 11–12
average hourly earnings index 99, 163

bandwagon effect 6
Baran, P.A. 52
Baranzini, M. xix, 19
Bartley, R.L. xvii, 96
basic innovations 6–7, 16
  Internet 153–4
Becker, G. 34, 35
Bleaney, M.F. 30
Bluestone, B. 135
bourgeoisie 4
business cycles see cycles

capacity utilization 99, 166
capitalism 3–4
  corporate 52
Cassel-Von Neumann-Leontief theory of
  growth 21
'characteristics' model 34
chemicals and allied products 103–4,
  175–6
Chenery, H.B. 20
Chipman, J.S. 36
choice
  directional 33–4
  instrumental 34
  rational 33–6, 48–51

see also preferences
Clark, J. 6, 7–8, 9, 10
clothing, accessories and jewelry
  expenditure 109–10, 113–14, 182,
  188, 194
clustering of innovations 6
commodification
  modes of life 76, 149–50
  new needs 149–51, 152
compensation 5
composite economic sector 133, 150–1
composite index of profitability 100, 164
construction 104
consumer demand 1–2
  see also demand
consumer durables see durables
consumer installment debt 98, 162
consumer theory 33–6
  criticism of 39–40
  limitations 48–51
consumption xv–xvi, xviii
  adaptive 35
  culture of 134–5
  Levine's approach 59–64
  mass 3–4, 138–9
  modes of 68–9, 76, 77
  need development and system of
    consumption 67–71
  patterns and social polarization 135–6
  personal consumption expenditure
    96–7, 161
  recovery and structural transformation
    in US 148–9
  relationship between microeconomic
    and macroeconomic theory 46–8
  spending and aggregate demand 97–9
  underconsumption 28–30, 52, 83
consumption composition xviii, 107–19,
  127–8, 180–99
  Engel law and theory of consumption
    110–11

evolution in post-war period 107–10,
        180–7
ex-post forecast of consumption shares
        111–14, 188–99
and new markets 115–17
structural transformation and 116, 129
consumption deepening xvii, 142–7
    intensive growth 144–6
    technology, innovation and market
        development 146–7
consumption function 37–8
consumption-growth relationship xvi–xvii,
        xviii, 53–6, 67–86
    consumption deepening 142–7
    demand-led growth 81–4
    empirical analysis 90–1
    market development process 78–80
    mass consumption 138–9
    need development and system of
        consumption 67–71
    new approach to consumption theory
        73–6
    theory of market creation 76–8
    transformation of consumption sphere
        71–3
consumption ratio 97–8, 161
consumption sphere *see* transformation
    of the consumption sphere
consumption theory 32–45
    demand composition and 23–6
    Duesenberry's theory of consumption
        and saving 39–43
    Engel law and 110–11
    macro models 37–9
    new approach to 73–6
    Pasinetti's theory 23–6, 32–3
consumption widening 138–42
    limits of 139–42
corporate capitalism 52
creative destruction 4, 15, 20
Cross, J.C. 35
culture of consumption 134–5
cycles 3, 15
    expansion cycle of 1990s 151–2
    growth and in the post–war period
        96–7
Cyert, R.M. 35

data series 121–2, 202
De Groot, M.H. 35

Debreu, G. 35
declining industries 100–2, 171
debt ratio 98, 162
defense expenditure 99, 168
demand xi–xii, xiv–xv, xvii–xviii, 54
    aggregate 97–9
    autonomous demand and growth 11–12
    composition and the theory of
        consumption 23–6
    development, structural change and
        18–19
    economic change and consumer
        demand 1–2
    effective 83–4
    Pasinetti's structural dynamics and
        demand theory xiv–xv, xvii–xviii,
        xix, 18–31, 32–3
    potential *see* potential demand
    productivity, output and 8–9
demand-creating technical progress 12–14
demand-led growth 11–14, 81–4
demonstration effect 41
developing sector 62, 82
development *see* economic development
differentiation, product 131, 133, 140
diffusion 6
directional choice 33–4
disequilibrium hypothesis 43–4
displacement 5
disposable income 96–7, 160
Duesenberry, J.S. xv, 38–43, 47–8
    Relative Income Hypothesis 38–9
        empirical test of 42–3
    theory of consumption and saving
        39–43
durables 42–3, 145
    consumption expenditure 107–8, 180

Earl, P.E. 36, 49
econometric testing 121–4
economic development x–xi, xiv, xvii,
        1–17, 50
    and consumer demand 1–2
    demand-led growth 11–14
    neo-Schumpeterian theory xx, 5–11
    potential demand and market creation
        14–16
    Schumpeter's theory xiv, xvii, 1–5,
        14–16, 18–19, 81–2, 116
    structural change and 18–19, 20

technology-driven economic growth
10–11
economic space 72
education expenditure 109–10, 113–14,
185, 191, 198
Edwards, R. xx, 10, 135
effective demand 83–4
electrical and electronic equipment
103–4, 178
Elster, J. 34
empirical analysis 87–128
consumption composition 107–19,
127–8, 180–99
consumption-growth relationship 90–1
industrial growth patterns 100–5, 127
long-term transformation and 1980s
recovery 91–2
macroeconomic trends 96–100, 126,
159–68
market development and output
composition 120–5, 127–8
recovery of Reagan years 93–5
employment
full 5, 22
and investment 7–8
endogenous preferences 36, 49
endogenous structural change 82–3
Engel law 24
and theory of consumption 110–11
entrepreneurship 2, 4, 15
exogenous preferences 49
expanding industries 100–1, 103–5, 127,
170–1
expansion, structure of xvi, 59–62, 70
expansion cycle of 1990s 151–2
exports 99, 167
extensive growth of the market 139–42

fabricated metal products 103–4, 177
federal government purchases 99, 167–8
Fishburn, P.C. 36
food and kindred products 103–4, 173
food and tobacco expenditure 109–10,
113–14, 182, 188, 194
Fordism 91
forecast model of consumption shares
111–13
results 113–14, 188–99
foreign travel and other expenditure
109–10, 113–14, 115, 187, 193, 199

free time 117
Freeman, C. 6, 7–8, 9, 10
Friedman, M. 37, 38
full employment 5, 22
furniture and fixtures 103–4, 175

Galbraith, J.K. 52
Gay, A. 34
generalized preference systems 39–40
Gershuny, J. 111
GNP 96–7, 126, 159
goal utility 35
Gordon, D.M. xx, 10, 135
government purchases 99, 167–8
Gronau, R. 35
gross hourly earnings of non-agricultural
production workers 99, 163
growing industries 101, 171
growth xiv–xv
autonomous demand and 11–12
consumption-growth relationship *see*
consumption-growth relationship
and cycles in post-war US 96–7
demand-led 11–14, 81–4
Levine's approach to consumption and
growth 59–64
long-term 154–6
market-limited 51–3
multisectoral growth model 20–1
proportional 21, 23
technology-driven economic growth
10–11
transformational xviii, xix–xx, 56–9
Gualerzi, D. xv, 15, 23, 26

habit formation 36, 40–1
Harris, D. 23
Harrison, B. 135
Harrod–Domar growth model 12
Harvey, D. 91
hierarchy of needs 24, 28, 36, 111
household operation expenditure 109–10,
113–14, 117, 183, 189, 195
household production function 35
housing expenditure 109–10, 113–14,
115, 183, 189, 195

imitation 144–6
income
disposable 96–7, 160

per capita 160
and needs satisfaction 24
potential demand and income creation 26–8
uncommitted 61, 80
income distribution 59, 141, 143
US 99–100, 126
consumption patterns and social polarization 135–6
self-limiting forces 149–51
increasing returns 11–12
individuation 67–71
industrial capitalism 52
industries grouping 169–79
three-digit 169–73
two-digit 173–9
industrial growth 100–5
manufacturing growth 100–2, 127, 129
patterns 102–5, 127, 128–9, 169–79
uneven industrial development 82–3
industrial transformation 130–3, 148
and consumption sphere 131–2
industrialization of services 133, 150
inferior needs 24, 110–11, 114
information and communication technologies (ICT) 152
basic innovation 153–4
market creation and coming of age of 156–7
innovation 148
basic innovations 6–7, 16, 153–4
in consumption 74–5
product innovation 144–5
Schumpeter's theory of economic development 2–3, 9
structure of expansion 62
technological systems 6–7
technology, market development and 146–7
institutional change xx, 10
instrument and related products 103–4, 178–9
instrumental choice 34
intensive growth of the market xvii, 144–6
interdependence
of needs 76–7
preferences 39, 49
Internet 153–4, 156
investment 61, 132, 200, 202

capacity-creating effect of 46–7
market development 77, 79, 79–80
in market development and output composition 121–5
pattern in US 98–9, 165
neo-Schumpeterian theory 6, 7–8
structure of expansion 60–2
US expansion cycle 148, 151–2
Ironmonger, D.S. 36, 48, 111

Japan 12, 13

Kaldor, N. 11, 83
Keynesian theory xi, 46
consumption function 37
Kondratiev, N. 10
Kornai, J. 35
Krause, U. 34
Kurz, H. xi
Kuznets, S.S. 20

labor market 71
segmentation 135–6
laborer: separation from work 88–9
Lancaster, K.J. 34
learning 22–3, 25–6, 29, 32, 74–5
leather and leather products 103–4, 176
Levine, D. xiii, xvi, xviii, xix, 71–2, 87–8
approach to consumption and growth 59–64
need development and system of consumption 67–71
Life Cycle Hypothesis 37
life style 49–50, 74
local government purchases 99, 168
long-term growth 154–6
long-term transformation 91–3
long wave xx, 10
Lowe, A. 29
lumber and wood products 103–4, 174–5
Luxemburg, R. 30, 52
luxuries 110–11, 114

machinery, except electrical 103–4, 177–8
macro models 37–9
macroeconomic theory of consumption 37–9
and microeconomic theory 46–8
macroeconomic trends xviii, 96–100, 126, 159–68

consumption and aggregate demand 97–9
  growth and cycles 96–7
  income distribution 99–100
Mankiw, N.G. xi
manufacturing 99
  growth patterns 100–2, 127, 129
  see also industrial growth
Marglin, S.A. 43–4, 149
market
  extensive growth 139–42
  intensive growth xvii, 144–6
  mass markets 52, 58, 92, 104
  potential market 78–9, 81–2
  social purpose of 64
  structure of expansion 59–62
market creation xii, 57–8, 69–70
  and coming of age of ICT 156–7
  consumption composition and 115–17
  demand-led growth and 82, 83–4
  economic development, potential demand and 14–16
  growth patterns and 130
  structural dynamics 87–90, 151–4
  theory of 76–8
  see also new markets
market development 78–80, 144–5
  and output composition in US xviii–xix, 120–5, 127–8
  stages of 79–80
  technology, innovation and 146–7
market-limited growth 51–3
Marx, K. 30, 52
mass consumption
  and accumulation 3–4
  consumption-growth regime 138–9
mass markets 52, 58, 92, 104
mass production 58
mature sector 62
medical care expenditure 109–10, 113–14, 117, 184, 190, 197
microeconomic theory of consumption 46–8
miscellaneous manufacturing industries 103–4, 179
modes of consumption 68–9, 76, 77
modes of life 68, 73, 76, 77–8
  commodification 76, 149–50
Modigliani, F. 37
multisectoral growth model 20–1

natural rate of growth 21
natural resources 104
natural system 22–3
natural trajectories 6
necessities 110–11, 114
needs 74–5, 76
  commodification of new needs in US 149–51, 152
  hierarchy 24, 28, 36, 111
  inferior 24, 110–11, 114
  intensive growth and new needs structures 144–6
  need development and culture of consumption 134–5
  need development and system of consumption 67–71
  need satisfaction and consumption deepening 143
  need satisfaction and consumption widening 140
  socially determined 62–4, 67, 73–4, 87–8
  superior 24, 110–11, 114, 129
  theory of market creation 76–8
'negative-growth' two-digit sectors 103–4
Nell, E.J. xviii, xx, 56–8, 156
Nelson, R. 6
neo-Schumpeterian theory xx, 5–11
  employment and investment 7–8
  productivity, output and demand 8–9
  technological systems 5–7
  technology-driven economic growth 10–11
New Economy 153–4
New Growth Theory xi
new industries 132–3
new markets xii
  consumption composition and 115–17
  trends of transformation 132–3
new products 27, 42–3, 61, 80
  investment in market development 121–5, 201, 202
  and market creation 77–8
  and needs development 69
  potential demand, income creation and 26–8
  and social status 75
  trends of transformation 132–3, 152
non-durables consumption expenditure 107–8, 181

'non-growth' two-digit sectors 103–4
non-neoclassical theory of saving 43–4
norm 141–2
novelty 141–2
    consumption deepening 143, 144–5,
        146–7

output 200, 202
    capacity 99, 166
    composition in US xviii–xix, 120–5,
        127–8
    productivity and 8–9, 11–12
overproduction 30, 55

Packard, V. 52
paper and allied products 103–4, 175
Parrinello, S. 35, 36
Pasinetti, L.L. 9, 46–7, 54–5
    structural dynamics and demand theory
        xiv–xv, xvii–xviii, xix, 18–31
    theory of consumption 23–6, 32–3
permanent income theory 38
personal business expenditure 109–10,
        113–14, 116–17, 186, 192, 196
personal care expenditure 109–10,
        113–14, 117, 184, 190, 196
personality development 76, 87–8, 140–1
    need development and system of
        consumption 67–71
    socially determined needs 63, 73–4
petroleum and coal products 103–4, 176
polarization
    consumption patterns 143–4
    social 135–6
policy 7, 29
Pollak, R.A. 35, 36
'positive-growth' two-digit sectors 102–4
potential demand xiv, 47, 78, 81, 87
    economic development, market
        creation and 14–16
    new products and income creation
        26–8
potential market 78–9
    and Schumpeter's theory of economic
        development 81–2
preferences
    consumer theory 33–6, 39–40
    discontinuity 36
    endogenous 36, 49
    exogenous 49

formation 24–6
    interdependence 39, 49
prices 8–9, 143
    and consumption shares 108, 115
primary metal industries 103–4, 177
printing and publishing 103–4, 175
private education and research
        expenditure 109–10, 113–14, 185,
        191, 198
process utility 35
producer's durable equipment 98, 165
product differentiation 131, 133, 140
product innovation 144–5
    see also new products
production
    mass 58
    overproduction 30, 55
    system 73
productivity 8–9, 11–12
profits 100, 164
proportional growth 21, 23

qualitative change 1–2
quality 132–3
quality of life 117

ratchet effect 38, 75
rational choice 33–6, 48–51
Reaganism 93–5, 135
recovering industries 100–1, 103–5, 127,
        169–70
recovery x–xi, xvi–xvii, 91–5
    structural transformation and 91–3,
        128–30, 147–9
recreation expenditure 109–10, 113–14,
        117, 185, 191, 197
Regulation School xx
Reich, M. xx, 10, 135
Reich, R. 135
religious and welfare activities
        expenditure 109–10, 113–14, 187,
        193, 199
Relative Income Hypothesis 38–9
    empirical test of 42–3
research and development (R&D)
        expenditure 121–5, 200, 202
return of preferences 34
Romer, D. xi
rubber and miscellaneous plastics
        products 103–4, 176

sales, growth of 120–5, 128
Salter, W.E.G. 11
Salvadori, N. xi
saturation of inferior needs 24, 110–11
saving 40–4
  empirical test of Relative Income
    Hypothesis 42–3
  non-neoclassical theory of 43–4
  theory of 40–2
saving ratio 98, 162
Scazzieri, R. xix, 19
Schefold, B. 36
Schelling, T.C. 34
Schumpeter, J. ix–x, 9, 19–20
  theory of economic development xiv,
    xvii, 1–5, 14–16, 18–19, 81–2,
    116
Scitovsky, T. 150
self-expansion 87–90
self-limiting forces 149–51
Sen, A. 36
services
  consumption expenditure 107–8, 181
  industrial transformation 130–1
  industrialization of 133, 150
Shapiro, N. 80
shrinking industries 101–2, 127, 172–3
Simon, H. 35, 49
social polarization 135–6
social status 41
social structure, changes in 58–9
social structures of accumulation xx, 10
socially determined needs 62–4, 67,
    73–4, 87–8
Soete, L. 6, 7–8, 9, 10
speculative bubble 153–4
stagnating industries 100–2, 171–2
stagnation 30, 51, 87–9
Stanback, T.M. 131
standardization 139–41
state government purchases 99, 168
status, social 41
steady state models 20–1
Steedman, J. 34
Steindl, J. 51
stock market 153–4
stone, clay and glass products 103–4,
    176–7
strong expanding industries 101, 170–1
strong recovering industries 101, 169

Strozt, R.H. 34
structural change xii–xiii, 54
  and consumption composition 116, 129
  demand-led growth and effective
    demand 83–4
  development, demand and 18–19
  endogenous and uneven industrial
    development 82–3
  market creation 87–90, 151–4
  and natural relations 18–23
  and the natural system 21–2
  Pasinetti's structural dynamics xiv–xv,
    xvii–xviii, xix, 18–31
  theory of 19–20
  US xix, 126–37, 151–4
    recovery and structural
      transformation 91–3, 128–30,
      147–9
    trends 130–6
structure of expansion xvi, 59–62, 70
structure of wealth 89
subject capabilities 36
superior needs 24, 110–11, 114, 129
swarming effect 6
Sweezy, P.M. 52
Syrquin, M. 20

taste formation 14, 27, 73–4
  see also preferences
Taylor, L. 20
technical change/progress
  demand-creating 12–14
  multisectoral growth model with 20–1
  needs satisfaction and 74–5
technological systems 5–7
technological unemployment 29
technologically sophisticated industries
    104–5
technology
  ICT 152, 153–4, 156–7
  industrial transformation 148
  innovation, market development and
    146–7
  transformation of the consumption
    sphere 132–3
technology-driven economic growth 10–11
teleological preferences 34
textile mill products 103–4, 174
three-digit industries groups 101–2,
    103–4, 169–73

tobacco manufacturers 103–4, 173–4
transformation of the consumption
　　sphere xvi–xvii, xix, 71–3
　　and potential market 78–9
　　US economy 131–6, 154–7
transformational growth xviii, xix–xx,
　　56–9
transportation equipment 103–4, 178
transportation expenditure 109–10,
　　113–14, 115, 186, 192, 198
trend factors 38
twin deficit 93
two-digit industries groups 102–4, 173–9

uncommitted income 61, 80
underconsumption 28–30, 52, 83
unemployment 4–5
uneven industrial development 82–3
United States (US) xvi–xvii, xviii–xix,
　　57, 87–158
　　consumption composition 107–19,
　　　127–8, 180–99
　　consumption deepening 142–7
　　consumption widening 138–42
　　data series 121–2, 202
　　data sources 200–1
　　empirical analysis of consumption-
　　　growth relationship 90–1
　　　results 126–8
　　expansion of 1980s 96–100, 126,
　　　159–68
　　industrial growth patterns 100–5, 127,
　　　169–79
　　long-term transformation 91–3
　　market development and output growth
　　　xviii–xix, 120–5, 127–8
　　recovery of 1980s x–xi, xvi–xvii, 91–5

and structural transformation 91–3,
　　128–30, 147–9
self-limiting forces 149–51
structural change *see* structural change
trends of transformation 130–6
unlimited growth 154–7
utility tree 34–5

Van Duijn, J.J. 3
Veblen, T. 49
vertically integrated sectors 23
Von Neumann model 21

Wachter, H. 35
wages 89, 138, 141, 142
　　average hourly earnings index 99, 163
　　gross hourly earnings of non-
　　　agricultural production workers
　　　99, 163
wants satisfaction 48–9
　　see also preferences
weak stagnating industries 102
wealth
　　and needs satisfaction 64, 71
　　new hierarchy of 138–9, 144–6, 148–9
　　structure of 89
Weisskopf, T.E. xx
welfare and religious expenditure 109–10,
　　113–14, 187, 193, 199
Winston, G.C. 35
Winter, S.G. 6

Yoshikawa, H. 12–14
Young, A.A. 11

Zamagni, S. 33–4, 36